THE
COLORADO
TRAIL

Tenth Edition

The Colorado Trail
Foundation

THE OFFICIAL GUIDEBOOK OF
The Colorado Trail Foundation

COLORADO
MOUNTAIN CLUB

The Colorado Mountain Club Press
Golden, Colorado

The Colorado Trail: The Official Guidebook of The Colorado Trail Foundation, Tenth edition

© 2024 by The Colorado Trail Foundation
122 Halley's Ave, Poncha Springs, CO 81201
(303) 384-3729 | ctf@ColoradoTrail.org | ColoradoTrail.org
Please alert the CTF to any errors or outdated information at the address above.

Published by:
The Colorado Mountain Club Press
710 10th Street, Suite #20, Golden, CO 80401
(303) 996-2743 | (800) 633-4417 | cmcpress@cmc.org

Founded in 1912, The Colorado Mountain Club is the largest outdoor recreation, education, and conservation organization in the Rocky Mountains. Look for our books at your local bookstore or outdoor retailer or online atcmc.org

Bill Manning, Tisha McCombs, and Brent Adams: authors
Jerry Brown, Bear Creek Survey Service, Inc.: GPS trail data
Bristlecone-Geo: creator of maps and elevation profiles
Brent Adams, Tim Burroughs, and Jared Champion: editors
Vicki Hopewell: design and composition

Front cover photo by William Baeder
Back cover photo by Katie Lyons

Distributed to the trade by:
Mountaineers Books
1001 SW Klickitat Way, Suite 201, Seattle, WA 98134
(800) 533-4453 | mountaineersbooks.org

We gratefully acknowledge the financial support of the people of Colorado through the Scientific and Cultural Facilities District of greater metropolitan Denver for our publishing activities.

ISBN 978-1-937052-89-8
Ebook ISBN 978-1-937052-90-4
Printed in Korea

24 25 26 / 10 9 8 7 6 5 4 3 2 1

WARNING AND DISCLAIMER
Read, Enjoy, and Proceed at your own Risk

OUTDOOR RECREATION IS HAZARDOUS AND CAN EVEN BE DANGEROUS AND LIFE-THREATENING. Weather and terrain conditions can change often, rapidly, and unpredictably. Techniques, routes, and equipment change and evolve, and in the case of equipment, can wear out or break. Participant skills, abilities, and physical conditioning can also change or be inadequate for weather and terrain. The users or readers of this and all other Colorado Mountain Club ("CMC") books, articles, videos, and websites are solely responsible for their own safety, including using common sense and fully understanding their own knowledge, skills, abilities, equipment, surroundings, and conditions, and proceed at their own risk.

The information in this and all other CMC books, articles, videos, and websites is general in nature; discrepancies may exist between the text and the trails or routes in the field. Land managers may change, alter, or close trails. Check with local land management agencies before proceeding to receive the latest information and warnings.

HIKING, BACKCOUNTRY TRAVEL, MOUNTAINEERING, ALPINE CLIMBING, BACKCOUNTRY SKIING, ROCK CLIMBING, BOULDERING, ICE CLIMBING, AND OTHER MOUNTAIN AND OUTDOOR RECREATIONAL ACTIVITIES ARE DANGEROUS AND MAY RESULT IN SEVERE AND/OR PERMANENT INJURY OR DEATH. The user of the information contained in this publication assumes all risks of the use and application of the information provided or discussed within it.

The authors and CMC expressly disclaim all liability arising out of or related to the content of this and all other CMC books, articles, videos, and websites. The authors and publishers make no representations or warranties, express or implied, of any kind regarding the contents of these publications. All representations and warranties, express or implied, regarding this and all other CMC books, articles, videos, and websites and the accuracy of the information therein and the results of the use thereof are expressly disclaimed, including but not limited to any and all warranties of Merchantability and Fitness for a Particular Purpose.

Early morning light in the
Weminuche Wilderness.
Photo courtesy of David Fanning

CONTRIBUTORS

This book is a collaborative effort by The Colorado Trail Foundation (CTF) and its volunteers, the builders and stewards of all 567 miles of The Colorado Trail. To find out more about the CTF or to join in preserving and maintaining The Colorado Trail, visit ColoradoTrail.org.

CTF volunteers work to clear the trail. Thousands of fallen trees are removed every year by CTF volunteers who maintain The Colorado Trail. Photo by Darin Radatz

Many people helped the CTF develop the tenth edition of The Colorado Trail Guidebook and the preceding editions, and we thank everyone. Jerry Brown surveyed the trail, completing it six times, gathering accurate trail data with professional survey-grade GPS equipment. Tim Burroughs donated his professional expertise and authored the five chapters for the Collegiate West alternative. Brent Adams compiled and updated trail features data for this edition of the guidebook and refined the guidebook's trail descriptions. Jared Champion used his extensive knowledge of the Trail to update reference points and travel tips. Paul Magnanti used his "triple-crowner" experience to write about lightweight backpacking. Tisha McCombs, CTF executive director, coordinated the entire effort for the tenth edition.

This edition relies on earlier editions developed by many volunteers, including George Miller, Steve Staley, Gudy Gaskill, Dan Cohen, Tom Easley, Ron Davis, David Dolton, Jodie Petersen, Dave Peters, Georgia Hoffman, Cindy Johnson, Victoria Klinger, Terry Root, Merle McDonald, Marilyn Eisele, Suzanne Reed, former CTF Executive Director Bill Manning, and others. Many Colorado Trail users also contributed photographs and reported about necessary refinements to the CTF office. The CTF needs, and is grateful for, all of our good Friends of The Colorado Trail, the CTF volunteers and donors whose involvement preserves The Colorado Trail.

Support from the US Forest Service, Department of Agriculture, Rocky Mountain Region, is acknowledged and appreciated.

CONTENTS

SEGMENTS 1–5
WATERTON CANYON TRAILHEAD TO KENOSHA PASS

SEGMENTS 6–10
KENOSHA PASS TO MOUNT MASSIVE TRAILHEAD

SEGMENTS 11–15
MOUNT MASSIVE TRAILHEAD TO MARSHALL PASS

SEGMENTS 16–20
MARSHALL PASS TO SAN LUIS PASS

SEGMENTS 21–28
SAN LUIS PASS TO JUNCTION CREEK TRAILHEAD

SEGMENTS CW01–CW05
COLLEGIATE WEST, TWIN LAKES TO SOUTH FOOSES RIDGE

For ease of navigation, sections of this guidebook are organized by color.

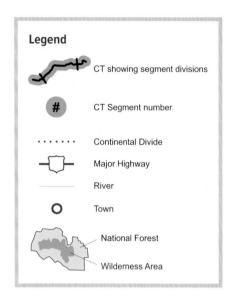

Legend

	CT showing segment divisions
#	CT Segment number
·······	Continental Divide
—⬡—	Major Highway
——	River
O	Town
	National Forest
	Wilderness Area

N

Miles

0   25

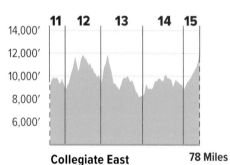

11   12   13   14   15

Segment

CW 01   CW 02   CW 03   CW 04   CW 05

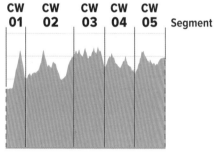

Collegiate East   78 Miles
Elevation Gain ~17,800'
(Southbound)

Collegiate West   83 Miles
Elevation Gain ~19,800'
(Southbound)

THE COLORADO TRAIL
Elevation Gain 89,354' (Southbound, Collegiate East)

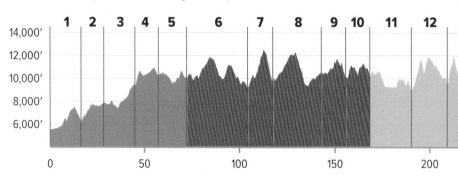

1   2   3   4   5   6   7   8   9   10   11   12

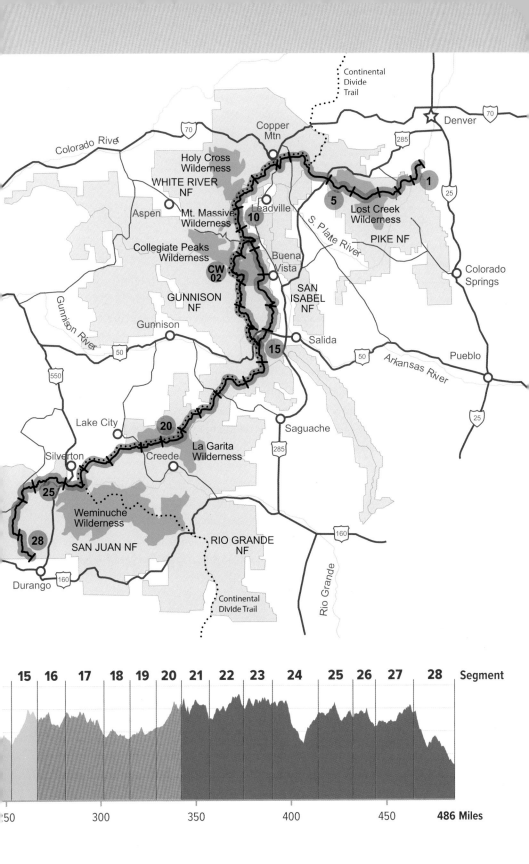

FOREWORD

After an up-and-down process spanning nearly fifteen years, volunteers finally succeeded in connecting The Colorado Trail (CT) end-to-end in 1987. It was a collaborative effort with the US Forest Service that connected existing routes with new trail built by hundreds of volunteers, primarily under the leadership of the late Gudy Gaskill, who afterwards became known as "The Mother of The Colorado Trail." Celebrations were held on Sept. 4, 1987, commemorating the Trail's official opening. The following trail season, intrepid hikers and runners endeavored to follow the still-poorly-signed route. The record shows a total of thirteen completers in 1988. The Trail was open for business. Today, after more than thirty-five years of improvements, the Trail is considered one of the best maintained trails anywhere in the world.

This guidebook details The Colorado Trail's more than 560 stunningly beautiful miles in both photos and words, giving readers a glimpse of its great geographic and geologic diversity. Day trippers, section-hikers, and thru-travelers alike will find this book useful in planning their adventures. From driving routes to each trailhead, to mile-by-mile descriptions of each of the Trail's thirty-three segments and five bicycle detours, this book has it all. Though some people carry this book with them on their excursions, others lighten their loads by removing just the pages covering their specific trips or by using it for planning purposes only and carrying with them instead the lighter and smaller *Colorado Trail Databook*, a companion volume that includes much of the same information in abbreviated form.

The Colorado Trail is a relatively short "long trail," making it ideal for hikers, bikers, and horse riders looking to set goals—from completing just a few miles at a time, to full segments, to the entire Trail in a summer. There is something for everyone. Bicyclists are allowed on roughly 75 percent of the Trail, excluded only from federally designated wilderness areas. Motorized users, including motorcycles and ATVs, are allowed on about 100 miles of the Trail's 567 total miles. Dogs are allowed on almost 99 percent of the Trail.

6   THE COLORADO TRAIL

Elevations on the CT range from about 5,500 feet to 13,300 feet, averaging around 10,300 feet. Traversing the high altitudes and an elevation gain of almost 90,000 feet from end to end offers an unusual challenge and a special sense of accomplishment.

CT completers often report that the Trail has changed their lives, giving them a new level of confidence. Others relate that their time on the Trail has enabled them to leave behind an old life chapter and experience a sense of renewal. Others say that the people they have met along the way have helped restore their trust in humanity. Even though most characterize the Trail as hard, nearly all describe their journeys as a lot of fun.

Volunteers who help build and maintain the CT report similar experiences, saying that

Bill Manning. Photo by Amy Nelson

although the work can be difficult, it is rewarding as well, and they love seeing the results of their labor and the friendships they make. Many return year after year.

The nonprofit organization that makes all of this possible is The Colorado Trail Foundation, which is headquartered in Poncha Springs, Colorado. Most of the Foundation's work is accomplished by volunteers and is funded primarily through individual donations. The organization's website is ColoradoTrail.org. It includes information for trail travelers, volunteers, and donors.

In our current times and with our hectic lifestyles, having access to recreational opportunities like The Colorado Trail has become more important than ever, both physically and mentally. The Trail offers a myriad of opportunities for personal growth. Those who travel it, volunteer to improve it, or donate to support it do so because they hold it in such high regard. We hope this guidebook will open the door to new adventures for all who read and use it. If you don't already love The Colorado Trail, we're sure you will after spending some time on it. Happy trails!

TRIBUTE TO GUDRUN "GUDY" GASKILL (1927–2016)
"Mother of The Colorado Trail"

By Tim Burroughs

> "
> It's an understatement to say that there would be no
> Colorado Trail if it weren't for Gudy. No person, man
> or woman, has ever single-handedly had a greater impact
> on the successful completion of a national treasure as
> Gudy has with the creation of The Colorado Trail.
>
> —**MERLE McDONALD**, former president of The Colorado Trail Foundation

In the many articles written about Gudy Gaskill over the years, she was often described as "a force of nature." Gudy was certainly that, but she was also a force "in" and "for" nature as well. Fortunately for her adopted and beloved home, Colorado was the chief beneficiary.

Gudy was most often recognized for spearheading the creation of The Colorado Trail, but she was far from single-minded. She was also a driving force in the Colorado Mountain Club; a devoted mother of four and wife to Dave Gaskill for more than 60 years; a prolific painter, potter, and sculptor; and an indefatigable hiker, climber, skier, and traveler, all while running her own real estate business.

She was born Gudrun E. Timmerhaus in 1927 in Palatine, Illinois. Her love for the Rocky Mountains began just a few years later when her father took the family along as he worked as a summer ranger in Rocky Mountain National Park. She eventually attended Western State College in Gunnison, Colorado, where she met Dave, and later earned a master's degree in industrial recreation from the University of New Mexico.

Gudy and Dave, a geologist with the US Geological Survey, spent time in Kansas, New Mexico, and California before returning to Colorado to stay. Both were active outdoors people and in 1952, they joined the Colorado Mountain Club. Gudy became one of the club's most active members, leading trips both in Colorado and around the world as well as chairing several committees, and in 1977 became the organization's first woman president.

It was as chair of the CMC Trails Committee that Gudy attended a planning meeting in 1973 to discuss the creation of a "Colorado trail" to be completed in time for Colorado's centennial celebration in 1976. As detailed in another chapter in this guidebook, that proved to be only a pipe dream, but Gudy clung to the concept, keeping it

Gudy Gaskill. Photo by Eric Wunrow

alive and moving it forward even as funding dried up and internal dissent on the committee threatened to scuttle the project altogether.

She led the effort to draw a detailed route for the Trail, incorporating existing trails and logging and mining roads where possible; almost single-handedly persuaded the US Forest Service and other federal entities to get behind the project; then recruited volunteers and led crews in building new trail to fill in the gaps along the route.

After the completion of the Trail in September 1987, and its official dedication on July 23, 1988, Gudy took on the role of president of the newly created Colorado Trail Foundation, whose mission to maintain and improve the Trail continues to this day. She held that position until 1998, then stayed on as a member of the CTF Board of Directors until near the end of her life. For many years, she also led educational programs along the Trail and at the Colorado Trail Cabin near American Basin in the San Juan Mountains of southwestern Colorado. An endowment in her name continues to support the Trail.

For her work to create this Colorado gem, she was recognized by President Ronald Reagan with a Take Pride in America Program award and by President George H.W. Bush through his Points of Light program. In 2002, she was inducted into the Colorado Women's Hall of Fame.

As you enjoy The Colorado Trail on foot, horseback, or the seat of a bike, you may encounter solid reminders of Gudy—the Gudy Gaskill Bridge over the South Platte River at the intersection of Segments 1 and 2, a bench near the southern terminus of the Trail outside Durango known as Gudy's Rest—but in essence, every step taken or turn of the wheel pays homage to the woman who refused to let a dream die.

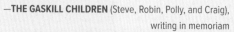

PRAISE FOR GUDY

"[She] was outstanding in every way. She was the best mother we children could have ever had. [She] taught us to love wandering in the mountains, the beauty of wildflowers, the chill of a waterfall shower. She was a painter, sculptor, artist, and always a leader. She was a leader who we all followed because she inspired everyone she met."

—**THE GASKILL CHILDREN** (Steve, Robin, Polly, and Craig), writing in memoriam

"She had such a bright spirit. It's not a stretch by any means to say The Colorado Trail is here because of Gudy."

—**BILL MANNING**, former executive director of The Colorado Trail Foundation

"Once she started a project, she was tenacious. She didn't quit. ... She believed the more people that enjoyed and understood the wilderness and the backcountry, the more people would be willing to protect it."

—**STEVE GASKILL**, professor at the University of Montana and one of Gudy's four children

THE COLORADO TRAIL FOUNDATION

THE COLORADO TRAIL

In 1984, the *Empire* magazine section of *The Denver Post* characterized The Colorado Trail as the "Trail to Nowhere." Initially, Bill Lucas of the US Forest Service and Merrill Hastings of *Colorado Magazine* conceived the idea of a long-distance trail between Denver and Durango in 1973. In 1974, several focus groups were held to develop a plan for building the trail.

Gudy Gaskill, an active member of The Colorado Mountain Club since 1952 and later the first woman president of the CMC, attended the first focus group. Subsequently, in those early years, she never missed a planning meeting. The Colorado Mountain Trails Foundation, predecessor to The Colorado Trail Foundation, was formed to plan, develop, and manage The Colorado Trail, and Gudy Gaskill was asked to chair the committee.

Roundup Riders of the Rockies were early CT advocates and remain involved today.

The task ahead was immense: A route had to be scouted through eleven Forest Service districts. Inquiries had to be sent to each district to get permission to build. Gudy emphasized that CTF volunteers were building the trail for about $500 per mile, compared with an estimated Forest Service cost of $25,000 per mile. She made numerous trips to persuade reluctant district rangers to buy into the idea of The Colorado Trail. After a year of intense work, most districts agreed to the plan. At the same time, Gudy was recruiting and training volunteers, leading trail crews, and purchasing supplies.

Despite the massive effort of Gudy and her "dirt-digging volunteers," The Colorado Trail seemed to languish. Hence the "Trail to Nowhere" designation by *Denver Post* writer Ed Quillen. (This article and others are posted at ColoradoTrail.org under Who We Are, Trail History.) That article was just what The Colorado Trail needed. It caught the attention of then-Governor Dick Lamm and his wife, Dottie. They joined a trail crew, hosted a fundraiser, and rekindled support and cooperation between the state and Forest Service.

In 1986, Gudy founded The Colorado Trail Foundation, whose nonprofit mission was to complete and maintain the trail. Gudy was a true visionary in realizing that volunteers were the heart, soul, and future of outdoor stewardship. With the Forest Service providing technical assistance, Gudy's volunteers provided the labor. The 486-mile-long trail between Denver and Durango was completed in 1987.

Gudy remained active in The Colorado Trail Foundation until her passing in 2016, and the organization continues to be volunteer driven. Its board of directors, Adopters, crew leaders, crew participants—hundreds of them from all over the world—volunteer their time each year to preserve and improve the trail.

The spirit of Gudy's inspiration and can-do attitude permeates this effort. For that, the "Mother of The Colorado Trail" has been honored by two US presidents and in 2002 was inducted into the Colorado Women's Hall of Fame.

VOLUNTEERS BUILD AND MAINTAIN THE TRAIL

Volunteers led by The Colorado Trail Foundation continue as primary stewards of The Colorado Trail. Work is done in cooperation with the US Forest Service, with such success that, in 2012, the agency requested the CTF add the 85-mile Collegiate West alternative and expand the volunteer stewardship.

Keeping the trail in good shape is a monumental task. Mother Nature has the greatest impact on the trail, toppling trees that block the path and sending runoff that erodes the tread. The toll is continuous, and without annual maintenance the trail would degrade quickly and become impassable in just a few years. Clearing

A volunteer trail crew, one of many that build and maintain The Colorado Trail. Photo by Dale Zoetewey

downed trees and diverting runoff to prevent erosion are just some of the tasks volunteers perform. Where plant growth is prolific, volunteers rework the edges and trim overgrowth. They build bridges and walkways. They clear new tread when needed. It has been a decades-long labor of love by the friends of Colorado's best-known trail, now totaling 567 miles.

There are many ways volunteers contribute:

Adopters: Colorado Trail Adopters carry out routine trail maintenance. Working through the CTF, they each take responsibility for an average of 8 miles of the trail. Each season, just after the snow melts, Adopters and their helpers embark on numerous trail maintenance excursions. Their goal is to clear the trail of fallen trees and debris and dig away the silt and rocks from water diversions. Typical Adopters spend several days each year on their section, working and camping until each is clear and in good shape. They also report to the CTF on trail conditions and any additional work needed.

Trail Crews: Volunteer trail crews take on larger trail improvements. For example, when a bridge needs rebuilding, some twenty or so volunteers team up to build a new

Left: CTF volunteers find joy in giving back to the trail. Photo by Carolyn Burtard **Right:** CT trekkers hike toward Searle Pass in Segment 8. Photo by Keith Evans

structure. Crews also build reroutes where needed, construct retaining walls, install signs, build cairns, and establish new and more durable water diversions. About twenty volunteer trail crews are scheduled each summer, usually from mid-June to mid-August. Crew schedules are usually announced in February, giving volunteers time to integrate one or more outings into their summer plans. Schedules are sent to those on the CTF mailing list and are posted on the CTF website (ColoradoTrail.org) as well. The typical volunteer enjoys traveling The Colorado Trail and finds working on a crew fun, rewarding, and a good way to meet new friends, as well as a great way to give back. Despite the hard work, many return year after year.

Trekking on The Colorado Trail: For three decades, the CTF has offered weeklong guided and supported treks, and many trail volunteers and supporters first experienced The Colorado Trail on one of these trips. Camping gear is transported ahead of the hikers and guides lead the way. After a day's hike, trekkers arrive at camp to appetizers, cold drinks, comfortable camp chairs, and a backcountry shower. They also enjoy backcountry gourmet meals prepared by the staff. Space is limited to about twelve participants each week, and spots fill quickly. For more information and to register, visit ColoradoTrail.org.

Funding: CTF funding comes primarily from private donations, which are essential to sustaining The Colorado Trail. Funding goes to trail maintenance, including volunteer food and equipment; publications about the trail; signs and bridges; insurance for trail volunteers; office expenses; and even thank-you cards for the many volunteers. The Foundation is able to accomplish great work with modest resources and is proud of its volunteer tradition and its ability to leverage donations into top-notch trail preservation. The organization is a 501(c)(3) nonprofit and donations are tax deductible.

HELP KEEP THE TRAIL CLEAR: THE CTF POCKET CHAINSAW

People frequently ask the CTF, "How can I get involved?" Beyond donating or becoming an Adopter or crew volunteer, here's a great way to contribute, one that you can begin on your next Colorado Trail excursion.

The trail continuously needs to be cleared of fallen trees; they topple with surprising frequency. While CT Adopters do their best and remove most of the fallen trees, they cannot monitor all 567 miles all the time. It is common for trail users to encounter fallen trees and, if carrying a pocket chainsaw, they can eliminate the blockage on the spot.

The CTF pocket chainsaw weighs less than 8 ounces including the carrying case. It is easy to take on every trail outing. Two people team up to make a cut and users find that cutting a log is unexpectedly easy, even one as big as 15 inches in diameter.

The more users who contribute to trail clearing, the clearer The Colorado Trail stays.

A pocket chainsaw is ultra-light, useful, and worth carrying.

HOW TO USE THIS GUIDE

The Colorado Trail is divided into 28 segments, plus the 5 segments of the Collegiate West alternative, each of which is covered by a chapter in this guide. Segments were established based on convenient access points to the trail. Most can be hiked in a day, although admittedly some require a very long day, even with a light pack. The map of The Colorado Trail on page 5 shows the entire length of the trail, plus major highways, towns, national forests, and wilderness areas along the route. The information presented is from Denver to Durango, in a southbound direction.

SEGMENT COLOR CODING

This guide is separated into color-coded sections, representing six multi-segment stretches of the trail. Look for the colored tabs to find the section you are interested in researching.

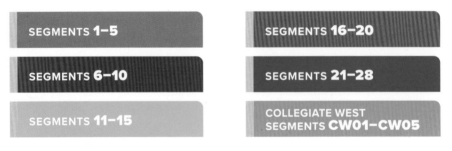

SEGMENTS **1–5**

SEGMENTS **6–10**

SEGMENTS **11–15**

SEGMENTS **16–20**

SEGMENTS **21–28**

COLLEGIATE WEST
SEGMENTS **CW01–CW05**

THE SEGMENTS

Each segment chapter begins with a short summary of pertinent information for the segment, including the starting and ending points, one-way distance, and approximate elevation gain and loss. The elevation gain (southbound) is the sum of the major ascending portions and, in addition to mileage, is a general indicator of how much effort is required to complete the segment. Elevation loss (southbound) is included as well.

Following that is a list of maps relating to the segment. The first, included in the guidebook, is a US Forest Service map, which is useful for general orientation purposes. These also provide road information and show trail access points. Listed next are relevant pages from the *Databook*, then topographic maps in *The Colorado Trail Map Book*, which is available at ColoradoTrail. org. These full-color maps show The Colorado Trail in detail. Next are the National Geographic Trails Illustrated maps that pertain to that segment. These waterproof, tear-resistant maps cover surrounding areas and trails as well. Pertinent Latitude 40° maps are also listed.

A trekker hops a stream in the San Juan Mountains. Courtesy of Colorado Mountain Expeditions

Beneath the map listings is the jurisdiction (the US Forest Service ranger district) for that segment. Contact addresses for the districts are listed on page 343. Because most of The Colorado Trail passes through federally managed public lands, contact the appropriate office if you have questions about regulations.

The symbols for access from Denver (right-facing car) and access from Durango (left-facing car) indicate the normal condition of access roads to the trail from the Denver and the Durango ends of that section. (For thru-travelers going from Denver to Durango, the first is the start of that segment and the latter is the end of that segment.) Please note that a dirt or gravel road listed as easily negotiable by a normal passenger car can become impassable in wet weather. Also, many of these secondary roads are not kept open during winter.

Next are symbols that indicate the likely availability of water in the segment during late summer. More detailed information about the location of water sources is provided in the trail description for each section.

Finally, there is a symbol that pertains to bicycling in that segment. If a mandatory bicycle detour applies, a page number for the detour is listed.

Key to Symbols

Paved or graded-dirt access road*	Rough, dirt access road*	Four-wheel-drive (4WD) access road*
Plentiful water sources	Scattered water sources	Water is difficult to obtain
Bicycles allowed	Bicycles prohibited	

*The symbols for access from Denver (right-facing car) and access from Durango (left-facing car) indicate the normal condition of access roads to the trail from the Denver and the Durango ends of that section.

About This Segment

This section provides general information, interesting facts, and local history about each segment.

Trailhead/Access Points

This section gives instructions for reaching the trailheads and trail access points, along with symbols that indicate normal road conditions. All of the beginning and ending points are accessible by vehicle. Many segments have additional trail access points, some of which are accessible by road, while some are not. Generally, a *trailhead* refers to an official access point with a parking area, though these are sometimes primitive. *Trail access* refers to a point where the trail crosses or approaches a road, but where no official parking is provided.

Services, Supplies, and Accommodations

This section describes nearby supply points and services. For major supply points, a town or city map is included, as well as a list of services such as grocery stores, showers, post offices, and laundries. Larger towns offer multiple lodging and dining options. Check with the local chamber of commerce for more information. It should be noted that on some remote segments of The Colorado Trail, no convenient points of resupply are available.

The Waterton Canyon Trailhead at the Denver end of the Colorado Trail. Photo by Ravi Nagarajan

Trail Description

Detailed trail descriptions progress from Denver to Durango. They indicate the distance between recognizable features (indicated in bold) from the beginning of the trail segment. The mileages were obtained using professional-grade GPS equipment.

Maps, Elevation Profiles, and GPS

Each segment chapter ends with a vicinity map. They were designed for this book and show all types of roads and road access reasonably well. A dashed line with bold yellow highlighting indicates the trail in this segment. A dashed line with lighter highlighting shows adjacent segments. Key features (usually trail intersections, creek crossings, or trail access points) also are shown.

Also included with each vicinity map is a trail elevation profile showing the ups and downs encountered along that segment. Note that the hill steepness is not consistent in each segment due to the variations in the scale of miles.

For those who like to have detailed topographical maps, The Colorado Trail Foundation recommends *The Colorado Trail Map Book*. The *Map Book* and other Colorado Trail guides are available at our CT Store, ColoradoTrail.org/shop.

Another valuable publication is *The Colorado Trail Databook*, available at the CT Store and many other retailers. It contains simple maps and many users find that the *Databook* is all they need for their CT excursion.

And There's More!

Additional information boxes provide interesting facts or useful information to help you get the most out of your Colorado Trail experience.

 WARNING: Be alert for this symbol and box. It highlights a particular caution or warning for that segment.

TRAVEL TIPS: Be sure to check out this useful insider information about the segment from the CTF Team.

 Indicates helpful tips for hikers and highlights other hikes or climbs in the segment.

 Indicates a special viewing opportunity in this segment.

 Indicates information for mountain bikers, including other rides in the area that might be of interest.

 Indicates services, supplies, and accommodations in the area.

PLANNING FOR THE COLORADO TRAIL

Winding 486 miles from Denver to Durango, 567 miles in all, through the magnificent heart of the southern Rockies, The Colorado Trail is one of the nation's most beautiful and varied long-distance trails. For recreationalists—hikers, backpackers, mountain bikers, and horseback riders—the CT offers an unparalleled path into the scenic wonders of Colorado's mountains, crossing eight mountain ranges, six national forests, and countless streams and rivers. The topography ranges from the high plains of eastern Colorado to the alpine peaks along the Continental Divide.

The enjoyment of the CT experience is dependent in large part on users' ability to respond to the demands, challenges, and even dangers imposed by this remarkable path through the backcountry. Relatively few people consider traveling the

A thru-hiker in Segment 23 above Silverton. Photo by Felecia Moran

entire trail—it's not an endeavor for the unprepared or out of shape. Most users opt instead for day trips or outings of a few days at a time. However long your excursion is, planning is crucial.

CONSIDER THE SEASON

The Colorado Trail traverses a landscape ranging in altitude from 5,522 feet at its eastern end to over 13,000 feet in the lofty San Juan Mountains in the southwestern corner of the state. Much of the trail is above 9,000 feet, where winters are long and extreme. Snow covers the trail for much of the year, usually persisting through June along high ridges or in shady ravines. For that reason, it is important to carefully consider the time of year for your trek or ride.

Furthermore, while it is possible to travel some segments of the CT in the winter (Segment 9 at Tennessee Pass, for instance, is the start of several classic ski tours), most of the secondary access roads mentioned in this guide are closed to traffic during the winter and well into the spring.

Unlike thru-travelers, day or short-term users can pick and choose among individual segments based on snow cover. Segments 1 through 3 can have scant snow cover (or none at all) between winter storms. By early May, these lower-elevation sections are often snow-free and showing their early wildflowers. Likewise, the first half of Segment 28 at the western end of the trail is low enough in altitude to be hiked in late spring.

An early-season hiker "postholes" through snow near Georgia Pass in Segment 6.
Photo courtesy of Colorado Mountain Expeditions

By early June, portions of the trail up to 9,000 feet are mostly free of snow, sometimes including Segments 4 and 5, as well as that part of the CT traversing the lower flanks of the Sawatch Range in Segments 13 and 14.

The eastern half of the trail holds late-melting snow on Georgia Pass, the Tenmile Range, Searle and Kokomo Passes, as well as the north-facing forested slopes nearby. The high reaches of the western half of the trail melt off even later, especially Segments 20 through 28 and the Collegiate West segments where snow can linger well into July.

Crossing significant snowpack can turn even a short trip into a monumental, even unsafe, outing. For one thing, The Colorado Trail is not signed for snow travel. Until the snows melt, many CT signs and trail markers are buried in the snow. Also, the signs are too infrequent to guide users traveling atop snow, with trail markers appearing at approximately half-mile intervals. Winter users can easily get off track.

Another hazard is "post-holing" (sinking deeply into the snowpack while hiking), which quickly becomes exhausting and presents the risk of sprained ankles (and worse) from stepping on branches and rocks hidden beneath the snow. Even if the snow is firm enough to walk atop, hikers can encounter slick, icy surfaces that are hard to negotiate safely.

Together, spring snowpack, icy slopes, and cornices make travel difficult and dangerous.

THRU-TRAVELING

So, when should thru-travelers start? The Colorado Trail near the Denver area is generally accessible by the end of the first week of June, sometimes earlier. Based on the average snowpack west of Kenosha Pass, however, thru-travelers hoping to avoid lengthy stretches of deep snowpack should not set out earlier than late June. Eastbound and Collegiate West hikers shouldn't take off from Durango until July because of the lingering snow at the higher elevations of the trail. Winter returns to the high country in October, so hikers should plan to finish their trek before September ends.

The Colorado Trail Foundation recommends that thru-travelers begin their trek from the eastern end, starting at Segment 1 and ending at Segment 28, as described in the pages of this guide. Not only does the trail tend to clear of snow a little earlier on the eastern end, but by starting at the lower-elevation Denver end of the trail, hikers do not encounter tree line until Georgia Pass in Segment 6, some 80 miles into the trek. Hikers starting from Durango, on the other hand, reach tree line much more quickly, barely 20 miles into Segment 28, which doesn't allow much time to acclimatize to higher elevations.

In addition, the average elevation overall for the eastern half of the CT is much lower than the western half, which is dominated by long alpine sections through the San Juan Range, some of the loftiest mountains in the state. The conditioning gained while hiking east to west can help hikers better handle the strenuous, higher-elevation western half.

FOOT CARE

Experienced hikers report that attention to your feet is most important, both in planning a hike and while on the trail, and that it is particularly important for those on

Happy trail feet and footwear, nearing completion of the CT. Photo by Jeff McGarvin

multiday hikes. Why? Because sore feet limit enjoyment, and blisters are common and painful. But, careful attention to your feet can help. Keep in mind that blisters result from a combination of friction, heat, and moisture; plan to minimize these.

Begin focusing on your feet when planning your trip and doing your training hikes. Carefully choose your footwear and socks. Consider lightweight and lower-height shoes that have proven adequate even for a thru-hike and offer advantages like less heat buildup. Cooler feet can mean drier feet and fewer blisters. Choose good-quality socks that help wick moisture and dry fast; avoid cotton. Try lighter-weight socks, as some find that they reduce heat buildup. Train in the shoe/sock combination you plan to take on your trip and refine your footwear until you're using what works best for you. Attempt to strengthen and toughen your feet; it will pay off on your CT hike. Some hikers have found that applying a preventative anti-friction/anti-chafing product (stick or cream) during training and even on the trail helps fend off blisters. Study foot care. A highly rated resource is *Fixing Your Feet: Injury Prevention and Treatments for Athletes* by John Vonhof. Secure supplies such as leukotape, moleskin, scissors, ointment, and skin-cleaning wipes and know how to use them. Consider carrying extra pairs of socks.

Employ your knowledge gained in training and planning at the very start of your journey, from your first steps on the trail. Tape your feet in advance if that's what works best. Keep your shoes and socks as dry as you can. If you feel a hot spot, stop right away and care for it to keep from forming blisters or allowing them to grow larger.

GETTING TO AND FROM THE TRAIL

Both Denver and Durango are served by several national and regional airlines. Express bus and van service is available between Denver International Airport and several resort communities close to The Colorado Trail, including Breckenridge, Frisco, and Copper Mountain. The Regional Transportation District (rtd-denver. com), a bus and light rail system serving the Denver metropolitan area, provides service trail users have found helpful.

Commercial bus lines run between some of the towns and cities listed as resupply points in this guide. Schedules and routes change frequently, however, so inquire about service before setting off on your trip. A few towns have shuttles that CT users can take between the trail and town; notably, the Summit Stage in Segments 6 and 7. Phone the chambers of commerce mentioned in the Services, Supplies, and Accommodations section of each chapter for information about local shuttle services or taxis.

A unique way to access Segment 24 from either Durango or Silverton is aboard the historic Durango & Silverton Narrow Gauge Railroad. You can book trips and check fares and schedules at durangotrain.com, or by calling 888-TRAIN07 (888-872-4607).

RESUPPLYING

For those planning an extended or thru-trip on The Colorado Trail, you'll probably want to resupply. While the entire trail has been traversed without resupply, not many will want to carry all the provisions (and weight) for such a trip. Resupply towns are noted in the Services, Supplies, and Accommodations section of each chapter. Many CT thru- and long-distance hikers have reported being able to resupply with relative ease by taking side trips to the nearby towns. However, planning is warranted as some of the small towns have limited supplies and lack the lightweight backpacking meals and gear many long-distance trekkers prefer.

Supplies also can be mailed ahead of time. Address parcels to yourself in care of "General Delivery," and send to the post offices listed in this guide. Or arrange to meet someone at points where the CT crosses a convenient access point. Bring along extras of any small, unique items that are crucial parts of your kit.

Also, please note that there are some long, remote stretches of the CT where convenient resupply is not possible.

Sisters loaded up for their CT thru-hike. Photo by Linda Jeffers

EQUIPMENT

The Colorado Trail traverses a wide range of life zones—from the hot, dry foothills of the Front Range to the harsh alpine tundra of the high mountains, where cold and wind can challenge anyone's gear. Effective, good-quality clothing and other gear can spell the difference between a safe, enjoyable day in the mountains and an unpleasant, or even potentially disastrous, experience.

When preparing for a hike on the CT, always start with the "ten essentials" as your foundation (see Equipment Checklist). Lightweight but sturdy shoes or boots are fine for most trips. Backpackers carrying traditional, heavy-weight loads will want heavier, stiffer boots for good ankle support. Others carrying lighter loads often find that trail shoes work best. For clothing, modern synthetics, such as polypropylene and fleece, are lightweight, insulate well, and dry quickly. But traditional wool clothing is also effective, even when damp. Avoid cotton entirely because it loses its insulating ability when wet. Rain gear should be waterproof and breathable.

Study the recommended equipment lists for both day and thru-hikes. For years, long-distance backpackers have been discovering that lighter-weight gear is as effective as older, more traditional gear without sacrificing safety or comfort. With its long segments and strenuous climbs, the CT lends itself well to this "going lighter" approach. An article on pages 28–31 offers tips and suggestions for the weight-conscious packer.

EQUIPMENT CHECKLIST

The Ten Essentials

- ☐ Food
- ☐ Water
- ☐ Emergency shelter
- ☐ Extra clothing
- ☐ First-aid kit
- ☐ Flashlight
- ☐ Map and compass or GPS
- ☐ Matches/fire starter
- ☐ Pocketknife
- ☐ Sunglasses/sunscreen

For Day Hikes

- ☐ Daypack: 1,500 to 3,000 cubic inches
- ☐ Insulating layer: synthetic or wool tops and bottoms
- ☐ Shirt or sweater: synthetic or wool
- ☐ Pants: synthetic or wool
- ☐ Parka shell: waterproof and windproof
- ☐ Pants shell: waterproof and windproof
- ☐ Hat: stocking cap or balaclava
- ☐ Gloves: synthetic or wool
- ☐ Shoes: broken in
- ☐ Extra socks: ones that dry quickly

For Backpacking

- ☐ Backpack: 3,500 cubic inches or more
- ☐ Insulating layer: synthetic or wool tops and bottoms
- ☐ Shirt or sweater: synthetic or wool
- ☐ Pants: synthetic or wool
- ☐ Parka shell: waterproof and windproof

- ☐ Pants shell: waterproof and windproof
- ☐ Hat: stocking cap or balaclava
- ☐ Gloves: Synthetic, wool, or waterproof
- ☐ Shoes: sturdy and broken in
- ☐ Extra socks: ones that dry quickly
- ☐ Waterproof pack cover
- ☐ Sleeping pad
- ☐ Stove and fuel
- ☐ Cooking gear
- ☐ Eating utensils
- ☐ Food and food bags
- ☐ Bear/critter food equip, e.g. bear canisters
- ☐ Tent, tarp, or bivy sack
- ☐ Waterproof ground cloth
- ☐ Personal toiletries
- ☐ Camp shoes
- ☐ Headlamp
- ☐ Repair kit and sewing kit
- ☐ Water filter and/or iodine tablets
- ☐ Plastic trowel for catholes
- ☐ Plastic bags for garbage
- ☐ Rope or cord

Optional

- ☐ Pillow
- ☐ Camera gear
- ☐ Reading material and/or journal
- ☐ Fishing gear
- ☐ Binoculars
- ☐ Camp chair
- ☐ Radio
- ☐ Cell phone or satellite messenger
- ☐ Walking stick/hiking poles

WHY AND HOW TO GO LIGHT

By Paul Magnanti

One sunny summer day in 1998, I summited Mount Katahdin in Maine. I not only had climbed one of the most majestic mountains in the East, but I had finished a thru-hike of the 2,175-mile Appalachian Trail. It was a memorable day, and one I look back on fondly. A week or so later, though, my knees were in pain. I was twenty-four years old, muscular, fit, and in terrific shape, but I was hobbling up and down stairs like an elderly man. It would take almost a month for my body to fully recover.

So, why did I suffer so much discomfort? Blame much of it on my weight—my pack weight.

Why Lighten Up?

Many people say the Appalachian Trail is more physically demanding than any other long-distance hiking trail. Parts of the AT are indeed steeper than anything found on The Colorado Trail, the Pacific Crest Trail, or Continental Divide National Scenic Trail. Nevertheless, when I later thru-hiked the 300-mile Benton MacKaye Trail, which has more difficult grades than on the nearby AT, I was steadily and comfortably hiking about 25 miles per day.

What changed? I was a more experienced hiker, for one. I also was in better shape mentally and physically than I was when I did my AT hike. And, finally, my gear was lighter.

After my AT hike, I vowed never to carry 50 pounds up and down mountains again. Over the next year, I read articles on how to reduce my backpack's weight. I went to a smaller pack. I made my own alcohol stove. I cut the size of my sleeping pad.

I did the physically demanding 273-mile Long Trail in Vermont in 1999 and felt great. The AT thru-hikers I met that year were a little surprised by my small pack. By the time I hiked the 2,650-mile Pacific Crest Trail in 2002, my base pack weight, or BPW (gear weight minus food, water, and fuel), was half that as on my AT hike.

The adventure of hiking the PCT was fantastic—incredible vistas, experiences I will not forget—and I felt great at the end of the journey. With lighter gear, the climbs were easier, I wasn't as tired at the end of the day, and the overall experience was much more enjoyable.

When I hiked The Colorado Trail, with its high elevations, big climbs, and long stretches far from resupply points, my lighter kit really came into its own. I was able to carry more food because of my lighter BPW. Inclement weather or

Two hikers head into Segment 3 with ultralight backpacking setups. Photo by Rachel Flunker

shortened days could be dealt with because of my faster pace. The trail was not something to survive, but an experience to revel in and enjoy.

My gear continues to evolve, but my basic setup has not changed since the PCT: frameless pack, trail runners instead of boots, a good down bag, a simple shelter in lieu of a tent, a cut-down foam pad, and so on. (See complete list at PMags.com.) I would not go on another hike with my Appalachian Trail gear.

The Ultra-light Philosophy

In the process of lightening my load, I've come to look more at why I should take a particular piece of gear rather than what I should take. I do not consider myself an "ultralighter." That term, to me, evokes too technical an image, one where the emphasis is on gear and not on enjoying the trail itself. While gear is important, I think it is the least important part of hiking. I use gear to hike, not hike to use gear.

What I consider before going out are personal safety, comfort, and fun. On three-season solo hikes, my gear list is pretty scant. A simple tarp and thin pad are part of my kit. The stove is left behind. On social backpacks (more camping, less hiking), I'll take the stove, along with a book, and perhaps a small libation to enjoy at night.

Why do I advocate this approach? Because it simplifies things; there is little to come between me and my enjoyment of the outdoors. The simple act of walking can be enjoyed without worrying about how heavy the gear is on my back. A backpacker who isn't exhausted at the end of the day can better appreciate the sunset over the mountains, the sound of the wind in the trees, and the hike just completed.

Over the years, my gear has changed and evolved. There has been a gradual decline in my BPW. I am now at a point where I can get lighter only by spending more money to shave ounces rather than pounds. I then have to ask myself, how much is it worth to lose that weight in my pack? Or, as one thru-hiker friend said to me, "Losing pounds is cheap; losing ounces is expensive." To me, that can refer to money, time, or comfort. Each hiker has to find that balance for themselves.

Some Simple Changes

There is more than one way to lighten one's load. Most backpackers can easily get to the 15- to 20-pound BPW range without making any radical changes in their hiking or camping styles. Today, there is lighter gear available that is functionally equivalent to more traditional equipment.

A good friend of mine is a prime example of how anyone can benefit from a lighter kit. Backpacking had become, for him, a trudge rather than a pleasure. He'd be achy, sore, and exhausted at the end of the day. He wanted to enjoy hiking again but also feel comfortable in camp. He asked me to look over his gear and give him some recommendations. That led to the purchase of a new frame pack, along with a good down sleeping bag and light synthetic jacket. A small pot, canister stove, lightweight two-person tent, and relatively light Therm-a-Rest sleeping pad completed the kit. We chose the gear based on his backpacking style, not mine.

The end result of this makeover? His BPW is now 17 pounds. Most people, if they are in the position to buy new gear, do not have to carry any more than that. His gear is functionally the same as his older, more traditional gear, but without the weight. It is not any less safe, nor does it require any more knowledge regarding its use, nor has he had to sacrifice any comfort. Actually, his comfort level is better now because he is no longer as tired and sore.

Going Even Lower?

As other experienced hikers have noted, it is difficult to go below 15 pounds BPW. The gear becomes more expensive and/or you need to become more of a minimalist. If you are the type of person who hikes all day and spends little time in camp, a minimalist kit may be for you. A cut-down foam pad instead of a Therm-a-Rest, a lined windshirt instead of a heavier jacket, and so on, might work well for you. But if you want more camp comforts and a more traditionalist setup, go for the 15- to 20-pound BPW range. Remember, there is no such thing as the "best" gear, only what works best for you.

Below 10-pound BPW? You had better be comfortable, knowledgeable, and experienced in a wide range of outdoor situations to go that light. As more than one hiker has found out, it is one thing to read about the joys of going below 10 pounds, but it is something entirely different in real-world situations. What is your experience level? Are you honestly capable of handling whatever Mother Nature may throw at you with only a very minimal kit?

It's best to find that out on a shorter trip before venturing out on a longer trek. Discovering that you do not know how to set up your tarp, that you hate going stoveless, or that you wish you'd brought a thicker sleeping pad is easier to deal with on a weekend outing than in a fall snowstorm deep in the San Juans.

My kit is at about 8 pounds, 12 ounces now. (Lose the camera equipment and it's right at 8 pounds.) I've pretty much reached my limit, and I'm comfortable with it.

Hiking all or part of The Colorado Trail is a wonderful experience. With lighter gear, hiking the CT can be an even more enjoyable experience. You'll have fewer aches and pains and find it less tiring. Buy gear that works for you, go out on some backpacking trips, adjust accordingly, and have fun on your journey!

Other Resources

Lighten Up!, by Don Ladigin: A good "meat and potatoes" guide for traditional backpackers who want to lighten their load. Not as detailed as other guides, but sometimes too many details get in the way of the overall goal. It's a good guide for the why of going lightweight rather than the specific what. Start with this book if you want to go from a 30-pound BPW to 15 pounds.

Lightweight Backpacking and Camping, edited by Ryan Jordan: A detailed, gear-oriented workshop in book form. This book is aimed more toward high-end gear for lightening your load. If you want diverse opinions from many different sources and wish to fine-tune your techniques, this book is a great guide. The editor is the publisher of backpackinglight.com.

Pmags.com: My website offers my take on the basics of backpacking and going light. Articles include: "Beginners Backpacking Primer," "Lightweight Backpacking 101," and "My Evolving Gear List."

It took many miles, many years, and much tweaking to get to my current level of gear. What I've learned may be instructive as you put together your own kit.

Volunteer trail surveyor Jerry Brown embarks on his fifth CT thru-trip. Photo by Carl Brown

SIGNS, PUBLICATIONS, AND NAVIGATING

The Colorado Trail is reasonably well marked. Alert trail users can generally navigate using the CT signs alone, including the double-peaked triangular logo markers on posts and trees. Nevertheless, things happen. Signs fall down, markers sometimes become souvenirs, and bad weather can cause travelers to lose their way. Trail confidence markers are not allowed in designated wilderness areas. It is not uncommon for a CT user to veer off trail unintentionally.

Whether out for just the day or committed to completing the entire route in a single trip, all CT users should carry at least one of the official guides to help them stay on the trail. These include *The Colorado Trail Guidebook*, *The Colorado Trail Databook*, and *The Colorado Trail Map Book*.

Many users have reported that the *Guidebook*, or portions of it, and a compass were adequate to navigate the trail. Others prefer carrying the *Databook*, partly because it is lighter and fits in a pocket. It includes mileages plus simple maps that indicate where water and campsites can be found. Still others appreciate the detail provided on topographic maps and choose the *Map Book* instead. A waypoint-programmed GPS unit or smartphone with app can be invaluable, especially when the trail is covered by snow.

An old-style CT marker shows the way. Photo by Aaron Locander

Over the years since The Colorado Trail was developed, a variety of signage has been used to mark the trail, from simple creosote posts to triangular plastic markers, from expensive redwood signs to reflective metal markers, and even to blazes on tree trunks. All have one thing in common: they display the instantly recognizable, mountain-shaped Colorado Trail logo.

In some segments, the CT's path coincides with another developed trail and shares signage with that trail. For instance, the CT is co-located with the Continental Divide National Scenic Trail for 319 miles, where markers for both are placed. In other sections, routes marked with blue diamonds denote cross-country ski trails that join the CT for short distances before veering off.

Unfortunately, both the tread itself and the signs marking it are susceptible to the elements, encroaching vegetation, downed trees, avalanches, and vandals. With the CT's many confusing intersections, indistinct or spotty tread in places, and the sporadic placing of trail signs, it is important to use the navigational aids available to the CT hiker.

A trail intersection sign at the south end of the Collegiate Loop atop the Continental Divide. Photo by David Dolton

USING GPS

A small, lightweight GPS receiver is a great tool for navigating The Colorado Trail. It can be loaded with waypoints, either manually or by electronic data transfer. Waypoints organized sequentially serve as a series of invisible cairns along the trail. Since a GPS receiver always knows exactly (to within a few meters) where it is, it can automatically calculate the bearing and distance to any waypoint stored in its memory. As a result, you can easily determine how far it is to a campsite, which fork you should follow, or what the bearing and distance are to a reliable water source. A GPS receiver can be particularly helpful early in the season when snow can obscure the trail and trail signage.

Volunteers obtained trail data using professional survey-grade GPS equipment. This guidebook lists the waypoints for some 500 features along the CT, including trail and road intersections, stream crossings, and other important features.

The waypoint database for The Colorado Trail is around 1,430 points. You can download these CT waypoints from bearcreeksurvey.com. On this site, you'll also find tips for setting your GPS to the correct units and coordinate system before you load any waypoint data.

Be sure to follow the instructions for your particular GPS manufacturer. Before entering UTM data into the GPS unit, set the GPS position format to UTM/UPS

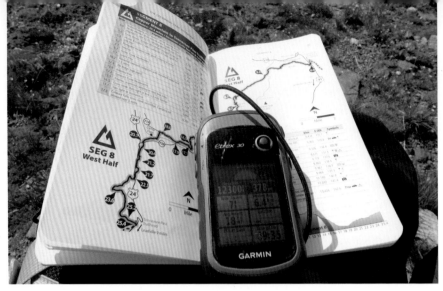

The Databook and a GPS are well-used CT navigation tools. Photo by Ed Hyatt

and set the datum (may be called spheroid) to either NAD83 or WGS84. Once the UTM waypoint has been entered, GPS users can easily convert to latitude-longitude, if desired, by switching the coordinate format. Waypoint users need to be aware that the UTM zone switches in Segment 27 from UTM Zone 13 to Zone 12 at the 108-degree longitude line. It returns to Zone 13 early in Segment 28. Most GPS receivers will make this transition automatically. If for some reason your GPS doesn't, turning it off then on again will usually do the trick.

USING CELL PHONES

Smartphones are becoming increasingly popular on the trail, not only for voice and text communication but for photography and navigation as well. Careful users protect their phone in a waterproof/shockproof bag or container to avoid calamities reported by travelers in previous seasons.

More and more trail users are using phone apps, such as FarOut, to supplement their hard copy guides and maps. They're available for download at reasonable cost. If you are planning to use FarOut for your CT travels, please download it through our website, ColoradoTrail.org, to ensure that a portion of your purchase goes back to supporting the Foundation.

There are drawbacks, however, to relying on a cell phone on the CT. Connectivity can be spotty all along the trail. Signal strength varies widely, sometimes allowing only voice or text communication, and often none at all. Signals tend to be stronger near urban areas and high points.

Another concern is battery life. Searching for a signal can quickly drain battery strength. Turning off the phone or putting it in airplane mode (in which the satellite and GPS functions still work) can alleviate this somewhat, but users should bring chargers and cords to use where outlets are available (primarily in stopover towns) and portable battery chargers (power banks) where they are not.

Users have reported some success with portable solar chargers, and they are sure to grow in popularity as those devices become lighter and more efficient. Be aware, however, that shaded areas and cloudy days can curtail their effectiveness.

WATER ALONG THE TRAIL

Drinking water is readily available along most segments of The Colorado Trail, and this guide points out many potential sources. On the first page of each segment, a symbol indicates whether water sources are scarce, abundant, or scattered in a typical year. There are some segments where careful water planning is strongly advised. In these cases, reliable sources may be up to 20 miles apart, especially during drought years or in late summer when many seasonal streams have dried up.

Except for water available at campgrounds, picnic areas, and the like that is clearly marked as potable, water from all sources should be purified before drinking. In addition to the abundance of wild critters in the backcountry, grazing livestock—mostly sheep and cattle—are very common, even at higher elevations. All can introduce protozoa and bacterial organisms to water sources. You should

Left: A hiker relaxes, refreshes, and replenishes his water supply at a creek along the trail. Photo by Aaron Locander **Right:** Chemically treating water obtained along the trail is one way to make it safe for drinking. Photo by Roger Forman

SAFE DRINKING WATER

In times past, one of the great outdoor pleasures for a hiker was to dip a Sierra cup into a fast-flowing stream for a long drink of ice-cold water. Today, hikers know that this can be an invitation for a nasty pathogen to invade your system.

While day-hikers on the CT typically carry adequate water for their needs, it is a constant daily chore for trail users to meet their need for safe drinking water. Most likely possibilities for contamination in the Colorado backcountry include *Giardia lamblia*, *Cryptosporidium*, and occasionally, some strains of bacteria and viruses in areas closer to towns.

While agricultural runoff is seldom a backcountry problem, chemical discharge from old mines is common in Colorado. The rule of thumb is to look in the stream for plants, insects, and other ample signs of life.

There are four proven methods for treating water to make it safe, and trail users will want to learn before deciding which method they choose:

- Boiling is the simplest, if you have adequate fuel, and kills most pathogens. While there is debate about boil times, a minimum of 5 minutes at a rolling boil is recommended.
- Chemical disinfection (including iodine, chlorine-based halazone tablets, and silver ion/chlorine dioxide tablets) is not as reliable as boiling, but provides some protection against *Giardia* and most bacteria, but not *Crypto*. Tablets are light and easy to carry, but don't reduce sediment from sources that are murky. Very cold water should be left to treat overnight.
- Filters are popular for backcountry water purification because they're relatively quick/easy and they remove sediments. Check the specifications for individual devices before buying one, and choose a filter with small enough pores to eliminate *Giardia* and *Crypto*. Many filters won't eliminate viruses, but some systems will. An advantage of filters is you can drink immediately after filtering and fill your containers again, which can reduce carried weight.
- Ultraviolet water purifiers treat water quickly. These battery-powered devices use UV light rays instead of chemicals or filters. They are effective when used in relatively clear water and can work well to eliminate *Giardia* and *Crypto* but don't always kill viruses. Pre-filtering can be required to reduce turbidity.

Hygiene is also worth mentioning. Backcountry experts agree, "Besides proper treatment of water, basic sanitation will help prevent gastro-intestinal illnesses hikers sometimes experience. After any bowel movements and before eating, be sure to wash your hands. Alcohol gel sanitizer is lightweight, effective, inexpensive and requires no water."

treat all drinking water by one of four recommended methods: boiling, filtration, chemical disinfectant, or ultraviolet water purifier.

In addition, always practice Leave No Trace principles to safeguard the water supply for other users. That includes camping at least 100 feet from any stream, lake, or spring.

BIKING

Mountain biking is popular in Colorado, including along the stretches of The Colorado Trail where it's allowed. The Buffalo Creek bicycle trails in the Pike National Forest around Segment 3 are particularly popular, along with the CT west of Kenosha Pass in Segment 6; the dramatic ride over Searle and Kokomo Passes in Segment 8; the nationally known Monarch Crest ride along the Continental Divide in Segments CW05, 15 and 16; the flower-filled meadows west of Molas Pass in Segment 25; and Segment 28 near Durango. In addition to cyclists enjoying day trips, there are some intrepid cyclists who "bikepack" the trail, carrying gear for multiday trips.

Cyclists roll atop Elk Ridge between Searle and Kokomo Passes in Segment 8. Photo by Dan Milner

Mountain bikers face many technical challenges.
Photo by Jesse Swift and Bill Turner

Cyclists need to be aware that portions of the trail that pass through federally designated wilderness areas, as well as other bike-regulated sections, are off-limits to cyclists and their bicycles. These include the Lost Creek Wilderness in Segments 4 and 5, the Holy Cross and Mount Massive Wilderness Areas in Segments 9 and 10, the Collegiate Peaks Wilderness in Segments 12, 13, and CW02, the La Garita Wilderness in Segments 19 through 21, the Weminuche Wilderness in Segment 24, and the entire Segment CW03 between Cottonwood Pass and Tincup Pass Road (which does not pass through a designated wilderness, but Forest Service rules prohibit bike travel on this section of trail). Riders are strongly urged not to violate these prohibitions; it is illegal and a real hot-button issue among trail users.

This guide notes the mandatory bicycle detours and describes carefully chosen detour routes around sections where bicycles are prohibited. While small portions of the detours involve riding on busy highways, the majority of the miles are spent on little-used back roads and jeep trails through country every bit as scenic as the main CT route.

Most mountain bicyclists are responsible trail users and their thoughtfulness is appreciated. Other trail users also appreciate the efforts of cyclists to be courteous to others, by slowing down and saying "hi" and "thank you" when encountering hikers and riders, as well as passing responsibly. It is especially important that cyclists converse with horse riders well in advance of passing to keep from spooking their animals. Cyclists who avoid skidding are also appreciated; skidding tires loosens the tread material, which fosters erosion and can create significant repair work for trail volunteers.

Those cycling on the CT, as on other trails, are cautioned to be properly prepared. Make sure your bike is in good working order before leaving and that you are capable of making basic repairs on the trail.

HORSEBACK RIDING

The Colorado Trail is open to horses for the entire 567 miles, with a few restrictions in wilderness areas, usually regarding group size and the need to use certified, weed-free feed. Check with the appropriate ranger district for specific regulations for each wilderness area.

While many riders have completed the CT without problems and have thoroughly enjoyed their trip, others have reported some difficulties to The Colorado Trail Foundation. The CTF's maintenance guidelines call for the trail corridor to be cleared of vegetation 4 feet on either side of the centerline of the tread and to a height of 10 feet. While we strive to meet these guidelines, 8 feet wide and 10 feet high has not been achieved everywhere.

Low branches can usually be avoided and down trees bypassed without too much trouble. However, riders may need to remove obstructions and should carry some sort of saw. There may be some places, however, where the trail corridor is too narrow for a heavily loaded packhorse to pass. Tight spots can typically be passed by off-loading the pack animal, proceeding through the narrow section, and reloading.

Roundup Riders on one of their group's Colorado Trail rides. Photo by Roy Berkeley

Riders enjoy the scenery while their horses focus on the trail. Photo by Bill Manning

Some horses become upset when encountering hikers and mountain bikers. Most trail users, if asked, are happy to move well clear of the trail while the horse passes.

Many of the streams that cross the CT have a suitable ford around the bridges. A few of the larger streams have sturdy wooden bridges suitable for horses. Some horses become agitated, though, at the sound of their steel shoes on a wooden bridge. Familiarization with these types of obstacles can reduce problems on the trail.

The Colorado Trail has proven to be much harder on horseshoes than one might suspect. In a group of twenty horses on a weeklong ride on the CT, at least one horse required shoe repair every evening for loose or lost shoes. Carrying repair tools is essential.

PHOTOGRAPHY ON THE TRAIL

Cell phones are the most popular cameras on The Colorado Trail. A growing number of optically excellent point-and-shoots are next. Some hikers carry DSLRs with interchangeable lenses. What camera you carry depends on your photographic intent, how light you pack, and the trip length. A day or section hiker can think differently about camera gear than a thru-hiker counting ounces.

Take spare batteries and cards. Consider carrying a portable charger. Trail towns have places where you can recharge, so be sure to pack your charging cord and USB adapter. To prolong battery life, turn cameras off when not in use and put cell phones in airplane mode. Keep batteries warm.

The Colorado Trail is rough on cameras. Protect them with suitable cases and plastic bags. Keep cameras accessible—around your neck, strapped to your chest, or in a pocket.

It's easy to forget where you took a picture. Taking notes helps, as does taking pictures of trail markers, road signs, trailheads, and distinctive landmarks.

Please share your photos with The Colorado Trail Foundation by way of our website, Facebook, and Instagram. We welcome full-resolution contributions to our photo library for use in newsletters, publications, and this guidebook.

Left: Indian Trail Ridge with the La Plata Mountains in the distance, Segment 27. Photo by Dean Krakel **Right:** Cascade Creek in Segment 25. Photo by Aaron Locander

SAFETY

Along the more isolated portions of The Colorado Trail, assistance may be many hours, even days, away. Travelers should keep the following things in mind:

- **Be aware of weather conditions:** Watch the sky and be alert. Hypothermia, dehydration, and lightning are all potential hazards.
- **Start early:** Summer afternoon thunderstorms are common in the high country. Start early and plan to be off exposed ridges before storms brew.
- **Don't travel alone:** It's safest to hike with companions; at the very least, make sure you leave a detailed itinerary with others.
- **Be in shape:** Get in condition and acclimatize to altitude before beginning your trek.
- **Use sun protection:** The UV radiation in Colorado can be very intense. Wear sunscreen and/or a long-sleeve shirt and pants and wide-brimmed hat. Sunglasses are strongly recommended.
- **Carry and use your map/guide/GPS:** Although the CT is generally well marked, travelers should always carry a guide or map, compass or GPS, and know how to use these tools.

A hiker assesses the weather to determine whether to proceed or stay put for a while.
Photo by Paul Croxton

- **Satellite messenger:** Consider buying/taking one of these, in part for its function to alert search and rescue. It can also keep loved ones informed and help with any rendezvous. Increasingly, cell phones are offering similar functionality and are worthy of consideration.

To activate a rescue group, contact the nearest county sheriff page 342 for a list of contact numbers. Counties and other jurisdictions may pass along the costs of a search-and-rescue to the people involved, which can often reach thousands of dollars. To keep search-and-rescue efforts at a high standard, The Colorado Trail Foundation recommends purchasing a Colorado Outdoor Recreation Search and Rescue "CORSAR" card. Proceeds go to the state's Search and Rescue Fund, which reimburses teams for some costs incurred in search-and-rescues. Funds remaining at the end of the year are used to help pay for training and equipment. Anyone with a current hunting or fishing license is already covered by the fund. The CORSAR card costs $3 for one year or $12 for five years. Cards are available at some Colorado retailers or online.

Be aware that cell phone connectivity is spotty in the Colorado backcountry, and users will find there is no signal at many locations. CT travelers sometimes find cell phone signal when they're near towns and at high points. Signal strength varies and at times is only sufficient to send a text.

BACKCOUNTRY ETHICS

The Colorado Trail runs almost entirely through national forest lands. In some areas, the trail crosses or is adjacent to private property or patented mining claims. Keep in mind that if problems arise, private landowners could withdraw rights. Please respect private property and no trespassing signs.

Remember also that federal law protects cultural and historic sites on public lands, such as old cabins, mines, and Native American sites. These assets are important to us all and should not be scavenged for personal gain or enjoyment.

Practicing the Leave No Trace principles listed on pages 345–347 will ensure that our public lands remain pristine well into the future. It is your responsibility to be aware of rules and regulations on public lands that the CT crosses. Contact the agencies listed on page 343 for more information.

ADDITIONAL RESOURCES

In addition to *The Colorado Trail Guidebook*, *Map Book*, and other available maps, the following resources may be helpful to those wishing to hike all or part of The Colorado Trail:

For on-the-trail use, the *Databook* is a great resource.

- *The Colorado Trail Databook* is a concise, inexpensive, pocket-sized guide that contains essential information such as mileage, water sources, and road crossings. After planning their trip using the *Guidebook*, many users choose to carry the lighter *Databook* on the trail. The *Databook* is available via the online CT Store, ColoradoTrail.org/shop.
- The Colorado Trail Foundation's website, ColoradoTrail.org, is the first place anyone interested in the CT should go. It answers many common questions and offers trail updates, including recent reroutes.
- The Colorado Trail Foundation's Facebook page, facebook.com/Colorado TrailFoundation, is a hub for CT info, tips, and photos.
- The Facebook group page for each new year's class of trail travelers has become a very active gathering place for Q&A and advice that's often trail tested. Search Facebook for group page titles such as "Colorado Trail Thru-Hike 2024."

WILDERNESS AREA REGULATIONS

Colorado has forty-four designated wilderness areas encompassing more than 3.7 million acres. The Colorado Trail passes through six of them. From north to south, they are the Lost Creek, Holy Cross, Mount Massive, Collegiate Peaks, La Garita, and Weminuche Wilderness Areas. Colorado Trail users may find a register at wilderness boundaries and may be asked to fill out a simple form and display their copy while passing through.

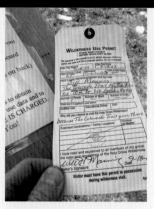

On entering wilderness areas, users encounter a register where they are asked to fill out a permit that helps the Forest Service gather usage information. Photo by Bill Manning

Trail enthusiasts can minimize their impact by adhering to the Leave No Trace principles outlined on pages 345–347 and by following these general rules governing wilderness areas:

- Camp at least 100 feet from lakes, streams, and trails
- Use a stove rather than building a fire
- Bury human waste 6 inches deep and 200 feet from water sources
- Pack out toilet paper and trash
- Keep dogs leashed or under voice control
- Detour around the area if you are on a bike. It is prohibited to ride or even carry (possess) a bicycle in a wilderness area

Each wilderness area may have additional rules specific to that area including group size limits, dog laws, equestrian feed parameters, dispersed camping specifications, and other regulations.

THE HERITAGE OF
THE COLORADO TRAIL

Sawatch Range. Photo by Roger O'Doherty

For thousands of years, this land belonged to the indigenous peoples—the towering peaks, the expansive intermountain parks full of game, the cool mountain streams. The southern Rockies were home to a succession of cultures that left little impact upon the land other than the paths through the mountains that defined their seasonal wanderings, some of which we still travel on today as part of The Colorado Trail.

By the 1600s, the Ute Indians, whose forebears probably arrived from the Great Basin a few centuries earlier, had established themselves in the mountains of west-central Colorado. Perhaps the first tribe to acquire horses, they pursued a nomadic existence following the movement of game, seeking spiritual guidance on mountaintop vision quests, and engaging in sporadic warfare with other tribes—the Arapahos, Navajos, and Comanches—who encroached on their mountain territory.

By the time white settlers arrived in the nineteenth century, two tribes of the several bands of Utes dominated western Colorado, the Tabeguache and the

View from Indian Trail Ridge in Segment 27.
Photo by Jeff Alvarez

Uncompahgre. A succession of mostly failed treaties were signed that eventually would exile these bands to a small corner in the southwest part of the state and a reservation in Utah.

One of those treaties, negotiated in 1858, prohibited the Utes from entering areas where valuable minerals had been discovered, in effect limiting them to western and southern Colorado. Soon after, as miners continued to push west, conflicts erupted, resulting in the so-called Kit Carson Treaty of 1868. It was negotiated by a delegation of Utes, including Chief Ouray, who were led to Washington, D.C. by Carson, the famed scout and American Indian fighter. This treaty pushed the Utes farther into an area west of the Continental Divide corresponding with the San Juan Mountains.

Two agencies were set up to distribute goods to the Indians: the White River Agency to the north and the Los Piños Agency west of Cochetopa Pass. But blatant trespassing continued as prospectors probed the mineral-rich lands of the San Juans. The infamous Brunot Agreement of 1873 (once again facilitated by Chief Ouray, assisted by his friend Otto Mears), tried to settle the matter. The precious San Juans were ceded to the eager miners and the Utes were settled on reservations, where they were expected to shift from their traditional nomadic lifestyle to an agrarian one.

Many resisted the change, however, continuing with their age-old ways. Coupled with continued pressure from white settlers who coveted land north of the San Juans, the Brunot Agreement began to unravel. The conflict boiled over, culminating in the Meeker Massacre of 1879 at the White River Agency that left eleven white men dead. A final treaty forced on the Utes by an enraged white populace banished the Uncompahgre band to a new reservation in Utah, and the long occupation of Colorado's mountain region by the Utes ceased.

Chief Ouray, who had attempted to walk a fine line between two clashing cultures, never saw the heartbreaking removal of the Utes from Colorado. He died while traveling to confer with other tribal leaders, and a mountain peak bearing his name along the Continental Divide near Marshall Pass commemorates his legacy.

THE FIRST EXPLORERS

The Spanish, whose knowledge of the vast region north of their empire was limited, were the first whites to explore the area that became Colorado. In 1765, Juan Maria de Rivera explored the San Juan country on his way to Utah, describing to his backers the mineral wealth of the region. Two friars, Fathers Domínguez and Escalante, followed in 1776. Charged with finding a route to California, their journeys throughout the Southwest, including the present-day Durango area, and the detailed maps they produced had a great influence on subsequent travelers.

A few years later, an expeditionary force led by Juan Bautista de Anza entered the region in pursuit of raiding Comanche bands. They traveled through the San Luis Valley, noting the topography of the eastern flank of the San Juan Mountains and the Cochetopa Hills, and crossed over Poncha Pass, viewing the skyscraping Sawatch Range. Others came after, and by the early 1800s the Spanish Trail wound through southwest Colorado as caravans carried goods from Santa Fe to California.

With the completion of the Louisiana Purchase in 1803 and the Treaty of Guadalupe Hidalgo following the war with Mexico in 1848, exploration of the region shifted to American interests. Trappers and mountain men penetrated the southern Rockies, following the ancient Native American trails and using the same low passes over the Continental Divide that would later see wagon roads, railways, highways, and The Colorado Trail.

Government-sponsored expeditions set out to discover the character of this new land—destined, many believed, to become part of the country—and what lay beyond the seemingly impenetrable barrier known then as the "Shining Mountains." An 1820 expedition led by Major Stephen Long crossed the plains and tentatively explored along the Rocky Mountain front, including present-day Waterton Canyon (the start of today's Colorado Trail), as it investigated the source of the South Platte River.

SCOUTING THE WAY

Soon after the conclusion of the Mexican War, Congress planned five expeditions to study proposed routes for a transcontinental railroad. Thomas Hart Benton, an influential senator and strong proponent of Manifest Destiny, provided financial backing for several subsequent expeditions led by his son-in-law, Captain John C. Frémont, already known for his trailblazing in California. His ill-fated fourth expedition in the winter of 1848 attempted to cross the Continental Divide at the Cochetopa Hills and ended in disaster in the snowy mountains.

Despite that setback, Benton and others pushed to find a feasible rail route through the southern Rockies. In 1853, Captain John W. Gunnison, an officer with considerable experience in exploring and surveying the West, was dispatched to explore a mid-latitude rail route that would cross the Sangre de Cristo Mountains, pass through the San Luis Valley, cross the Continental Divide via one of the low passes in the Cochetopa Hills, and continue on to Utah and the Great Basin.

After great difficulty hacking a wagon road over Cochetopa Pass from a scant Indian trail—felling trees, moving huge rocks, and lowering wagons on ropes down the steep, western side—Gunnison's party emerged only to find the way blocked by an impassable gorge, now known as the Black Canyon of the Gunnison. Convinced that a rail route through the area was not practical, Gunnison nevertheless pushed on into Utah, only to be killed with several of his companions by a band of Paiutes. His second-in-command, Lieutenant E. G. Beckwith, continued westward, completing the survey the following year.

While the Gunnison Expedition met with tragedy, it was to have an important impact: providing information about the country that would influence future settlement. Eventually, rails would cross the Divide at Marshall Pass, just a few miles east of Gunnison's crossing.

Following the Civil War, the government turned its attention to the settlement of the West. It sent out surveys to explore the country's resources and produce maps that would be useful to the miners, farmers, ranchers, and town builders who were clamoring for information. The two most important of these in Colorado were the War Department–led Wheeler and civilian-based Hayden Surveys.

Both surveys ranged widely over the Colorado mountains, scaling summits to set up triangulation stations, naming topographic features, analyzing the geology and mineral deposits, and studying the agricultural potential. Many of the prominent features encountered today by Colorado Trail users—including scores of peaks, rivers and streams, and mountain passes—bear names recorded by the men of these surveys.

LAND OF RICHES

Most of The Colorado Trail through the southern Rockies winds along the so-called "Mineral Belt," a geologic band trending from the northeast to southwest that contains the riches that attracted early prospectors and miners. After gold was discovered in Colorado in 1858, boom towns sprang up overnight, with many fading just as quickly as the next big strike occurred.

By the early 1870s, when big silver discoveries began to stabilize the mining industry in the state, more permanent towns and cities began to thrive. Although the eventual collapse of silver prices in the late 1890s threatened the economy

An old miner's cabin in Elk Creek in Segment 24. Photo by Pete Kartsounes

of these young settlements, many live on to this day—places like Breckenridge, Leadville, Creede, Lake City, and Silverton—offering resupply points to The Colorado Trail user. Others left their rusting and fallen relics behind for the CT hiker to explore and ponder. What was fortuitous in the eventual creation of The Colorado Trail was the network of footpaths, wagon roads, and rail lines linking remote communities.

RAILROADS COME AND GO

Railroads quickly became the key to the development of the state's mining towns and cities, and entrepreneurs vied to be the first to penetrate the mountain barriers and reach the new diggings.

In the early 1880s, the competition was fierce between two narrow-gauge lines, John Evans' Denver South Park & Pacific and General William J. Palmer's Denver & Rio Grande Western, to reach the quickly growing Gunnison and San Juan mining districts. Today's CT user follows the original path of the DSP&P as it once chugged into Waterton Canyon, then catches up with it again at Kenosha Pass. CT users also encounter the old roadbed left behind at Chalk Creek, where the line once snaked up the valley to bore under the Continental Divide through the Alpine Tunnel. Likewise, users cross the old roadbed of the D&RGW at Tennessee and Marshall Passes.

While these lines are long gone, a remnant of the D&RGW, rechristened the Durango & Silverton Narrow Gauge Railroad, still crosses the CT in the scenic

A rusting steam boiler and windlass sit next to an abandoned mine near Carson Saddle in Segment 22. Photo by Andrew Skurka

Animas Canyon as a tourist train. The Colorado Midland Railway was another short-lived line whose remains the CT visits near Mount Massive, where the Hagerman Tunnel once took the rails under the Continental Divide at approximately 11,500 feet.

With the waning of mining in the first half of the twentieth century, the rails were torn up and a colorful time in the state's history vanished forever. Many of those abandoned railbeds and old wagon roads have become the roads and highways that today serve as CT access routes.

In the 1930s, workers from the Civilian Conservation Corps and other Depression-era programs began a wave of trail building in the state that lasted into the 1950s, providing the tread for many miles of the current CT. These trails were built primarily for fire management, often paralleling mountain ranges and sending off numerous side trails. One example, the Main Range Trail, coincides with large sections of The Colorado Trail on the eastern slope of the Sawatch Range. Other trails were built to facilitate fish stocking of high-country lakes and streams.

With the spectacular growth in backpacking, hiking, and other recreational pursuits starting in the 1960s, these forgotten Native American trails, wagon roads, logging tracks, abandoned railbeds, and fire trails became the new highways into Colorado's spectacular backcountry. Linked by miles of new tread built by thousands of dedicated volunteers, The Colorado Trail has become part of this rich heritage.

Here is a sampling of historical highlights found along each of the six sections of The Colorado Trail.

▨ Waterton Canyon TH to Kenosha Pass (SEGMENTS 1–5)

In the first few miles of Waterton Canyon, The Colorado Trail follows the roadbed of the Denver South Park & Pacific Railroad. Just downstream of the Gudy Gaskill Bridge sits the shuttered South Platte Hotel, once a busy stopover for travelers on their way to the mines of Leadville and Gunnison. Trail users encounter the DSP&P again at Kenosha Pass, where an interpretive display notes where the switchyard and maintenance shops once stood in the meadows atop the pass. The tracks over the pass were torn up in the 1930s. The DSP&P lost its race to reach Gunnison to the Denver & Rio Grande Western and achieved its loftier goal of reaching the Pacific only after it was sold in foreclosure to the Union Pacific Railroad.

▨ Kenosha Pass to Mount Massive TH (SEGMENTS 6–10)

In 1942, a new city sprang up practically overnight in the mountain wilderness of Colorado. Camp Hale was established in the East Fork valley as a winter and mountain training site for soldiers during World War II. The large, flat valley, surrounded by steep hillsides, proved ideal for teaching skiing, rock climbing, and cold weather survival skills. The famed 10th Mountain Division trained here. Few people know that from 1959 to 1965, when the camp was deactivated, the site was used by the CIA to secretly train Tibetan rebels. This area is now a national monument (see page 136), and a display atop Tennessee Pass and at nearby Ski Cooper commemorates its legacy, as well as the 10th Mountain Division hut system.

▨ Mount Massive TH to Marshall Pass (SEGMENTS 11–15)

Three distinct peaks frame the view on the route to Marshall Pass: Mount Ouray, named for Chief Ouray; Chipeta Mountain, named for Ouray's wife; and Pahlone Peak, named after their son. From this point west, The Colorado Trail largely travels through the ancestral lands of the Utes, whose story is one of great freedom and loss, as whites ignored treaties and eventually pushed them out and onto reservations. Ouray attempted to straddle a middle path between the conflicting cultures but, in the end, mostly gave in to white demands. Today, he is considered one of Colorado's pioneers, remembered with a portrait at the State Capitol and the lofty peak that bears his name.

▨ Marshall Pass to San Luis Pass (SEGMENTS 16–20)

Winding along the long section of the Continental Divide known as the Cochetopa Hills, The Colorado Trail crosses several historic passes. For centuries, these low points on the continent's backbone were used by both Native Americans and animals. "Cochetopa" means buffalo, presumably because the beasts migrated to and from the San Luis Valley through the area. Whites also were attracted to these easier crossings, sometimes with bad results. Explorer John C. Frémont's expedition to cross the Divide in the winter of 1848 led to disaster, with rumors of cannibalism—not the last time that charge was heard in these mountains. In 1874, a party of miners disappeared in nearly the same area. Months later, only Alfred G. Packer emerged. Packer was later convicted of murdering and dining on his companions.

▮▮ San Luis Pass to Junction Creek Trailhead (SEGMENTS 21–28)

You'll hear the long, mournful whistle of the Durango & Silverton Narrow Gauge Railroad long before you reach the bottom of Elk Creek and the Animas River Canyon in Segment 24. Completed in 1881, only nine months after construction began out of Durango, the railroad, then known as the Denver & Rio Grande Western, carried passengers and freight to the booming silver mines at Silverton. Through the years, slides, floods, snow, war, and financial instability threatened the line. Tourism saved the rail line, and it continues to operate today, carrying passengers in vintage railcars pulled by historic steam locomotives.

▮▮ Collegiate West, Twin Lakes to South Fooses Ridge (SEGMENTS CW01–CW05)

The five Collegiate West segments, like those in the Collegiate East, are rich in mining, railroad, and cultural history dating back thousands of years to the land's early occupants. Starting on the south shore of Twin Lakes, trail users can wander through the remains of the nineteenth century Interlaken Resort, where tourists once arrived by train and stagecoach. Across Hope Pass stands the ghost town of Winfield, one of many local reminders of the state's rich mining heritage, along with the scattered remnants of several played-out mines. Hikers follow a former roadbed for the narrow-gauge Denver South Park & Pacific Railroad to the now-rock-covered entrance to the 1,800-foot Alpine Tunnel—the first tunnel built under the Continental Divide in Colorado. On approaching Monarch Pass from the south, the CT passes by the low boulder walls of a "game drive" built by prehistoric hunters as early as 3000 B.C. and used until as late as A.D. 1800.

THE NATURAL HISTORY
OF THE COLORADO TRAIL

By Hugo A. Ferchau
Past Thornton Professor of Botany, Western State College

This brief look at Rocky Mountain ecology is intended for both those new to Colorado Trail country and those locals who have rarely ventured into its vastness. Veterans of these wilds could probably write an equally good account. Regardless, there is no question that the natural history of this region is the prize, the reward for making the effort to hike the CT, and I would underscore the value of walking, not running, as you pass through it.

Over many years of leading groups of students through the Rockies, it has been my experience that those who reach camp well ahead of the rest can rarely relate any interesting observations. They might as well have worked out in a gym.

To get the most out of your Colorado Trail experience, take the time to look, to sit, to let nature present itself to you, and to soak up all that it has to offer. You may pass this way but once.

OBSERVING WILDLIFE

For some reason, we commonly use the term "wildlife" to refer only to animals. Plants, evidently, are considered to be somewhat trapped or tamed, or at least subdued. There is less drama associated with plants because we can prepare for our encounters with them, whereas animals tend to take us by surprise—there all of a sudden, gone just as quickly. As a botanist, I recognize that most people would rather talk about a bear than about the bearberry.

Having been over most of The Colorado Trail, I cannot think of a single day that did not reveal

Marmot on rock, common at high elevations along the CT. Photo by Tom Hodge

much about the Rocky Mountain fauna. By the same token, I have seen students hike for days without seeing a single animal. This apparent contradiction can be explained by the fact that native animals are not in a zoo. They have instinctual and learned behaviors that enable them to avoid potential or perceived threats, such as hikers.

To see these animals, you must meet them on their own terms. Several general rules apply:

- Dawn and dusk are when animals tend to be most active, so rise early and get on the trail ahead of other hikers.
- Animals require water regularly, so look to their sources.
- Many animals will ignore you if you become part of the scenery, which means being quiet and still.
- Familiarizing yourself with the behavior of the animal, or animals, you wish to observe will increase your chances for success. Nocturnal rodents, for example, can be spotted at night by a patient observer with a flashlight.

Moose in pond along Elk Creek, Segment 24 near Silverton. Photo by Felecia Moran

A mountain goat wanders along the CT above tree line. Photo by Tom Parchman

Early-season trail users should note that deer and elk give birth in June. Try to avoid being disruptive if traveling at this time of year. Though some may be fearful of wildlife encounters, there is little need for concern. In years of student trips, we have experienced no attacks. I have seen mountain lion and bear from reasonable distances, and I am sure they have observed me from distances that would have excited me had I known about them. I have seen bear droppings on the trail on a cold morning that were so fresh that steam was still rising from them. My wife woke up from a nap one afternoon and found fresh bear claw marks on a tree above her head. Good judgment will help you avoid being molested. An animal seeks food, not your company. If you have no food in your presence, you will generally not be bothered. If you choose to keep food (even nuts or a candy bar) in your tent, you may wake up to find a hole chewed in the floor and the steely eyes of a mouse or pack rat staring back. After arriving in camp, hang your food away from your sleeping area—75 to 100 yards is a good distance.

PLANTS

The highly variable topography of the central Rocky Mountains hosts a kaleido-scopic variety of vegetation. The accompanying diagrams indicate the types of veg-etation encountered on The Colorado Trail, as well as their relationship to each other. Note that the zones are not defined by elevation alone, but also depend on local climatic factors.

The Natural History of The Colorado Trail

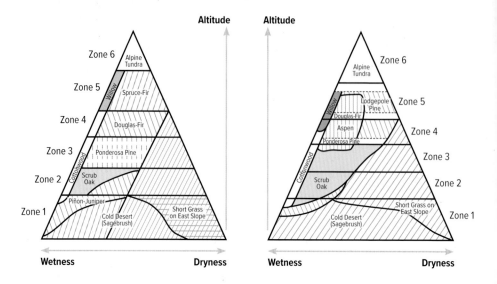

DIAGRAM 1. Climax Vegetation

Altitude

Zone 6 — Alpine Tundra
Zone 5 — Willow / Spruce-Fir
Zone 4 — Douglas-Fir
Zone 3 — Cottonwood / Ponderosa Pine
Zone 2 — Scrub Oak
Zone 1 — Piñon-Juniper / Cold Desert (Sagebrush) / Short Grass on East Slope

Wetness — Dryness

DIAGRAM 2. Successional Vegetation

Altitude

Zone 6 — Alpine Tundra
Zone 5 — Lodgepole Pine
Zone 4 — Willow / Douglas-Fir / Aspen
Zone 3 — Cottonwood / Ponderosa Pine
Zone 2 — Scrub Oak
Zone 1 — Cold Desert (Sagebrush) / Short Grass on East Slope

Wetness — Dryness

In the field, of course, things can be more complicated. In areas that have been disturbed by fire or logging, for instance, different types of vegetation will exist in different relationships. Diagram 1 shows the relationship between various plant communities in a climax situation—that is, in an ecologically stable, undisturbed environment. When the land has been disturbed, the plants proceed through a succession phase before eventually evolving back into a climax state.

Diagram 2 shows the relationship between various types of vegetation during succession. Because of the severe climate and short growing season in the Rockies, successional vegetation patterns may persist for more than a hundred years. In addition, a single hillside may be covered with successional vegetation in one place and climax vegetation in another.

Riparian Vegetation: This is the vegetation found along stream banks, and it plays a variety of important roles, such as controlling erosion and providing cover and feed for wildlife. On the Western Slope, the area of Colorado on the western side of the Continental Divide, lower-elevation stream banks are dominated by a variety of trees, primarily cottonwood, alder, maple, and red osier dogwood. With increasing elevation, the cottonwoods become less evident, while the shrubs persist, eventually becoming dominated by willows. East of the Divide, cottonwoods are not as evident, but, as on the Western Slope, a mixture of shrubs prevails, becoming increasingly dominated by willows at higher elevations.

Despite what appears to be very aggressive growth by riparian species, they are among the most sensitive to human activity. And because of their proximity to water, they are typically among the most threatened and endangered.

Sagebrush: Sagebrush, common to the cold, dry desert scrubland of the Rockies, is found from low to surprisingly high elevations. Interspersed with grasses, it predominates the primary grazing land of central and western Colorado.

Scrub Oak and Piñon-Juniper Woodland: This dryland plant community is most evident on The Colorado Trail where it climbs through the foothills above Denver. It also is seen occasionally at higher elevations, on the driest and most stressed sites, as the trail approaches Kenosha Pass. Junipers tend to be widely spaced, interspersed by grasses, while scrub oak tends to clump together so closely as to be almost impenetrable.

Forest in Segment 12, CT Collegiate East. Photo by David Dolton

This vegetation makes for good game habitat, and hikers should be prepared for deer to pop up almost anywhere, particularly in early June. In late summer, this woodland is prone to wildfire, which can move rapidly through dry terrain. Such fires are often started by lightning strikes, and occasionally by hikers, who are reminded to pay attention to their campfires.

Ponderosa Pine: This is the lowest-elevation timber tree. Because of its good lumber quality and proximity to civilization, it has been the most extensively cut. Thus you may see large old ponderosa stumps among woodland vegetation, indicating a logged ponderosa forest where the tall pines have not yet returned. These long-needled pines tend to grow well spaced, with grasses flourishing in between. As a result, ranchers like to graze their stock among ponderosa, particularly in early spring. On the East Slope, ponderosa pine is found on less-stressed south-facing hillsides. On the Western Slope, it is encountered above the open, arid countryside of the sagebrush community.

Douglas Fir: Though related, this predominant tree is not to be confused with the giant firs of the Pacific Northwest. In the Rockies, these are the runts of the litter. The Douglas fir occupies moist, cool sites. East of the Divide, these trees are found on the slopes opposite of ponderosa pine, and on the Western Slope they grow above the level of the ponderosa. In both regions, Douglas fir tend to grow closer together with little ground cover underneath. Because Douglas fir is the tree type most likely to burn, much of its habitat is occupied by successional vegetation.

Spruce-Fir Forest: This, the highest-elevation forest, is composed of Engelmann spruce and subalpine fir. Because of the late snowmelt, moist summertime conditions, and early snowfall, this vegetation has been the least altered by fire. Many of the spruce-fir forests in the Rockies are 400 years old. These dense forests tend to contain many fallen logs, which can be a real deterrent to hiking. The logs are typically moist, and hikers walking over them may be surprised when the bark slips off and they lose their footing. Ground cover may be lacking and a thick humus layer may be present.

Approaching timberline, the spruce-fir stands tend to be more open. The trees are clustered, with grasses and beautiful wildflowers interspersed between. These clusters provide refuge for elk at night. At timberline, the trees are bushlike, weather-beaten, and windshorn. They often grow in very dense clumps, which can provide ideal refuge for hikers. Animals are aware of this, too, and thus, while waiting out a storm, you may have the pleasure of observing a great deal of small mammal activity.

Lodgepole Pine and Aspen: These are ordinarily successional species that can occupy a given site for up to 200 years. The lodgepole pine often succeeds disturbed Douglas fir and spruce-fir communities and grows on the driest sites. Its seeds are opened by fire. A wildfire will cause the deposition of thousands of seeds, and, a few years later, dense stands of seedlings and saplings appear. There is virtually no ground cover in the deep shade beneath the saplings and competition is fierce between the closely spaced trees. The dryness of such sites encourages repeated fires.

Aspens occupy moister sites. A clump of aspen among lodgepole pines suggests a potential source of water. Aspens reproduce from root suckers, and any ground disturbance such as a fire causes a multitude of saplings to appear. On drier sites aspens are typically interspersed with Thurber fescue, a large bunchgrass. In moderately moist sites, the ground cover will consist of a multitude of grasses, forbs, and shrubs. In wet aspen sites, ground cover is often dominated by bracken fern.

Alpine Tundra: Though it strikes many people as odd, the tundra can be likened to a desert because it sees only minimal precipitation. During winters, fierce winds prevent snow from accumulating in depth anywhere except in depressions. During summers, the snowmelt drains quickly off the steeper slopes, leaving the vegetation to depend on regular afternoon showers for survival.

Despite the harsh conditions, alpine tundra is quite diverse, and includes such different environments as meadows, boulder fields, fell fields, talus, and both temporary and permanent ponds. The cushionlike meadows are a favorite site for elk herds. Boulder fields are home to pikas, marmots, and other animals, and the protected spaces between the boulders can produce some of the most beautiful wildflowers. Fell fields are windswept sites from which virtually all mineral soil has been blown away, leaving behind a "pavement" that, despite its austerity, can produce some interesting plants. Talus fields consist of loose rock, and also host some interesting plants and animals. Tundra ponds often teem with invertebrates and are good sites for observing the fascinating bird known as the ptarmigan.

WILDFLOWERS

Who can resist the elegant grace of Colorado's state flower, the blue columbine, or not be moved by nature's showy display blanketing the slopes astride The Colorado Trail in mid-summer? There are hundreds of species of flowering plants of conspicuous varieties (actually thousands, including inconspicuous plants such as grasses and sedges) along the CT as it winds its way through all five of the major Colorado lifezones.

The diversity of plant life is spectacular in the Colorado mountains. Photo by Felecia Moran

Lifezones are delineated by elevation and are defined by their unique ecosystems and plant communities. Beginning on the margin of the high plains at 5,800 feet at Waterton Canyon (Segment 1), The Colorado Trail climbs to a lofty 13,264 feet on the slopes of Coney Summit (Segment 22). In the process, it ascends through these lifezones: plains (3,500–6,000 feet), foothills (6,000–8,000 feet), montane (8,000–10,000 feet), sub-alpine (10,000–11,500 feet), and alpine (11,500–14,400 feet). An alert hiker will notice the progression of plant communities along the way, which is driven by changes in climate, soil chemistry, snow accumulation, and other factors.

As the season unfolds, the colorful pageantry climbs up the slopes along with The Colorado Trail hiker. A Durango-bound thru-traveler starting among late-May blooming cactus and the bright, spring-green slopes in Waterton Canyon will reach tree line at Georgia Pass still blanketed by snow. But by the time hikers climb atop Indian Trail Ridge near the end of their trek in mid-July, they will stroll through the tundra carpeted with an incredibly colorful display of alpine flowers.

The next two pages offer a sampling of some of the more common wildflowers prevalent in each of the six sections of The Colorado Trail delineated in this guide. In general, each section has characteristics that dictate the types of flowering plants a trail user may encounter. However, most of these plants are not unique to any one portion of the CT and may be found in any suitable habitat along the trail. (For

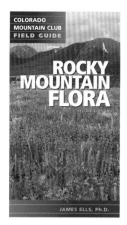

Left: A trekker identifies wildflowers in Segment 20. Photo by Don Wallace **Right:** *Rocky Mountain Flora*

instance, the many species and subspecies of Indian paintbrush exist throughout the state in a variety of habitats.)

Each plant listed here is identified by one of its common names, along with its scientific name. A plant can have several different common names, often varying by region, and the existence of a myriad of subspecies can frustrate precise identification for the amateur. You'll need to get a good hand lens for close examination of biological features as well as an excellent flower guide for Colorado plants. *Rocky Mountain Flora* by James Ells (Colorado Mountain Club Press) is an excellent field guide with more than 1,200 color photos.

Left: Lush flowering bluebells in Segment 24 sparkling with morning dew. Photo by Roger Forman **Middle:** Pasqueflower. Photo by Joe Brummer **Right:** Globeflower. Photo by Lori Brummer

The Natural History of The Colorado Trail

Red columbine. Photo by Lori Brummer

▨▨▨ Waterton Canyon TH to Kenosha Pass (SEGMENTS 1–5)

Most of this section is at lower elevations. Plants from the plains zone merge in Platte Canyon with foothills zone residents. Blooms begin as early as late April and extend well into June. Look for prickly pear cactus (*Opuntia macrorhiza*), yucca (*Yucca glauca*), tiny filaree (*Erodium caepitosa*), and showy prickly poppy (*Argemone polyanthemos*). The dry, gravelly soils beyond the canyon support sand lily (*Leucocrinum montanum*), while you may find pasqueflower (*Anemone patens*) in the damp ravines. Close to Kenosha Pass, wild iris (*Iris missouriensis*) bursts forth in the meadows of South Park.

▨▨▨ Kenosha Pass to Mount Massive TH (SEGMENTS 6–10)

Most southbound thru-travelers cross the high passes of the Continental Divide and Tenmile Range too early for most flowers to appear. Look, however, for sweet-smelling alpine forget-me-not (*Eritrichium elongatum*) and alpine spring beauty (*Claytonia megarhiza*) in the fell fields and rock crevices. As the snow melts along the trail, snow buttercup (*Ranunculus adoneus*) and globeflower (*Trollius albiflorus*) spring out of retreating snowbanks. Once in the shadow of Mount Massive, alpine wallflower (*Erysimum capitatum*) and Ryberg penstemon (*Penstemon rydbergii*) are common.

Elephantheads. Photo by Bill Manning

Mount Massive TH to Marshall Pass (SEGMENTS 11–15)

In this section, The Colorado Trail runs largely through thick montane forests, alternating between rather barren lodgepole stands and some lovely aspen forests. In aspen glens and forest clearings, tall heart-leaved arnica (*Arnica cordifolia*), larkspur (*Delphinium nuttallianum*), red columbine (*Aquilegia elegantula*), and monkshood (*Aconitum columbianum*) rise above the undergrowth. Sharing the sunny benches above reservoirs with the ubiquitous sage are shrubby cinquefoil (*Pentaphylloides floribunda*) and rabbitbrush (*Chrysothamnus nauseosus*). The latter is a late bloomer and harbinger of fall.

Marshall Pass to San Luis Pass (SEGMENTS 16–20)

On this high, lonely section along the Divide, the midsummer wildflowers are a cheerful companion to the CT hiker. Grasses and sedges dominate the sweeping ridgetop panoramas, punctuated by alpine sunflower (*Rydbergia grandiflora*), with its huge heads turned to the rising sun, and the more understated American bistort (*Bistorta bistortoides*). Farther west, the Divide rises to true alpine tundra near San Luis Peak, and the slopes are carpeted with dwarf plants like alpine avens (*Acomastylis rossii turbinata*), alpine phlox (*Phlox condensata*), and moss campion (*Silene acaulis subacaulescens*).

Left: Kingscrown. Photo by Lori Brummer **Right:** Alpine sunflower. Photo by Joe Brummer

San Luis Pass to Junction Creek Trailhead (SEGMENTS 21–28)

For the southbound thru-traveler, the best is saved for last. West of Molas Pass, The Colorado Trail enters a verdant landscape of rolling mountains, rising above lush subalpine meadows and culminating in mid-July in spectacular displays on Indian Trail Ridge. Blue columbine (*Aquilegia coerulea*), wild geranium (*Geranium caespitosum*), and silky phacelia (*Phaecelia sericea*) nod in the breeze. Along the rushing streams, monkeyflower (*Mimulus guttatus*), Parry primrose (*Primula parryi*), and kingscrown (*Rhodiola integriflia*) dip roots in cold melt water.

Collegiate West, Twin Lakes to South Fooses Ridge (SEGMENTS CW01–CW05)

Look for these wildflower varieties as you pass through this newest addition to the CT: the purple-hued elephant heads (*Pedicularis groenlandica*) (you may be lucky enough to spot the less common white variety as well); rose paintbrush (*Castilleja rhexifolia*), which are quite common and come in several varieties and colors; glacial daisy (*Erigeron glacialis*), with its lavender petals with yellow centers; and the purple Hall's penstemon (*Penstemon hallii*).

GEOLOGY ALONG THE COLORADO TRAIL

By Jack Reed

A GEOLOGIC CHRONICLE

The diverse collage of landscapes traversed by The Colorado Trail is the result of the complex geologic history of western Colorado. At first the ages and types of rocks along the trail seem almost random, but if we study them carefully and try to decipher their stories, we find that they record a fascinating chronicle of geologic events that began 1.8 billion years ago and continue today. They tell of the slow shift of continents, the rise and destruction of mountain ranges, the ebb and flow of ancient seas, and the tireless work of wind, water, and glacial ice in shaping the ever-changing landscape. The geologic story of the rocks along the trail can be condensed into eight major chapters.

Typical outcropping of Pikes Peak granite in Segment 3. Photo by Julie Vida and Mark Tabb

CHAPTER 1: The Basement Rocks

The oldest rocks in the Colorado mountains are metamorphic and igneous rocks, the oldest of which formed between 1.8 and 1.6 billion years ago during the consolidation of the part of the continental plate that ultimately would include Colorado. Those rocks are collectively called "basement rocks" because they formed first and underlie all of the other rocks of the region.

The metamorphic rocks are chiefly gneiss and schist derived from volcanic and sedimentary rocks that were subjected to high temperatures and enormous pressure during burial to depths as great as eight miles below the surface. The metamorphic rocks were intruded by extensive bodies of granite several times: once when they were being metamorphosed, once about 1.4 billion years ago, and once again about 1.1 billion years ago. Basement rocks are exposed along the CT, particularly in the Front Range, the Sawatch Range, and the Needle Mountains.

CHAPTER 2: Rocks of the Western Seas

Following their formation, the basement rocks were uplifted and eroded to a nearly flat land surface. Then, about 515 million years ago during the early part of the Paleozoic Era, the western edge of North America began to subside and shallow seas flooded eastward onto the continent.

Eroded formations of volcanic air-fall ash near Snow Mesa in Segment 21.
Photo by Aaron Locander

As those seas ebbed and flowed across the Colorado region for the next 150 million years or so, extensive, relatively thin layers of sandstone, shale, and limestone were deposited within them. The CT crosses those beds in only a few places, once in Segment 9 just before Tennessee Pass and again in Segments 24 and 25 near Molas Pass, but they are spectacularly exposed in Glenwood Canyon.

CHAPTER 3: The Ancestral Rocky Mountains, the Mountains No One Knew

About 320 million years ago in the late Paleozoic Era, plate tectonic movement brought North America together with South America and Africa. One of the results of that collision was the uplift of great mountain ranges in the Colorado

Sloping beds of sedimentary rocks at Section Point along Segment 26. Photo by Nate Hebenstreit

region. Those ancestral ranges were probably just as rugged as our modern Rocky Mountains, but their bases lay at or near sea level.

As those ancient mountains rose, the early Paleozoic sedimentary rocks that once blanketed the basement were stripped by erosion, and debris from the rising mountains was swept into basins between the ranges where it accumulated to thicknesses of thousands of feet. The peaks that formed those Ancestral Rocky Mountains are now completely gone, but the thick layers of red conglomerate, sandstone, and shale that were deposited in the basins that flanked them are now widely exposed and make up some of the most spectacular modern ranges. You can see them near the start of the CT on the eastern flank of the Front Range, in Segment 8 between Copper Mountain and Tennessee Pass, and in Segments 25–28 between Molas Pass and Junction Creek.

CHAPTER 4: The Great Cretaceous Seaway

Following the leveling of the Ancestral Rockies, extensive layers of sandstone and shale were deposited across their eroded stumps. Those rocks were originally laid down as windblown desert sands, and as sand and mud along sluggish streams and in shallow lakes. Then, about 100 million years ago in the Cretaceous Period of the Mesozoic Era, waters of a great seaway that covered much of central North America began to spread westward across the future site of Colorado. Sand from the beaches that flanked the advancing seaway formed what is now called the Dakota Sandstone.

Chalk Cliffs at the south end of Segment 13. The cliffs are not actually chalk, but 34 million-year-old granite altered by hot springs waters. Photo by Carl Brown

As the water deepened, thick deposits of black mud accumulated and are now preserved as thousands of feet of black shale that overlie the Dakota Sandstone. Seaway deposits are exposed along the CT only on the ridges north of Swan River in the western part of Segment 6. Some of the deposits that immediately predated the seaway cap the high ridge that the CT follows in Segments 27 and 28.

CHAPTER 5: The Laramide Orogeny

As the Cretaceous seaway was beginning to withdraw about 75 million years ago, the first stirrings of the Laramide Orogeny began. This was the episode of mountain building that laid the foundations for most of the present mountain ranges. Plate movements along the western edge of the continent began to buckle the Earth's crust, raising domes and elongate welts, most of which were bounded by folds or faults along which slabs of rock were moved several miles relative to the rocks beneath them.

During the orogeny, extensive bodies of granite and porphyry (a light-colored, fine-grained rock studded with large rectangular crystals of feldspar) intruded both the basement rocks and the overlying sedimentary strata. Many of those intrusions took place along the Colorado Mineral Belt, a northeast-to-southwest trending belt that extends from the western San Juan Mountains to the Front Range near Boulder and contains most of the important gold and silver mining camps in Colorado.

Erosion began to attack the uplifts as soon as they began to rise, carving mountain ranges from the more resistant rocks and depositing debris in the intervening basins. Uplift continued for as long as 30 million years, but as it waned erosion largely reduced the Laramide mountains to low rounded hills and a few low mountains separated by flat, sediment-filled basins. Parts of this post-Laramide landscape are preserved today, particularly in the area where the CT crosses the Front Range.

CHAPTER 6: The Great Volcanic Flare-Up

Igneous activity dwindled after the Laramide Orogeny, but about 36 million years ago, during development of the subdued post-Laramide landscape, it resumed with a vengeance. Volcanoes spewed huge volumes of lava, volcanic ash, and related deposits over large parts of the post-Laramide landscape, and many bodies of granite and porphyry were emplaced at depth beneath them. Those eruptions continued for about 10 million years, from the Eocene into the Oligocene Epoch of the Tertiary Period. Most of the San Juan Mountains are carved from a remnant of the extensive volcanic field that was built during that time.

CHAPTER 7: Uplift and Erosion

The penultimate episode in the shaping of the present mountain landscape began about 26 million years ago during the late Oligocene Epoch, when the tectonic forces that had compressed and shortened the Earth's crust during the Laramide changed direction and began to pull the crust apart. As the crust extended, a number of faults developed. The most significant are the faults bounding the Rio Grande Rift, which is a series of fault-bounded basins that extends southward from Leadville through

Left: Conglomerate boulder in CT Segment 25. Photo by Linda Jeffers **Right:** Redbeds along Indian Trail Ridge in Segment 27. Photo by Jesse Swift and Bill Turner

View of Lake San Cristobal and Slumgullion Slide showing the curved river valley that follows the outer wall of the Lake City caldera. At left, Red Mountain is in a lava dome within the caldera. Courtesy of Colorado Mountain Expeditions

the Upper Arkansas and San Luis valleys, and through New Mexico all the way to El Paso, Texas. Some of those faults are still active today.

Development of the faults was accompanied by regional uplift of the post-Laramide landscape, which originally stood only a few thousand feet above sea level, to its present elevation of 8,000 to more than 10,000 feet. During this uplift, which may still be continuing, all of the major canyons were incised into the post-Laramide surface, and the present mountain ranges were carved from the uplifted roots of the Laramide mountains and from the volcanic rocks of the San Juan volcanic field. During erosion, the more resistant rocks, such as the basement rocks, some of the sedimentary rocks from the Ancestral Rockies, the younger granite and porphyry, and some of the volcanic rocks, tended to form mountains, whereas softer, less-resistant rocks formed valleys and basins.

CHAPTER 8: The Ice Ages

Most of the erosion of the uplifted roots of the Laramide mountains was the work of the weathering of the rocks and the removal of material by streams and rivers. In the last 2 million years, however, since the advent of the Quaternary Epoch, glaciers have played a major role in the developing mountain landscape. Although there were several earlier periods of glaciation in the Colorado mountains, the principal glacial advances that shaped the present landscape were the Bull Lake glaciation, between about 170,000 and 120,000 years ago, and the Pinedale glaciation, between about 30,000 and 12,000 years ago. They carved the spectacular glacial amphitheaters, gouged out the U-shaped glacial valleys, deposited the conspicuous moraines, and shaped the basins that hold many of the jewel-like mountain lakes.

SOURCES AND ADDITIONAL READING

Blair, Rob. "Origin of Landscapes." In *The Western San Juan Mountains: Their Geology, Ecology, and Human History*, edited by Rob Blair, 3–17. Niwot, CO: University Press of Colorado, 1996.

Hopkins, Ralph Lee, and Lindy Birkel Hopkins. *Hiking Colorado's Geology*. Seattle, WA: The Mountaineers, 2000.

Mathews, Vincent, ed. *Messages in Stone: Colorado's Colorful Geology*. 2nd ed. Denver, CO: Colorado Geological Survey, 2009.

Raup, Omer B. *Colorado Geologic Highway Map*. 1:1,000,000 scale. Denver, CO: Colorado Geological Survey, 1991.

Reed, Jack, and Gene Ellis. *Rocks Above the Clouds: A Hiker's and Climber's Guide to Colorado Mountain Geology*. Colorado Mountain Club Press, Golden CO, 2009.

Tweto, Ogden. *Geologic Map of Colorado*. 1:500,000 scale. US Geological Survey, 1979.

Williams, Felicie, and Halka Chronic. *Roadside Geology of Colorado*. 2nd ed. Missoula, MT: Mountain Press, 2002.

Red Mountain and neighboring peaks in the Lake City caldera near Segment 22. Photo by Roger Forman

SEGMENT 1

Waterton Canyon Trailhead to South Platte River Trailhead

Waterton Canyon and the South Platte River. Photo by Chris Voisinet

Distance	16.5 miles
Elevation Gain	Approx. 2,830 feet
Elevation Loss	Approx. 2,239 feet
USFS Maps	Pike National Forest
The CT Databook, 8th Edition	Pages 10–11
The CT Map Book	Pages 9–10
Trails Illustrated Maps	No. 135, 1202
Jurisdiction	South Platte Ranger District, Pike National Forest

ACCESS FROM
DENVER END

ACCESS FROM
DURANGO END

AVAILABILITY
OF WATER

BICYCLING

ABOUT THIS SEGMENT: The first segment of The Colorado Trail begins at the Waterton Canyon Trailhead on the South Platte River. The trail follows a well-maintained dirt road for the first 6.6 miles, climbing an average of 63 feet per mile. There are mileage signs every half-mile. Enjoy the moderate walking and biking—it won't last for long! The canyon was carved in 1.7 billion-year-old metamorphic rocks from the Front Range uplift during the Laramide Orogeny.

Because of its proximity to the Denver metro area, this is by far the busiest section of The Colorado Trail. In spite of its popularity, this portion of the trail is very enjoyable, offering the potential for spotting deer and bighorn sheep that scramble along the canyon walls. Since this road is used by the Denver Water Board to access Strontia Springs Dam, there are several restrictions: Motor vehicle access is limited to official vehicles, no dogs are allowed on this stretch of trail, and there is no camping until after the single-track trail begins at **mile 6.7**. The road is open from a half-hour before sunrise to a half-hour after sunset.

Lenny's Rest at **mile 7.9** is a great place to stop for lunch or a snack after the first challenging climb on the CT. There are nice displays of wildflowers, including Colorado's state flower, the blue columbine, along the small creeks and in the drainages the trail passes.

The best camping in Segment 1 is found along Bear Creek at **mile 8.7**. There are several good spots available there. Once past the creek, however, there are few good

Bighorn sheep are often seen in Waterton Canyon, where their habitat is protected. Photo by Sean Riley

A volunteer improves a water diversion to stem trail erosion. Photo by Bill Manning

sites. Plan your day with this in mind. If you do plan to continue beyond this point, be aware that the next reliable water source is nearly 8 miles away when you reach the South Platte River again.

Trail users who want to travel with their dogs will be happy to know that the first 6.6 miles of Segment 1 is the only stretch of the CT where dogs are prohibited, although the first practical point to join the CT with dogs is at Lenny's Rest, **mile 7.9**, via the Indian Creek start to the CT (see sidebar on page 76).

The Waterton Canyon road is occasionally closed to all recreational use for maintenance and other reasons. During road closure periods, trail users can consider the Indian Creek start to the CT (see sidebar on page 76) or begin their CT travels at the start of Segment 2 at the South Platte River Trailhead.

TRAILHEAD/ACCESS POINTS

Waterton Canyon Trailhead: Take I-25 south out of Denver to the C-470 exit. Go west on C-470 for 12.5 miles and take the Wadsworth Boulevard (CO Highway 121) exit. Go left (south) on Wadsworth for 4.5 miles, then turn left onto Waterton Canyon Road. Continue 0.3 mile to the large trailhead parking area on the left. If this parking area is full, there is another parking area a quarter mile north up the road. It is connected to the lower parking lot by a trail.

Indian Creek Trailhead (Alternate Segment 1 Start): From the intersection of Highways 85 and 67 in Sedalia, south of Denver, go southeast on CO Highway 67 for 10.3 miles, paved most of the way and then gravel. Turn right for the Indian Creek Trailhead. The trailhead is a day-use fee area with limited parking that fills up frequently, particularly on weekends. Overnight parking is limited to 10 days and payment of the daily fee is required for each day a vehicle is parked, making it unsuitable for long-term parking. There is also a fee campground near the trailhead. Separate trailhead and campground facilities are also available for equestrians.

South Platte River Trailhead: See Segment 2 on page 81.

VIEWING BIGHORN SHEEP

The Rocky Mountain bighorn sheep, the state mammal, is a fitting symbol of Colorado. With their massive curving horns, rams present a majestic silhouette that matches the grandeur of their rugged surroundings. Waterton Canyon is home to a band of bighorn that has been increasingly threatened by encroaching human activities.

Bighorns in Waterton Canyon present an opportunity for photographers.
Photo by Mike Bollinger

The Waterton band is unusual because of its existence at such a low elevation and so close to a major city. Before human settlement, however, bighorns often wintered in the foothills and even ventured out onto the plains. Today, they are found mostly at higher elevations, often near or above tree line, usually avoiding forested country and civilization.

Bighorn are susceptible to lungworm and pneumonia, the spread of which appears to be tied to the stress of human pressure. Also, traditional routes to salt licks, important to the animals' mineral requirements, are being cut off. The construction of the Strontia Springs Dam in the 1980s severely impacted the Waterton band, which has recovered somewhat since then.

Visitors frequently spot the sheep, sometimes right along the service road. CT users should not harry, startle, or attempt to feed the animals. Trail users have several chances to view this magnificent animal along the CT, usually near or at tree line in open, rolling terrain, such as along the Continental Divide in Segments 15 and 16, and then again in the La Garita and Weminuche Wilderness Areas.

SERVICES, SUPPLIES, AND ACCOMMODATIONS: Denver and its suburbs have a full array of services.

TRAIL DESCRIPTION: The Colorado Trail begins across the road from the parking lot on Waterton Canyon Road at **mile 0.0.** Continue past the interpretive display and through another parking area that is closed to the public. Bear right at a fork in the road at **mile 0.4,** staying on the main dirt road for the next 6.2 miles. There is no camping permitted along this stretch of trail and dogs are not allowed.

> **(!) WARNING:** Camping is *not* permitted within sight of the river along the first 7 miles of Segment 1. Dogs are also prohibited on the Denver Water Board Road, and trail users with dogs will need to use alternate access through Indian Creek.

At **mile 6.2**, the Bighorn Sheep Rest Area provides a view of Strontia Springs Dam and a vault toilet. The CT bears to the left. Go straight at the intersection with a side road on the left that is the Roxborough Connection Trail at **mile 6.4**. This trail provides another alternate start to the CT from Roxborough State Park but only for hikers, as dogs, bikes, and horses are not allowed on trails within the Park. At **mile 6.6**, where the main road curves sharply to the right, leave the main road and go left onto an old roadbed. At **mile 6.7**, bear to the left and follow the single-track trail. The trail begins to climb more steeply from here.

The first potential campsite is at **mile 7.0**, but it is small and does not have a nearby water source. The trail continues climbing, following a series of switchbacks until reaching a bench known as Lenny's Rest at **mile 7.9**. There is a junction here with a connector trail leading to the Indian Creek Trail and Trailhead, which provides an alternate start to Segment 1 that can be used by all trail users. The trail then descends, crossing Bear Creek at **mile 8.7**. This is the last reliable water source for nearly 8 miles until the end of Segment 1 at the South Platte River. There are several good campsites in this area.

At **mile 10.0** the CT begins to parallel and then occasionally cross seasonal West Bear Creek. There is a good, dry campsite at **mile 11.8** near leaning rocks.

The trail continues climbing to a ridge at **mile 12.7**, the segment's highest point. From here, the CT descends nearly 4 miles to reach County Road 97 and the South Platte River Trailhead, the end of Segment 1, at **mile 16.5**.

Camping is prohibited at the trailhead and near the river and the trail, but there is some camping potential on the grassy slopes before reaching the trailhead. Look for markers designating approved dispersed campsites, or if selecting a site without a marker, make sure that it is at least 200 feet from the trail, the road, and the river and that "No Camping" signs don't prohibit camping at that location.

INDIAN CREEK ALTERNATE SEGMENT 1 START

HIKING TIPS

From the Indian Creek Trailhead, travel west and downhill on FS Road 513.A (also Indian Creek Trail) to the equestrian trailhead and campground. Continue on the single-track Indian Creek Trail departing from the end of the road loop at **mile 0.3**. Reach Bear Creek at mile 1.2, where there is camping potential over the next ¾-mile. At **mile 1.9**, cross a powerline right-of-way, then begin climbing to a forested ridge and follow the ridge for about a mile. At **mile 4.1**, turn left onto the Colorado Trail Connection Trail and follow it for 0.3 mile to reach Lenny's Rest, **mile 7.9** of CT Segment 1.

WATERTON CANYON

A favorite with hikers, bicyclists, anglers, birders, and others, Waterton Canyon can be a sometimes crowd-filled beginning to a 486-mile trek through the heart of the Colorado Rockies. The Colorado Trail follows a Denver Water Board service road for the first 6.6 miles, itself once a roadbed for the Denver South Park & Pacific Railroad, built in 1877.

Water was the driving force in the development of the canyon. Explorer Stephen Long, an Army major charged with finding the headwaters of the Platte

Strontia Springs Dam. Photo by Lawton "Disco" Grinter

River, camped here in 1820. Years later, the town of Waterton sprang up, serving as headquarters for the Denver Water Board's decades-long effort to harness the resource for the thirsty city that was developing on the plains nearby. Near the mouth of the canyon is the Kassler Treatment Plant, a national landmark noted for its technologically advanced slow-sand filtration system. Farther up the road, you can see the original diversion dam for the 140-year-old High Line Canal, a 71-mile irrigation canal that snakes its way through the Denver metro area. Other diversion dams also take water from the Platte to Marston Reservoir, a few miles to the north.

At **mile 6.2**, the 243-foot-high Strontia Springs Dam soars above the river. Finished in 1983, its 1.7-mile-long reservoir and extensive tunnel system tie together elements of the huge metro-area water delivery network.

If water developers had had their way, an even more immense reservoir, Two Forks, would have been built upstream, threatening the canyon and inundating a portion of the CT. The proposal was defeated in 1990, and for now, once past the dam, civilization is left behind and the canyon remains much as Stephen Long must have found it, with fir and pine sheltering the slopes and elusive bighorn sheep often seen on the crags.

Blisters are common for hikers, especially early in Waterton where a flat walk allows a brisk pace. Be sure to treat any "hot spots" early with moleskin or leukotape to prevent nagging injuries.

 TRAVEL TIPS

If you are a thru-traveler, you need to make sure your **gear** is in top shape. Although this guide points out towns along the way for resupply, they are few and far between. Carry spares of small, critical items.

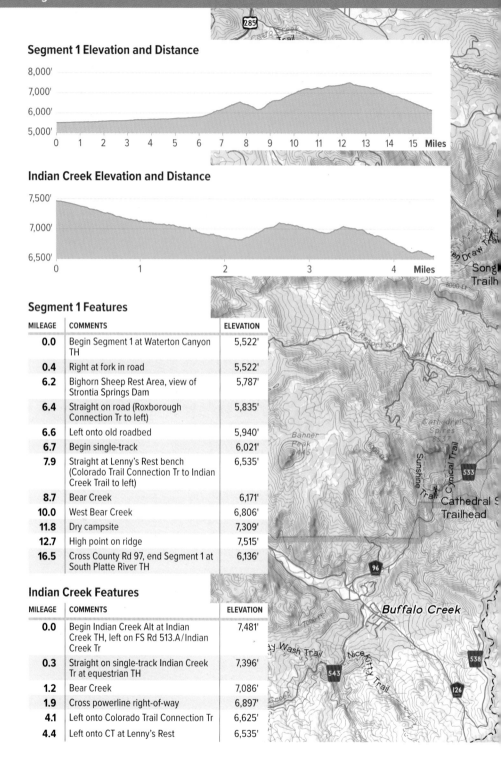

Segment 1 Elevation and Distance

Indian Creek Elevation and Distance

Segment 1 Features

MILEAGE	COMMENTS	ELEVATION
0.0	Begin Segment 1 at Waterton Canyon TH	5,522'
0.4	Right at fork in road	5,522'
6.2	Bighorn Sheep Rest Area, view of Strontia Springs Dam	5,787'
6.4	Straight on road (Roxborough Connection Tr to left)	5,835'
6.6	Left onto old roadbed	5,940'
6.7	Begin single-track	6,021'
7.9	Straight at Lenny's Rest bench (Colorado Trail Connection Tr to Indian Creek Trail to left)	6,535'
8.7	Bear Creek	6,171'
10.0	West Bear Creek	6,806'
11.8	Dry campsite	7,309'
12.7	High point on ridge	7,515'
16.5	Cross County Rd 97, end Segment 1 at South Platte River TH	6,136'

Indian Creek Features

MILEAGE	COMMENTS	ELEVATION
0.0	Begin Indian Creek Alt at Indian Creek TH, left on FS Rd 513.A / Indian Creek Tr	7,481'
0.3	Straight on single-track Indian Creek Tr at equestrian TH	7,396'
1.2	Bear Creek	7,086'
1.9	Cross powerline right-of-way	6,897'
4.1	Left onto Colorado Trail Connection Tr	6,625'
4.4	Left onto CT at Lenny's Rest	6,535'

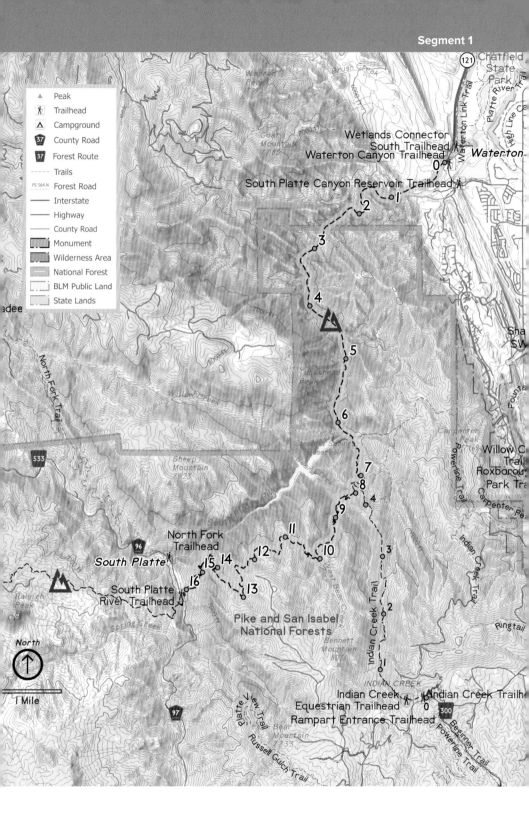

SEGMENT 2

South Platte River Trailhead
to Little Scraggy Trailhead

The evening sun illuminates Raleigh Peak. Photo by Bill Bloomquist

Distance	11.7 miles
Elevation Gain	Approx. 2,482 feet
Elevation Loss	Approx. 753 feet
USFS Map	Pike National Forest
The CT Databook, 8th Edition	Pages 12–13
The CT Map Book	Pages 10–11
Trails Illustrated Maps	No. 135, 1202
Jurisdiction	South Platte Ranger District, Pike National Forest

ACCESS FROM
DENVER END

ACCESS FROM
DURANGO END

AVAILABILITY
OF WATER

BICYCLING

> **TRAVEL TIP**
>
> When you reach the South Platte River (at the end of Segment 1),
> **fill up on water** because it is a long, dry climb to Top of the World ridge.
> This segment is relatively low in elevation and shade is scarce due to a
> wildfire in 1996. As a result, it can be brutally hot. Use your water carefully and hike early
> in the day when it is cooler.

> ⚠ **WARNING:** There is *emergency* drinking water available at an unmanned fire station a short walk north of where the CT first approaches County Road 126. There is a water faucet at the rear of the building. Fill your water bottle, *turn off the water*, and leave the area immediately.
> **One other caution:** Property owners along this segment tend to zealously guard their privacy. Don't trespass or park your vehicle on private land.

ABOUT THIS SEGMENT: As it crosses the South Platte River, the trail passes from metamorphic basement rocks into coarse-grained 1.1 billion-year-old Pikes Peak granite. This granite erodes to form spectacular spires, rounded domes, and smooth rocky faces. It decomposes into coarse, porous mineral soil that holds little water. Forests that grow on this dry loose soil are especially prone to wildfires.

The effects of the 1996 Buffalo Creek Fire are the dominating feature of Segment 2 and provide a great learning opportunity. The fire burned more than 12,000 acres and the impacts are still obvious. There are long stretches of the segment that have no shade because all of the trees were burned. The landscape is revegetating nicely, however, and many plants that love disturbances such as fire have taken hold. Keep your eyes open for paintbrush, buckwheat, yucca, and sunflowers, which bloom extensively in the summer.

It is imperative to be well prepared when heading into Segment 2. Users won't find water after the South Platte River until the faucet at the fire station building visible from the trail near **mile 10.0 and County** Road 126. The lack of trees exposes trail users to the direct sun, making the temperature feel much warmer than in a shaded forest. In addition, there is no camping allowed along the South Platte River and all campsites in Segment 2 are after starting the climb away from the river and will be dry. Keep this in mind when beginning the section. Carry plenty of water and hike early or late to avoid the heat of the day.

TRAILHEAD/ACCESS POINTS

South Platte River Trailhead: From the C-470–US Highway 285 interchange on the southwest side of the Denver area, drive southwest on US 285 for about 14 miles to the mountain town of Conifer. One-quarter mile past the end of town, exit the highway to your right, signed for Foxton Road. At the stop sign turn left on Foxton Road/County Road 97, proceed under the highway, follow the curve to the right, proceed 0.1 mile to a stop sign, and turn left. Proceed about 8 miles on Foxton Road/County Road 97 to a stop sign at an intersection with County Road 96. Turn left on County Road 96 and go 5.5 miles to the boarded-up South Platte Hotel.

Cross the bridge and the road becomes Douglas County Road 97. Seven-tenths of a mile on, you will see the Gudy Gaskill Bridge on the right. This is the South Platte River Trailhead, the start of Segment 2 of The Colorado Trail.

This trailhead also can be reached from the south via Woodland Park and north on CO Highway 67 to Deckers (a one-store town). Follow the river via CO 67, then County Road 97 to the trailhead.

Little Scraggy Trailhead: See Segment 3 on page 87.

TRAIL DESCRIPTION: Segment 2 begins by crossing the South Platte River on the 141-foot-long Gudy Gaskill Bridge, **mile 0.0**, the last water source for over 10 miles. Camping is not allowed at the trailhead or along the South Platte River, but numerous dry camping options can be found after **mile 0.7**. At the end of the bridge, the trail makes right turns and goes under the bridge along the river. Soon after, the trail veers right, leaving the river, and begins climbing steadily up several switchbacks. At **mile 1.1**, pass an abandoned quartz mine and enter the Buffalo Creek Fire area. Note how the forest is beginning to regenerate.

There are several good, dry campsites along the next stretch of the trail, including near a viewpoint between boulders at the top of a ridge at **mile 5.2**. From this scenic location, the Chair Rocks are visible to the west, Raleigh Peak (8,183') is about a mile to the southeast, and Long Scraggy Peak (8,812') is about 4 miles to the south.

After a slight downhill, the trail crosses Raleigh Peak Road at **mile 6.0**. Many potential dry campsites can be found in the next few miles. Continue left at **mile 6.2**, where a side trail leads right to Chair Rocks (0.6 mile one-way). After passing through forested sections, the trail then continues through the burned area. Near **mile 10,** the metal building that houses the unmanned fire station with an exterior water spigot is visible uphill and to the right. Turn sharply left at **mile 10.1** and parallel County Road 126 for the next 0.3 mile, crossing paved Spring Creek Trail and paved Spring Creek Road. Cross County Road 126 at **mile 10.4**, bypass a closed gate, and follow the gated road. Turn left at **mile 10.5** and continue on the dirt road. Many dry campsites can be found in the area, although the trail is very busy with mountain bikers and hikers from here through Segment 3.

Continue straight at two junctions with the Buffalo Burn Trail, one at **mile 10.6** and the second at **mile 11.5**. Segment 2 ends at **mile 11.7** when the trail reaches a large parking area at the Little Scraggy Trailhead on the left. There is a toilet and an information display here but no water. This trailhead is a Forest Service fee area. Camping is not allowed in the parking area, but is permissible outside this area in the vicinity of The Colorado Trail.

FIRE!

On May 18, 1996, the human-induced Buffalo Creek Fire burned nearly 12,000 acres of the Pike National Forest, including most of the western half of Segment 2, and nearly destroyed the small mountain community of Buffalo Creek. Following the wildfire, several torrential rainstorms swept the area, including one on July 12 that dumped almost 5 inches of rain on the denuded slopes, causing severe flash flooding. Two people died and millions of dollars in property damage occurred. Downstream, some 300,000 cubic yards of sediment were swept into Strontia Springs Reservoir and miles of habitat were lost along area creeks and rivers.

The fire burned the Top of the World Campground (permanently closed) and other features along the CT, dramatically changing the character of the landscape. Once a walk through pleasant pine forests, the CT in Segment 2 now has expansive views. Today, grasses and small plants are well established, but few trees survived the inferno, and it will be centuries before the area recovers to become a mature forest again.

It's little consolation to the victims, but a wildfire can be a good thing. Before human settlement, such fires occurred on a frequent basis,

Top: A hiker passes through a landscape recovering from fire. Photo by Andrew Skurka **Bottom:** Pincushion cactus in bloom. Photo by Bill Bloomquist

clearing out debris, rejuvenating the soil with nutrients, and keeping the amount of fuel low, which meant that rarely would a fire burn large or hot enough to destroy mature trees. Decades of fire suppression, and perhaps a decrease in logging, contributed to a disaster in the making. The Buffalo Creek area, in fact, is part of an almost continuous 2,500-square-mile swath of ponderosa pine forest that is primed for catastrophic fires, as was borne out only a few years later by the even more apocalyptic 138,000-acre Hayman Fire, which struck only a few miles to the south.

If there is an unintended boon for the CT hiker or rider, it is the vistas that have opened up in the area. The weathered domes of rough Pikes Peak granite—including the Cathedral Spires, Raleigh Peak, and Long Scraggy Peak—are striking sights from the trail. Early-season CT users are rewarded with acres of wildflowers in the opened-up slopes, including sand lily and paintbrush in the dry, gravelly areas and pasqueflower and spring beauty in the damper ravines.

BUFFALO CREEK

SERVICES, SUPPLIES, AND ACCOMMODATIONS

The town of Buffalo Creek, on County Road 126, is 3.2 miles north of the trail at **mile 10.1**. Once a whistle stop on the Denver, South Park & Pacific Railroad, the town survives with a few cabins, a small general store (unique!), a pay phone, and a Forest Service fire station.

Distance from CT: 3.2 miles
Elevation: 6,750 feet
Zip code: 80425
Area code: 303

Snacks/Post Office (limited hours)
J. W. Green Mercantile Co.
17706 County Road 96
(303) 838-5587

▲	Peak
🚶	Trailhead
⛺	Campground
37	County Road
37	Forest Route
-----	Trails
FS 564.N	Forest Road
——	Interstate
——	Highway
——	County Road
	Monument
	Wilderness Area
	National Forest
	BLM Public Land
	State Lands

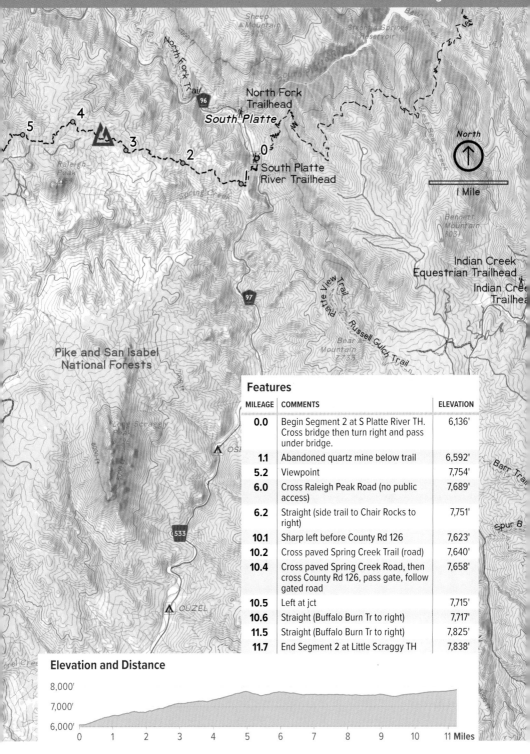

North Fork
Trailhead

South Platte

South Platte
River Trailhead

North Fork Trail

96

North

↑

I Mile

Sheep
Mountain

Strontia Springs
Reservoir

Raleigh
Peak

4

5

3

2

0
P

Bennett
Mountain

Spring Creek

Indian Creek
Equestrian Trailhead

Indian Creek
Trailhead

Platte View Trail

Russell Gulch Trail

Bear
Mountain

97

Pike and San Isabel
National Forests

Long Scraggy
Peak

OSP

533

OUZEL

Bear Trail

Spur B

Features

MILEAGE	COMMENTS	ELEVATION
0.0	Begin Segment 2 at S Platte River TH. Cross bridge then turn right and pass under bridge.	6,136'
1.1	Abandoned quartz mine below trail	6,592'
5.2	Viewpoint	7,754'
6.0	Cross Raleigh Peak Road (no public access)	7,689'
6.2	Straight (side trail to Chair Rocks to right)	7,751'
10.1	Sharp left before County Rd 126	7,623'
10.2	Cross paved Spring Creek Trail (road)	7,640'
10.4	Cross paved Spring Creek Road, then cross County Rd 126, pass gate, follow gated road	7,658'
10.5	Left at jct	7,715'
10.6	Straight (Buffalo Burn Tr to right)	7,717'
11.5	Straight (Buffalo Burn Tr to right)	7,825'
11.7	End Segment 2 at Little Scraggy TH	7,838'

Elevation and Distance

8,000'
7,000'
6,000'

0   1   2   3   4   5   6   7   8   9   10   11 **Miles**

SEGMENT 3
Little Scraggy Trailhead to Rolling Creek Trailhead

Granite outcrops good for camping and photo ops.
Photo by Bill Manning

Distance	12.5 miles
Elevation Gain	Approx. 1,975 feet
Elevation Loss	Approx. 1,549 feet
USFS Map	Pike National Forest
The CT Databook, 8th Edition	Pages 14–15
The CT Map Book	Pages 11–13
Trails Illustrated Maps	Nos. 105, 135, 1202
Jurisdiction	South Platte Ranger District, Pike National Forest

ACCESS FROM
DENVER END

ACCESS FROM
DURANGO END

AVAILABILITY
OF WATER

BICYCLING

ABOUT THIS SEGMENT: Segment 3 is very popular with mountain bikers and hikers due to its proximity to Denver and extensive network of interconnected trails. The pine and fir forests, along with many small creeks, make this segment quite inviting. In addition, winter snow usually melts by early spring, allowing for this segment to be accessible earlier than many of the higher portions of the CT. Trail users will appreciate the plentiful water sources and shaded portions of the trail after making it through the previous segment, which is very dry and often brutally hot. While most of this section is relatively flat, the climbs should not be taken for granted, especially considering the trail eclipses the 8,000-foot mark at the end of the segment.

TRAILHEAD/ACCESS POINTS

The beginning of Segment 3 has a parking lot and bathroom. There is a parking fee. Photo by Julie Vida and Mark Tabb

Little Scraggy Trailhead: From the C-470–US Highway 285 interchange on the southwest side of the Denver area, drive southwest on US 285 for approximately 21 miles to the traffic light in Pine Junction. Turn left (southeast) on County Road 126/Pine Valley Road and proceed approximately 9 miles, through the community of Pine, to the intersection with County Road 96/South Platte River Road. Continue 3.4 miles from the intersection, crossing the bridge over the South Platte River and passing through the community of Buffalo Creek, to the intersection with FS Road 550. This intersection is also one mile past Spring Creek Road. Turn right (west) on FS Road 550 and drive 0.1 mile to the trailhead. The Colorado Trail leaves the trailhead at the northwest end of the parking area. A daily fee is required each day to park a vehicle.

Rolling Creek Trailhead: See Segment 4 on page 93.

SERVICES, SUPPLIES, AND ACCOMMODATIONS: These amenities are available in Buffalo Creek, see Segment 2 on page 84, and in Bailey, see Segment 4 on page 95.

Mountain bikers love Segment 3, so if you are a hiker, talk loudly and often so bicyclists know you are there. If you are a cyclist, watch for hikers, especially around blind corners.

Little Scraggy has become a **popular trailhead**, especially on weekends. For a daily use fee, a toilet and picnic tables are provided, but there is no water available.

 TRAVEL TIPS

Aspen alight in the early morning.
Photo by Morgan and Robyn Wilkinson

TRAIL DESCRIPTION: Segment 3 begins at the Little Scraggy Trailhead next to the interpretive display at the northwest end of the parking area, **mile 0.0**. Head west on the trail. The CT and side trails in Segment 3 are part of the Buffalo Creek trails network popular with mountain bikers. At **mile 0.6**, the trail crosses FS Road 550, then passes the Shinglemill Trail at **mile 1.9**.

The trail crosses a small bridge over an intermittent stream with marginal camping at **mile 2.3**, then crosses Morrison Creek and a closed two-track with camping in the vicinity at **mile 3.0**. Pass the Little Scraggy Trail on the left at the top of a ridge at **mile 3.2**, then drop down and cross another small bridge over a stream at **mile 3.5**. Cross Tramway Creek at **mile 5.3**, where there are some good campsites. After crossing two more small streams at **miles 5.7** and **6.0**, pass the Green Mountain and Tramway Trails at a 4-way junction at **mile 6.3**. Cross a seasonal stream at **mile 6.6**. From here, the trail descends slightly to a junction at **mile 7.1**, where a side trail leads to Buffalo Creek Campground, a fee area about a quarter mile north. Go straight and continue on to another junction with the Green Mountain Trail at **mile 7.6**, where the CT turns downhill to the right.

At **mile 7.9**, cross a stream, then cross FS Road 543.F to the Meadows Group Campground shortly after. Veer left at **mile 8.0** where a connector trail to the Buffalo Trailhead continues straight ahead. After a pleasant section along Buffalo Creek,

BUFFALO CREEK RECREATION AREA

Trail users and the Forest Service have collaborated to establish a network of trails popular with cyclists on and around Segment 3 of the CT, designated as the **Buffalo Creek Recreation Area**. Due to the extensive trail network that connects to the CT, as well as its proximity to the Front Range, Segment 3 is one of the most heavily mountain biked sections of the CT, particularly on weekends.

The Monarch Crest Trail, coinciding with portions of Segments 15, 16, and CW05, from Monarch Pass to just south of Marshall Pass, can also be very busy with mountain bikers. Trail users may want to consider avoiding these sections on weekends, when possible, for greater trail enjoyment.

MOUNTAIN BIKING

MOUNTAIN BIKING

Bicyclists, the trail user group that travels the fastest, have sometimes been singled out, especially for their potentially startling interaction with other users. IMBA, the International Mountain Bicycling Association, has been a leader in making recommendations for responsible riding, including these useful tips:

- **Yield to Others and Pass with Courtesy:** Mountain bikers should yield to hikers and equestrians. Slow down when approaching other trail users and respectfully make others aware you are approaching. Pass with care and be prepared to stop if necessary.

Cyclists enjoy an extensive network of side trails in Segment 3. Photo by Peter Morales

- **Equestrians:** Because horses can spook easily and the chance for injury is high, use extra caution around equestrians. If you want to pass a horse, establish voice contact with the rider. Begin speaking with something like, "cyclists here, may we pass?" Your voice can calm both horse and rider, helping prevent horses from being spooked. Be prepared to stop until asked to proceed.
- **Ride Slowly on Crowded Trails:** Just like a busy highway, when trails are crowded you must move slowly to ensure safety for all trail users.
- **Say No to Mud:** Riding a muddy trail can cause unnecessary trail widening and erosion that may lead to long-lasting damage.
- **Respect the Trail, Wildlife, and Environment:** Be sensitive to the trail and its surroundings by riding softly and never skidding. Skidding through turns or while braking loosens trail soil and fosters trail erosion.

cross FS Road 543/Wellington Lake Road and the creek at **mile 8.2**. Turn sharply left at an intersection with Redskin Creek Trail at **mile 8.4**. Ahead is a shooting range south of the trail and it's common to hear shots; stay on the trail. The trail climbs to **mile 9.9**, where it crosses FS Road 550.C/Rifle Range Road, leading to the Camp Fickes Shooting Range. At **mile 12.1**, cross a small stream where there's good camping. After a short but steep climb, cross County Road 68/Wellington Lake Road and arrive at Rolling Creek Trailhead, the end of Segment 3 at **mile 12.5** .

The Lost Creek Wilderness Bike Detour begins here and rejoins the CT at the Rock Creek Trailhead midway through Segment 5. See page 96 for a description of the route.

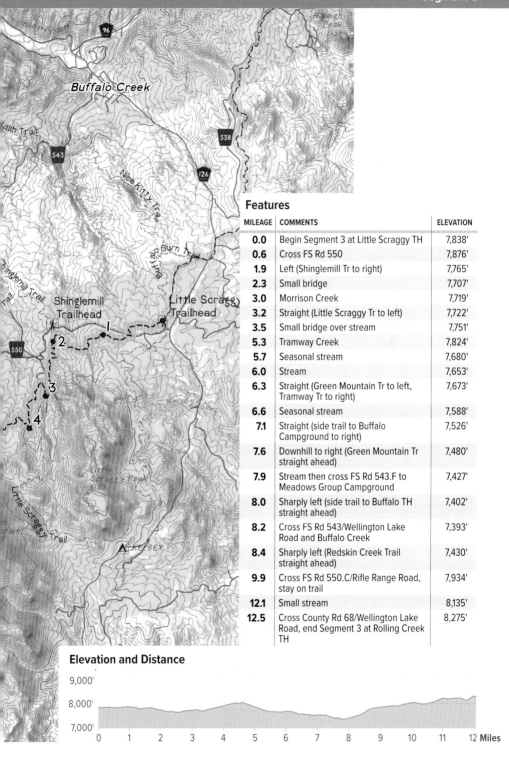

Features

MILEAGE	COMMENTS	ELEVATION
0.0	Begin Segment 3 at Little Scraggy TH	7,838'
0.6	Cross FS Rd 550	7,876'
1.9	Left (Shinglemill Tr to right)	7,765'
2.3	Small bridge	7,707'
3.0	Morrison Creek	7,719'
3.2	Straight (Little Scraggy Tr to left)	7,722'
3.5	Small bridge over stream	7,751'
5.3	Tramway Creek	7,824'
5.7	Seasonal stream	7,680'
6.0	Stream	7,653'
6.3	Straight (Green Mountain Tr to left, Tramway Tr to right)	7,673'
6.6	Seasonal stream	7,588'
7.1	Straight (side trail to Buffalo Campground to right)	7,526'
7.6	Downhill to right (Green Mountain Tr straight ahead)	7,480'
7.9	Stream then cross FS Rd 543.F to Meadows Group Campground	7,427'
8.0	Sharply left (side trail to Buffalo TH straight ahead)	7,402'
8.2	Cross FS Rd 543/Wellington Lake Road and Buffalo Creek	7,393'
8.4	Sharply left (Redskin Creek Trail straight ahead)	7,430'
9.9	Cross FS Rd 550.C/Rifle Range Road, stay on trail	7,934'
12.1	Small stream	8,135'
12.5	Cross County Rd 68/Wellington Lake Road, end Segment 3 at Rolling Creek TH	8,275'

Elevation and Distance

SEGMENT 4
Rolling Creek Trailhead to Long Gulch

Looking east down Long Gulch. Photo by Julie Vida and Mark Tabb

Distance	16.4 miles
Elevation Gain	Approx. 3,271 feet
Elevation Loss	Approx. 1,373 feet
USFS Map	Pike National Forest
The CT Databook, 8th Edition	Pages 16–17
The CT Map Book	Pages 13–15
Trails Illustrated Maps	No. 105, 1202
Jurisdiction	South Park and South Platte Ranger Districts, Pike National Forest

ACCESS FROM
DENVER END

ACCESS FROM
DURANGO END

AVAILABILITY
OF WATER

BICYCLING

See pages
96–97

Left: Mules are loaded with heavy culverts that volunteers will install to help keep the trail dry. **Right:** Volunteers improve one of many boggy sections in Long Gulch. Photos by Chuck Lawson

ABOUT THIS SEGMENT: Segment 4 enters the Lost Creek Wilderness shortly after the trail leaves the trailhead. At **mile 1.5**, the trail passes out of Pikes Peak granite and back into metamorphic rocks. There are abundant water sources and a lot of potential campsites along this section. The meadows along the North Fork of Lost Creek are great places to spot wildlife, including deer and bears. Be sure to keep your eyes and ears open!

The first half of this segment (and the first half of Segment 5) passes through the Lost Creek Wilderness, where bikes are not allowed. Mountain bikers rejoin the CT at the Rock Creek Trailhead, midway through Segment 5, at the end of the Lost Creek Wilderness Bike Detour. See page 96 for a description of the route.

TRAILHEAD/ACCESS POINTS

Rolling Creek Trailhead: 🚗 From the C-470–US Highway 285 interchange on the southwest side of the Denver area, drive southwest on US 285 for 27.5 miles to Bailey. Turn left and head southeast on County Road 68/Wellington Lake Road at the main intersection in town. After about 5 miles, you come to a Y in the road. Take the right branch, which continues as County Road 68. Two miles farther on, continue straight on County Road 68 at a 4-way intersection. Continue another mile to the Rolling Creek Trailhead, a small parking area on the right.

Segments 1 through 3 and Segment 5 see heavy use by day-hikers and cyclists. You'll find **peace and solitude** in the Lost Creek Wilderness Area.

This is the first of six **designated wilderness areas** the CT passes through on its 486-mile route. Review the wilderness regulations on page 44; especially note that bicycles are prohibited and dogs should be leashed.

 TRAVEL TIPS

Hiking west in Long Gulch, an open meadow that extends for nearly seven miles. Photo by Bernie Krausse

North Fork Trailhead: This trailhead is remote and the last 4 miles of the road are seldom used (except during hunting season). It is suitable only for 4WD vehicles with high clearance. From the C-470–US Highway 285 interchange on the southwest side of the Denver area, drive southwest on US 285 for 46 miles to Kenosha Pass. Continue another 3.2 miles to a gravel side road on the left marked Lost Park Road (County Road 56, then FS Road 56). Proceed nearly 16 miles to a side road (FS Road 134) that angles back to the left and starts to climb. Follow it about 4 miles to its end. The CT is just a short walk across a bridge over the North Fork of Lost Creek.

Lost Park Trailhead: An alternate way to access the midpoint of Segment 4 in a 2WD vehicle is to follow the directions above to the North Fork Trailhead, but pass by the left turn to FS Road 134 and continue on FS Road 56/Lost Park Road four more miles to its end at Lost Park Campground and Trailhead (limited trailhead parking). Follow the Brookside-McCurdy Trail to the north for 1.7 miles, joining the CT at the North Fork Trailhead.

Long Gulch Trailhead: See Segment 5 on page 101.

TRAIL DESCRIPTION: Segment 4 begins at the Rolling Creek Trailhead, **mile 0.0**. Go west on a two-track to a small parking area at **mile 0.3**. The CT leaves the parking area to the right in a northwesterly direction. At **mile 0.9**, take a left when the trail joins an old roadbed. After passing a fence, where there is a possible dry campsite, continue uphill to **mile 1.9**, where the trail enters the Lost Creek Wilderness. As with all wilderness areas, bikes and motorized vehicles are not permitted. Expect none of the triangular CT confidence markers you're used to seeing, as metal and plastic markers are not allowed in wilderness areas; in rare instances, wood markers, which are allowed, have been installed at potentially confusing locations.

There are small seasonal streams, including one at **mile 2.6**, and potential campsites in the next two miles. Pass the Payne Creek Trail on the right at **mile 3.2** and continue straight ahead. Cross a substantial stream at **mile 4.6** with good campsites nearby. At **mile 5.5**, turn left off of the roadbed onto single-track and

BAILEY

Bailey, west of Denver on busy US Highway 285 (approximately 8 miles northwest of the Rolling Creek Trailhead using County Road 68), has a small business center.

Distance from CT: 8 miles
Elevation: 7,750 feet
Zip code: 80421
Area code: 303

Dining, several places including:
Coney Island
10 Old Stage Coach Rd.
(303) 918-9527

Cutthroat Café
157 Main Street
(303) 816-5099

Gear (including fuel canisters)
Sasquatch Outpost
149 Main St.
(303) 816-9383

Platte River Outfitters
41 County Rd 68
(303) 838-8590

Groceries (convenience-store type)
Conoco Bailey Self-Service
US Highway 285
(303) 838-5170

Info
Chamber of Commerce
PO Box 477
(303) 838-9080

Laundry
Sudz Laundromat
29 Road P68 (Near US Highway 285)
(303) 838-4809

Lodging
Two Bridges Lodge and Hostel
59786 S. US Highway 285
(303) 800-4864

Bailey Lodge
57920 US Highway 285
(303) 838-2450

Post Office
Bailey Post Office
24 River Dr.
(800) 275-8777

begin a steep climb. Reaching a saddle at **mile 7.3**, the trail rejoins the old road-bed, crosses a small stream at **mile 8.1**, then leaves the Lost Creek Wilderness. The trail enters the large, grassy valley of the North Fork of Lost Creek, which will be followed for over 6 miles upstream. There are many side streams and potential campsites along the way.

The CT joins the Brookside-McCurdy Trail at **mile 8.8**; left across the bridge over the North Fork of Lost Creek is the North Fork Trailhead. The Brookside-McCurdy Trail leaves the CT to the right at **mile 11.2**, while the CT continues straight. Reach a fence at a saddle at **mile 14.4**, then leave the North Fork of Lost Creek valley and enter the forest, descending steeply from here. Reach the end of Segment 4 at **mile 16.4** at a junction with a connector trail to the Long Gulch Trailhead.

THE HAYMAN FIRE

Beginning in a campfire circle on the morning of June 8, 2002, the Hayman Fire quickly escaped to become the largest wildfire (at the time) in Colorado's recorded history. Drought conditions, high winds, and record hot weather spurred the blaze, which burned nearly 138,000 acres over three weeks. The fire destroyed 133 homes and cost nearly $40 million. The fire leapt highways, clear-cuts, and pre-scribed burn areas, pushing into the heavy underbrush and timber in the southern portion of the Lost Creek Wilderness Area, stopping just a few miles short of the CT. Thus, CT hikers will see little evidence of this catastrophe. But mountain bikers, who have to bypass to the south of the wilderness on Forest Service roads, will see firsthand the result of nature's fury. Campers in the wilderness are reminded to use a stove and forgo building fires.

LOST CREEK WILDERNESS BIKE DETOUR

MOUNTAIN
BIKING

This long, mandatory bike detour of Segment 4 and part of Segment 5 bypasses the Lost Creek Wilderness to the south. A shorter detour north of the wilderness exists, following US Highway 285, but cyclists have reported the uphill and curvy ride as dangerous due to the almost nonexistent highway shoulder and fast speeds of sometimes-inattentive drivers.

The standard detour can be very hot because of the relatively low elevation, potentially intense sun, and lack of shade, due to the loss of tree cover as a result of the Hayman Fire and because of the limited high desert vegetation.

Riders begin this detour at the end of Segment 3 at the Rolling Creek Trailhead. At **mile 0.0**, turn southeast and follow Wellington Lake Road, which starts as County

Road 68 then soon becomes County Road 105 (gravel). Alongside Welling-ton Lake at an intersection at **mile 2.9**, continue straight toward Stoney Pass onto FS Road 560/Stoney Pass Road (gravel). At **mile 5.2**, reach the top of Stoney Pass. At **mile 8.1**, cross Cabin Creek, where the route enters the burn scar from the Hayman Fire, then cross another stream at **mile 8.5**. At **mile 9.5**, continue straight ahead, ignoring FS Road 545 on the right. At an intersec-tion with FS Road 541 at **mile 12.1**, go left (east), staying on FS Road 560.

Riders in Segment 3 prior to the Lost Creek detour. Photo by Jesse Swift and Bill Turner

At **mile 13.6**, leave FS Road 560, take a sharp right (west) onto FS Road 211/Matukat Road (gravel). At **mile 18.7**, cross a stream. At **mile 18.8**, turn right, continu-ing on FS Road 211, ignoring the left fork to Lost Valley Ranch. At **mile 21.8**, cross Goose Creek. After about 0.1 mile, continue straight at the entrance to Goose Creek Campground on the left (fee, potable water, toilet, no reservations). Around **mile 26**, the road changes jurisdiction and becomes County Road 211.

At **mile 35.1**, turn right (northwest) onto County Road 77/Tarryall Road (paved) and exit the perimeter of the Hayman Fire. Much of the land adjacent to County Road 77 over the next 20+ miles is privately owned, with limited exceptions. If plan-ning on dispersed camping along this section, be sure to determine that the loca-tion is on public, and not private, land.

At **mile 40.3**, cycle through the nearly abandoned town of Tarryall. At **mile 41.7**, pass the entrance to the Spruce Grove Campground (fee, potable water, toi-let, reservations recommended), then at **mile 43.4**, pass the entrance to the less developed Twin Eagles Campground (fee, no water, toilet, no reservations).

At **mile 52.8**, cycle past Tarryall Reservoir. At **mile 61.4**, turn right onto County Road 39/Rock Creek Hills Road (gravel), which becomes FS Road 39 shortly after. Just before the turnoff, limited food and beverage options may be available at the Stagestop Store and Saloon (limited hours). Water is likely scarce for the remainder of the detour, and, if Johnson Gulch is dry, the next available water on route may be at Segment 6, **mile 3.1**, over 18 miles away. A generally reliable source not far off route is Rock Creek, 0.6 mile past the turnoff to the Rock Creek Trailhead at **mile 68.9**, described below.

At **mile 66.9**, turn right (east) onto FS Road 56/Lost Park Road (gravel). At **mile 68.9**, at a sign for the CT and Rock Creek Trailhead, turn left (northwest) onto FS Road 133 (dirt) (straight ahead 0.6 mile to reliable water at Rock Creek). At **mile 69.8**, cyclists rejoin CT Segment 5 at **mile 7.9** near Rock Creek Trailhead. The trail-head is just north of the CT.

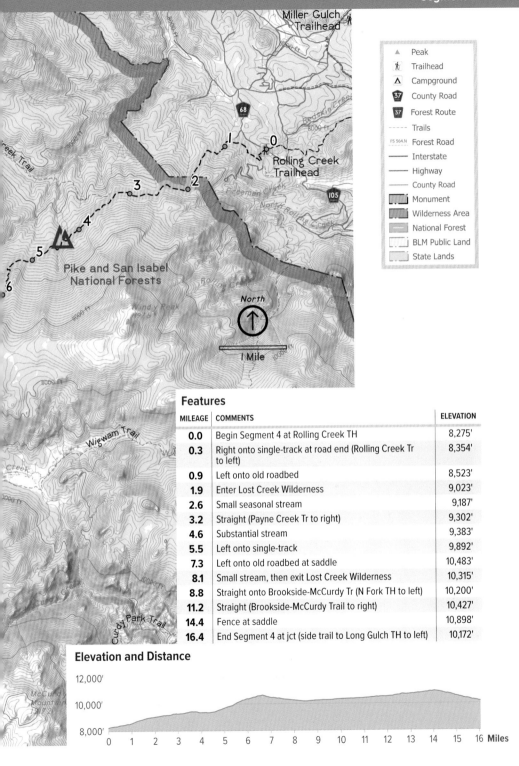

Features

MILEAGE	COMMENTS	ELEVATION
0.0	Begin Segment 4 at Rolling Creek TH	8,275'
0.3	Right onto single-track at road end (Rolling Creek Tr to left)	8,354'
0.9	Left onto old roadbed	8,523'
1.9	Enter Lost Creek Wilderness	9,023'
2.6	Small seasonal stream	9,187'
3.2	Straight (Payne Creek Tr to right)	9,302'
4.6	Substantial stream	9,383'
5.5	Left onto single-track	9,892'
7.3	Left onto old roadbed at saddle	10,483'
8.1	Small stream, then exit Lost Creek Wilderness	10,315'
8.8	Straight onto Brookside-McCurdy Tr (N Fork TH to left)	10,200'
11.2	Straight (Brookside-McCurdy Trail to right)	10,427'
14.4	Fence at saddle	10,898'
16.4	End Segment 4 at jct (side trail to Long Gulch TH to left)	10,172'

Elevation and Distance

SEGMENT 5
Long Gulch to Kenosha Pass

South Park near the west end of Segment 5 offers expansive views and fall color. Courtesy of the Colorado Trail Foundation

Distance	14.6 miles
Elevation Gain	Approx. 1,858 feet
Elevation Loss	Approx. 2,055 feet
USFS Map	Pike National Forest
The CT Databook, 8th Edition	Pages 18–19
The CT Map Book	Pages 15–17
Trails Illustrated Maps	No. 105, 1202
Jurisdiction	South Platte and South Park Ranger Districts, Pike National Forest

ACCESS FROM
DENVER END

ACCESS FROM
DURANGO END

AVAILABILITY
OF WATER

BICYCLING

See pages
96–97

ABOUT THIS SEGMENT: The trees are one of the highlights of Segment 5. The trail passes through several spectacular stands of aspen, a species that shares extensive root systems, producing colonies that can live thousands of years. The CT also passes by bristlecone pines. This five-needled pine lives at high elevations, and despite the poor soil and long winters, hearty individual bristlecones can live up to 5,000 years. If you are not familiar with the trees along the CT, be sure to bring a guidebook specifically for this section. Toward the end of the segment, views of the Continental Divide open up, giving trail users a good idea of the change in terrain to come.

The first half of this segment passes through the Lost Creek Wilderness, where bikes are not allowed. Mountain bikers rejoin the CT at the Rock Creek Trailhead, midway through the segment, at the end of the Lost Creek Wilderness Bike Detour. See pages 96–97 for a description of the route.

TRAILHEAD/ACCESS POINTS

Long Gulch Trailhead: From the C-470–US Highway 285 interchange on the southwest side of the Denver area, drive southwest on US 285 for about 46 miles to Kenosha Pass. Continue another 3.1 miles to a turnoff on the left side of the road marked Lost Park Road. Follow this road for nearly 11 miles (County Road 56, then FS Road 56). Look for a gully on the left side and a road marked FS Road 817. Follow this road for 0.1 mile to its end at the very small Long Gulch Trailhead (no facilities). Reach the CT by crossing the adjacent creek on a small bridge and follow the trail uphill for 0.2 mile to reach a well-signed intersection and the start of Segment 5.

Rock Creek Trailhead: Follow the aforementioned Long Gulch Trailhead instructions to Lost Park Road. Drive 7.2 miles on Lost Park Road to FS Road 133/ Rock Creek Road, a steep two-track that branches off to the left. Follow this uphill 0.9 mile to the CT crossing of the road and the trailhead just beyond on the right.

Between Black Canyon and Kenosha Pass, stop to take in the **incredible vistas** of South Park and the mountainous backdrop.

TRAVEL TIPS

South Park is a fault-bounded basin filled with sedimentary rocks that date from the time of the Ancestral Rocky Mountains and Cretaceous seaway. These rocks are overlain with younger sediments deposited during erosion of the mountains formed during the Laramide Orogeny. In this segment, travelers reach the **Continental Divide**, dominated by a lofty pyramid, **Mount Guyot** (pronounced gee-oh). Note **Georgia Pass**, the low point between Mount Guyot and the CT, where the trail enters the alpine ecosystem for the first time as it crosses the Continental Divide in Segment 6.

Mid-June snowpack lies ahead at Georgia Pass.
Photo by Bernard Wolf

Kenosha Pass West Trailhead: See Segment 6 on page 108.

SERVICES, SUPPLIES, AND ACCOMMODATIONS: The town of Jefferson is approximately 4.5 miles southwest of Kenosha Pass on US 285. See Segment 6 on page 109.

TRAIL DESCRIPTION: Segment 5 begins at the well-marked intersection with the connector trail to the Long Gulch Trailhead, **mile 0.0**. Cross a small creek on a bridge about 300 feet past the trail junction, where there is camping nearby. The trail enters the Lost Creek Wilderness at **mile 0.2**, shortly entering a mixed aspen-fir forest with some bristlecone pines. Cross a seasonal stream at **mile 2.9**. There is a good campsite nearby. Cross more streams at **mile 3.3**, **mile 3.9**, and **mile 4.4**. There is another creek at **mile 5.2** with several good campsites.

The trail leaves the Lost Creek Wilderness at **mile 6.5** and crosses two narrow bridges over Rock Creek at **mile 7.3**, the last reliable water for over 10 miles. Shortly after, angle left onto a closed two-track at the junction with the Ben Tyler Trail, then leave the two-track to the right onto single-track at **mile 7.4**. Pass through a gate at **mile 7.5**, then cross FS Road 133/Rock Creek Road at **mile 7.9** near the Rock Creek Trailhead. **Mountain bikers completing the Lost Creek Wilderness Bike Detour rejoin the CT at this point.**

Descend to Johnson Gulch and cross a seasonal stream on a narrow bridge at **mile 8.4**. This possible water source has room to camp nearby, although cattle may be grazing in the area. Just past the stream, the CT crosses an old two-track and eventually passes through a stand of large aspen trees. At **mile 10.8** continue straight across a two-track. The trail passes by more bristlecone pines with views to the south and west, including toward the first alpine pass on the CT, Georgia Pass. After passing through a large stand of aspens, the trail reaches FS Road 126/ Twin Cone Road near a parking area with a vault toilet at **mile 14.3**. The trail continues to the left onto FS Road 126, and after carefully crossing US 285 (can be busy with traffic at times), reaches the end of Segment 5 at Kenosha Pass West Trailhead, **mile 14.6**.

LOST CREEK WILDERNESS AREA

The name Lost Creek conjures up an image of an enigmatic place. And indeed, this 119,790-acre wilderness area has a fascinating history of lost gold, vanished dreams, and hidden places.

Lost Creek begins in the open meadows of Lost Park, sandwiched between the granite knobs of the Kenosha and Tarryall Mountains. The last native bison killed in Colorado fell in Lost Park in 1897. From here, the creek descends into a deeply etched canyon, vanishing among tumbled boulders and underground tunnels, and reappearing nine times. The "lost" stream eventually re-emerges as Goose Creek at the southeast end of the wilderness area.

The entrance to the Lost Creek Wilderness Area near the beginning of Segment 5. Photo by Lawton "Disco" Grinter

More than a century ago, the notorious Reynolds Gang terrorized nearby South Park, holding up stagecoaches and lone riders for their gold. The stories vary, but some say the gang stashed their lost cache in Handcart Gulch, north of Kenosha Pass, while others claim it is hidden among the strange granite outcrops that dot the hills above Lost Park, a frequent hideout for the gang.

Dreamers often vanished into the recesses of Lost Creek looking for riches. Both the Lost Jackman Mine and the Indian Mine were supposed to be fabulously rich in gold, but if they ever existed at all, they are lost forever to time.

Perhaps the most ambitious scheme was an early twentieth-century attempt to build an unusual subterranean dam on Goose Creek, which would have flooded a major valley, to meet the water needs of Denver. Fortunately, this effort failed, and Denver citizens have benefited more by having this magnificent wilderness preserved at their doorstep.

The Lost Creek Wilderness Area was established in 1980. Despite heavy use by recreationalists, there are still some unexplored corners and hidden places in the Lost Creek. In the early 1990s, prolific peak-bagger Bob Martin frequently visited the area in his quest to climb every peak in Colorado over 11,000 feet. He discovered a half-dozen remote "eleveners" tucked away in the wilderness area without signs of previous ascent. He reports that most were difficult scrambles, some requiring the assistance of a rope.

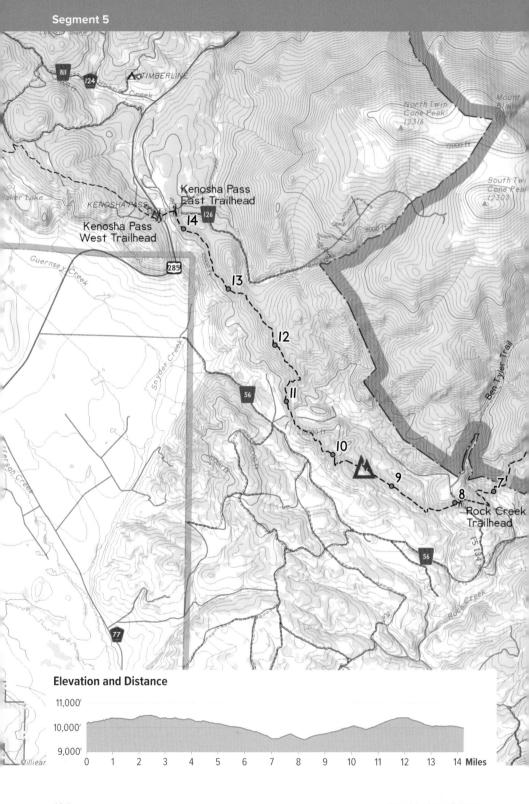

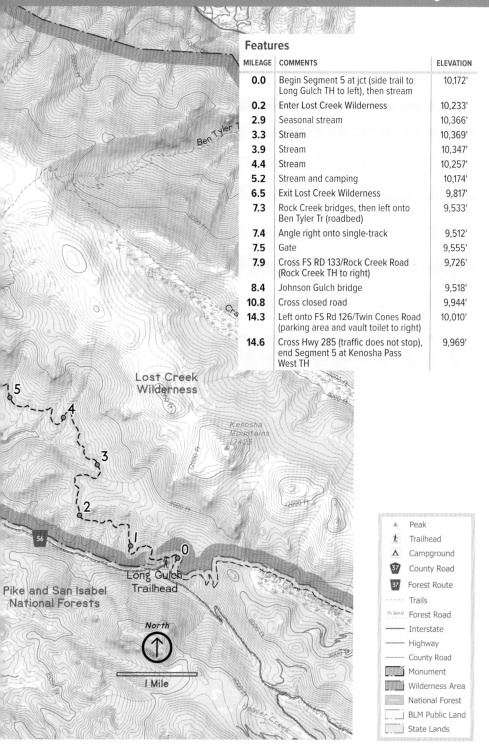

Features

MILEAGE	COMMENTS	ELEVATION
0.0	Begin Segment 5 at jct (side trail to Long Gulch TH to left), then stream	10,172'
0.2	Enter Lost Creek Wilderness	10,233'
2.9	Seasonal stream	10,366'
3.3	Stream	10,369'
3.9	Stream	10,347'
4.4	Stream	10,257'
5.2	Stream and camping	10,174'
6.5	Exit Lost Creek Wilderness	9,817'
7.3	Rock Creek bridges, then left onto Ben Tyler Tr (roadbed)	9,533'
7.4	Angle right onto single-track	9,512'
7.5	Gate	9,555'
7.9	Cross FS RD 133/Rock Creek Road (Rock Creek TH to right)	9,726'
8.4	Johnson Gulch bridge	9,518'
10.8	Cross closed road	9,944'
14.3	Left onto FS Rd 126/Twin Cones Road (parking area and vault toilet to right)	10,010'
14.6	Cross Hwy 285 (traffic does not stop), end Segment 5 at Kenosha Pass West TH	9,969'

Peak
Trailhead
Campground
County Road
Forest Route
Trails
Forest Road
Interstate
Highway
County Road
Monument
Wilderness Area
National Forest
BLM Public Land
State Lands

SEGMENT 6
Kenosha Pass West Trailhead to Gold Hill Trailhead

A cyclist pedals through golden aspen west of Kenosha Pass.
Photo by Nick Wilde

Distance	32.4 miles
Elevation Gain	Approx. 5,196 feet
Elevation Loss	Approx. 5,968 feet
USFS Map	Pike and White River National Forests
The CT Databook, 8th Edition	Pages 20–23
The CT Map Book	Pages 17–20
Trails Illustrated Maps	Nos. 104, 105, 108, 109, 1202
Latitude 40° Map	Summit County Trails
Jurisdiction	South Park and Dillon Ranger Districts, Pike and White River National Forests

ACCESS FROM
DENVER END

ACCESS FROM
DURANGO END

AVAILABILITY
OF WATER

BICYCLING

ABOUT THIS SEGMENT: Segment 6 is the longest segment on The Colorado Trail. Along its 32.4 miles, it reaches the Continental Divide, passes through several distinct watersheds, runs along a ridge near Keystone Ski Resort, and ends near the resort town of Breckenridge. There are lots of good places to camp near the major streams and many other potential campsites between water sources and near small streams.

The trail passes through many stands of aspens, with plentiful wildflowers in wet years on the way to the Continental Divide. There are great views to the south and north when crossing the Continental Divide above Georgia Pass, and southbound users first encounter the Continental Divide National Scenic Trail (CDNST, commonly referred to as the CDT). The CT shares a total of 235.4 miles with the CDT in two lengthy sections if traveling the CT Collegiate East, and a total of 319 miles in one lengthy section if traveling the CT Collegiate West (see page 161 for more detail on the CT Collegiate East and West routes).

It is not uncommon to encounter snowdrifts above tree line well into July, so be prepared. In addition to snow, summer thunderstorms can move in quickly and catch people off guard. Keep track of the time and weather conditions when heading into alpine areas. At about **mile 25.0**, the CT crosses from metamorphic basement rocks into black shale deposited in the Cretaceous seaway. The two types of rock are separated by the Elkhorn Mountain thrust, a Laramide fault along which the basement rocks have been carried westward more than 5 miles across the younger shale. The same fault forms the eastern margin of South Park.

The view toward Georgia Pass and the Continental Divide at the beginning of Segment 6.
Photo by Morgan and Robyn Wilkinson

Evening light over South Park after a rainy day. Photo by Mick Gigone

The Middle and North forks of the Swan River have several great campsites, but this part of the trail is accessible to motor vehicles via the roads near the rivers. Keep this in mind when choosing campsites because there may be other campers there as well.

The last few miles of Segment 6 go through large areas where trees have been killed by mountain pine beetles and the character has changed dramatically. Fire suppression and relatively warm winters have aided the beetles in proliferating and wreaking havoc. To reduce the risk of catastrophic wildfire and dead trees falling on trail users, many large areas of trees along the trail corridor have been cut down. Cut trees remain on the ground in many of the open areas, but these landscapes have begun to revegetate nicely.

Travelers on this segment may be exposed to severe weather for a couple of miles above tree line while crossing the Continental Divide, **mile 10.5 to mile 12.5**.

TRAILHEAD/ACCESS POINTS

Kenosha Pass West Trailhead: From the C-470–US Highway 285 interchange on the southwest side of the Denver area, drive southwest on US 285 for about 46 miles to Kenosha Pass. Kenosha Pass Campground is on the right and the Kenosha East Campground is 0.2 mile on FS Road 126 to the left. Both are fee areas. You may park alongside the highway, however, without paying the fee. The beginning of Segment 6 is on the right-hand (northwest) side of the highway, just past the entrance to the Kenosha Pass Campground. The CT begins at a trailhead sign near a gap in the fence.

Jefferson Lake Road Trail Access: This access requires a fee payment. From Kenosha Pass, continue southwest on US 285 for 4.3 miles to the town of Jefferson. Turn right on County Road 35/Michigan Creek Road. Drive 2.1 miles to an intersection. Turn right onto County Road 37/Jefferson Lake Road and proceed about a mile, where the road changes to FS Road 37 just before reaching a fee collection booth. Continue 2.1 miles to where the CT crosses the road. A small parking area is 0.1 mile farther on the left. Another larger parking area is 0.6 mile down the road, near the Jefferson Lake Campground.

One of many small, refreshing creeks in the segment. Photo by Bernard Wolf

Georgia Pass Trail Access: From Kenosha Pass, continue southwest on US 285 for 4.3 miles to the town of Jefferson. Turn right on County Road 35/Michigan

---

JEFFERSON

SERVICES, SUPPLIES, AND ACCOMMODATIONS

The town of Jefferson is approximately 4.5 miles southwest of Kenosha Pass on Highway 285. Historically, it was a train stop and now has a population of 18 with a tiny market in a 100-year-old building.

Distance from CT: 4.5 miles to Jefferson
Elevation: 9,499 feet
Zip code: 80456
Area code: 719

Basic Supplies
The Jefferson Market
38600 Highway 285
(719) 836-4919

Post Office (limited hours)
38588 Highway 285
(800) 275-8777

Dining
Hungry Moose Caboose
38539 Highway 285
(719) 839-5828

The Jefferson Market
38600 Highway 285
(719) 836-4919

Kenosha Pass West Trailhead to Gold Hill Trailhead

Southbound hikers move **above tree line** for the first time at Georgia Pass, so watch for imminent storms before crossing the exposed crest.

TRAVEL
TIP

Creek Road. At an intersection after 2.1 miles, continue straight on Michigan Creek Road, becoming FS Road 54, for 10 miles to Georgia Pass where there's a parking area. The last 2 miles are a little rough, but most vehicles with reasonable ground clearance can make it. From the pass and parking area, find the CT to the northeast and up the very rough 4WD FS Road 258.1/Glacier Ridge Road 0.4 mile.

North Fork Swan River Trail Access: From the C-470–I-70 interchange on the west side of the Denver area, travel west on I-70 for about 57 miles to exit 203 (Frisco/Breckenridge). Proceed south on CO Highway 9 for 6.6 miles to a traffic light at Tiger Road/Shores Lane. Turn left on Tiger Road/County Road 6 and drive 5.7 miles to an intersection with FS Road 354.1/North Swan Road. Turn left onto the dirt FS Road 354.1 (sometimes rutted) and follow it up the North Fork Swan River valley for 0.5 mile to an open area. The CT crosses FS Road 354.1 about 800 feet up the road beyond a seasonal closure gate.

White globeflower near Georgia Pass. Photo by Dave Jones

HIGHWAY 9 CROSSING OPTIONS

HIKING TIPS

An option that avoids crossing the busy highway is to cross Revette Drive at **mile 31.9** and head northwest through a large gravel area. Single-track then leads under the Highway 9 bridge adjacent to the Blue River. From there the trail leads to the paved path and turns right to reach the Gold Hill Trailhead. This option is not suitable for stock or during high water.

The safest option for stock is to cross at the signalized intersection of Highway 9 and Tiger Road south of the Revette Drive intersection. To reach the intersection, continue on the single-track on the south side of Revette Drive, then turn left and travel south for 0.4 mile on the east side of Highway 9 to reach Tiger Road. Turn right on Tiger Road, wait for the traffic light, and cross the highway to reach a paved path on the west side of the intersection. Turn right and follow the path to the Gold Hill Trailhead.

Middle Fork Swan River Trail Access: Follow the aforementioned instructions for the North Fork access then continue one-half mile beyond the intersection with FS Road 354.1 to a 3-way intersection. Continue straight onto County Road 310/Middle Fork Swan Road and follow the road as it curves to the left and becomes FS Road 6.2/Middle Fork of the Swan Road. Continue up the rougher road for slightly over a mile to where the CT crosses the road. Watch closely for signs and markers because the CT crossing is not obvious.

Gold Hill Trailhead: See Segment 7 on page 119.

TRAIL DESCRIPTION: Segment 6 begins on the west side of Kenosha Pass at **mile 0.0**, at the Kenosha Pass West Trailhead. Travel into the forest where the trail crosses a service road at **mile 0.3**, then crosses a powerline right-of-way at **mile 0.6**, and reaches a ridge shortly afterward with great views to the west. After passing through a stand of aspen trees and open meadows, the trail crosses an irrigation ditch at **mile 3.1**, then FS Road 809/Wahl Road. Just past the road, cross a small bridge over Guernsey Creek. There are several good campsites in this area, although some have vehicle access and may be occupied, particularly on weekends.

The trail continues west, crossing FS Road 427/Deadman Road at **mile 4.5** and Deadman Creek on a small bridge at **mile 4.6**. Gain a saddle and pass through a gate at **mile 5.4**. Cross County Road 37/Jefferson Lake Road at **mile 6.0** and a bridge over Jefferson Creek at **mile 6.1**. Turn right onto the West Jefferson Trail at **mile**

Snow remains through June on the high peaks. Photo by Bernard Wolf

6.2, then cross a small stream. Leave the West Jefferson Trail to the left at **mile 6.3** and begin the climb to the Continental Divide.

Continue straight at **mile 7.9** where the faint Michigan Creek Road Trail angles sharply left. After the trail leaves a subalpine fir forest and emerges above tree line, pass the West Jefferson Trail on the right at **mile 11.3** and cross a closed two-track at **mile 11.7**. Be aware of changing weather patterns when above tree line. Reach the Continental Divide above Georgia Pass at **mile 11.9** and the high point of the segment (11,876').

Reach FS Road 258.1/Glacier Ridge Road at **mile 12.1**, where the CT merges with the CDT, which joins from the north. The CT and CDT are co-located for the next 319 miles (via the CT Collegiate West option) into Segment 24 where the two trails diverge. Cross the road and descend on single-track as it turns right. After entering the trees, cross several closed roads then pass by a seasonal pond at **mile 15.9**. Keep descending, passing a small stream just above the bottom of the canyon with good campsites in the area. Cross the bridge over the Middle Fork of the Swan River and go right for 50 feet on FS Road 6.2/Middle Fork of the Swan Road at **mile 16.8**. The trail then leaves the road to the left into the woods onto single-track.

The trail crosses a small stream and curves right in the next 2 miles. You may hear barking dogs on this section coming from a commercial dogsled facility located below the CT. Reach a marshy area, crossed on a raised walkway, and a bridge over the North Fork Swan River at **mile 19.0**; there is good camping beyond the bridge, although it can be busy due to nearby vehicle access. The trail turns right and then curves left as it follows the perimeter of the camping area. Angle left across FS Road 354.1/North Swan Road at **mile 19.3** as the trail begins the climb of what is locally referred to as "West Ridge." Cross a seasonal creek twice, the second time on a low bridge, in the next mile; this may be the last water for the next 8 miles.

CONTINENTAL DIVIDE NATIONAL SCENIC TRAIL (CDNST)

HIKING TIPS

The Continental Divide National Scenic Trail, commonly known as the Continental Divide Trail (CDT), passes through five western states as it winds through the majestic Rocky Mountains from Canada to Mexico, encountering some of America's most dramatic scenery.

The Colorado Trail and the CDT are co-located for about 319 miles. The two trails join from Georgia Pass in CT Segment 6, continue as co-located along the entire CT Collegiate West, and finally diverge in CT Segment 24 atop the Divide near the Elk Creek descent.

First envisioned by several far-sighted groups and individuals, including Benton MacKaye, founder of the Appalachian Trail, the 3,100-mile CDT is about 95 percent complete today. The Colorado portion has one of the highest completion rates at 98 percent. The trail achieves its highest point in Colorado, passing over 14,270-foot Grays Peak, and includes a network of trails 759 miles long, beginning in the Mount Zirkel Wilderness Area on the Wyoming border and entering New Mexico through the spectacular San Juans.

The Continental Divide Trail Coalition (CDTC) estimates that about 300 people undertake the entire 5-month journey from Canada to Mexico each year but far fewer finish. As with The Colorado Trail, thousands more enjoy CDT day hikes or multiday backpack trips on sections of it.

The first complete hike of the Colorado portion of the Continental Divide Trail was done by Carl Melzer, his son Bob, and Julius Johnson in 1936. This was truly a pioneering trip, considering the incomplete maps and sketchy information available to them at that time. (The Melzers had a string of accomplishments. They also were the first to climb all of Colorado's fourteeners in one summer [1937] and the first to climb all of the fourteeners in the 48 states [1939]—all before Bob was 11 years old!)

For more information about the CDT, contact the CDTC at (303) 996-2759 or visit their website at continentaldividetrail.org.

Keystone Ski Resort eventually comes into view to the northeast after reaching the high point of the ridge. The trail intersects the West Ridge Loop Trail (from Keystone Gulch) twice, first at **mile 22.2** and then at **mile 23.4**, staying left at each junction. After a long descent on a series of switchbacks, the trail continues sharply left at the junction with the Red Trail at **mile 25.7**.

Angle left across the two-track Horseshoe Gulch Trail then cross a bridge over a seasonal stream at **mile 28.4** and follow the trail as it heads north with dry camping potential ahead. Go straight at trail junctions with Blair Witch Trail at **mile 29.2** and at Hippo Trail at **mile 29.5**. Descend several switchbacks above the Tiger Run RV Resort, passing the Campion Trail junction at the end of the bottom switchback at **mile 31.5**. Continue between a condominium complex and a pond and cross a substantial bridge over the pond inlet stream. Angle right across Revette Drive and a large gravel shoulder then cross a substantial bridge over the Swan River at **mile 31.7**.

At **mile 31.9**, reach Revette Drive and continue west on the path on the south

MOUNTAIN PINE BEETLES

VIEWING
OPPORTUNITY

On approaching the town of Breckenridge, it becomes apparent there is something amiss with the local forests. The needles of many of the pine trees are red, indicating the trees have died or are dying. Other pines have large popcorn-shaped masses of resin called "pitch tubes." On still others you can see wood dust from boring insects in the crevices of the bark or on the ground at the base of the tree. Some of the trees have foliage that is turning yellow, and will eventually turn red. These all are signs of infestation by the mountain pine beetle (*Dendroctonus ponderosae*), an insect native to Colorado's pine forests.

The beetle is only about the size of a grain of rice and has a one-year life cycle, but it has been able to kill millions of acres of Colorado forest. The mountain pine beetle normally attacks trees that are under stress from injury, poor soil conditions, root damage, or old age. In addition to these problems, forests in Colorado and Wyoming have become overcrowded due to fire suppression, enabling the beetles to proliferate and move easily from tree to tree.

The beetle population is normally held in check by cold winter temperatures, but relatively warm winters in recent years have not killed off sufficient amounts of beetles to stop the outbreak, which has been building over the past two decades. Now, nearly all of the pine trees in the area are dead or dying. The risk of fire in these tracts of forests is incredibly high and potentially devastating to local communities. Eventually, the dead trees will burn or be blown over in windstorms, thinning out the forests and beginning a new cycle of life in the region.

THE LEGACY OF TWO PASSES

The Colorado Trail crosses two historic mountain passes in Segment 6. Kenosha Pass—which isn't especially high by Colorado standards, never reaching tree line—has been an important crossing for centuries. It was first used by bands of Ute Indians, then white trappers, to reach hunting grounds in South Park. Explorer John C. Frémont crossed the pass in the 1840s. During the Colorado gold rush in the mid-1800s, prospectors used the pass to reach placer diggings around Fairplay.

Sign points to Georgia Pass. Photo by Anthony Sloan

When a toll road was built to the new diggings, a stagecoach driver, Clark Herbert, named Kenosha Pass after his Wisconsin hometown. The silver boom of the 1870s brought the narrow-gauge tracks of the Denver South Park & Pacific Railroad through Kenosha Pass. A switchyard was built on its flat meadows. When the tracks were removed in 1937, a modern highway, essentially following the old rail route, was built and contin-

Atop Georgia Pass with Mount Guyot behind. Photo by Pete Turner

ues to bring visitors and commerce over Kenosha Pass into South Park.

With the discovery of gold in 1860 near present-day Breckenridge, miners poured over the Continental Divide at another relatively low point, christening it Georgia Pass. With the coming of the railroad, the wagon road over Georgia Pass fell into disuse, becoming the obscure jeep track that it is today.

side of the road to the unsignalized intersection with CO Highway 9. Carefully cross Highway 9, which can be busy with traffic, at **mile 32.2**, just south of the free Summit Stage bus stop. Go right on the paved path, cross the Blue River on a large bridge at **mile 32.3**, then reach the Gold Hill Trailhead and the end of Segment 6 at **mile 32.4**.

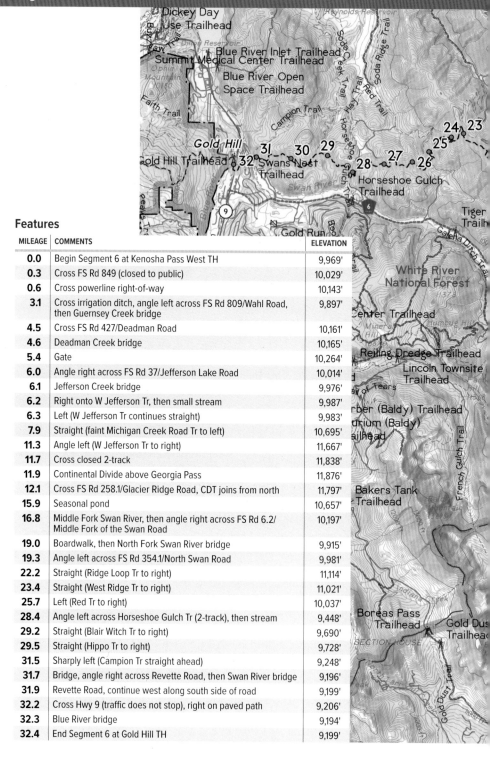

Features

MILEAGE	COMMENTS	ELEVATION
0.0	Begin Segment 6 at Kenosha Pass West TH	9,969'
0.3	Cross FS Rd 849 (closed to public)	10,029'
0.6	Cross powerline right-of-way	10,143'
3.1	Cross irrigation ditch, angle left across FS Rd 809/Wahl Road, then Guernsey Creek bridge	9,897'
4.5	Cross FS Rd 427/Deadman Road	10,161'
4.6	Deadman Creek bridge	10,165'
5.4	Gate	10,264'
6.0	Angle right across FS Rd 37/Jefferson Lake Road	10,014'
6.1	Jefferson Creek bridge	9,976'
6.2	Right onto W Jefferson Tr, then small stream	9,987'
6.3	Left (W Jefferson Tr continues straight)	9,983'
7.9	Straight (faint Michigan Creek Road Tr to left)	10,695'
11.3	Angle left (W Jefferson Tr to right)	11,667'
11.7	Cross closed 2-track	11,838'
11.9	Continental Divide above Georgia Pass	11,876'
12.1	Cross FS Rd 258.1/Glacier Ridge Road, CDT joins from north	11,797'
15.9	Seasonal pond	10,657'
16.8	Middle Fork Swan River, then angle right across FS Rd 6.2/Middle Fork of the Swan Road	10,197'
19.0	Boardwalk, then North Fork Swan River bridge	9,915'
19.3	Angle left across FS Rd 354.1/North Swan Road	9,981'
22.2	Straight (Ridge Loop Tr to right)	11,114'
23.4	Straight (West Ridge Tr to right)	11,021'
25.7	Left (Red Tr to right)	10,037'
28.4	Angle left across Horseshoe Gulch Tr (2-track), then stream	9,448'
29.2	Straight (Blair Witch Tr to right)	9,690'
29.5	Straight (Hippo Tr to right)	9,728'
31.5	Sharply left (Campion Tr straight ahead)	9,248'
31.7	Bridge, angle right across Revette Road, then Swan River bridge	9,196'
31.9	Revette Road, continue west along south side of road	9,199'
32.2	Cross Hwy 9 (traffic does not stop), right on paved path	9,206'
32.3	Blue River bridge	9,194'
32.4	End Segment 6 at Gold Hill TH	9,199'

Elevation and Distance

SEGMENT 7
Gold Hill Trailhead to Copper Mountain

An exhilarating view of the Tenmile Range. Photo by Bernard Wolf

Distance	13.8 miles
Elevation Gain	Approx. 3,674 feet
Elevation Loss	Approx. 3,053 feet
USFS Map	White River National Forest
The CT Databook, 8th Edition	Pages 24–25
The CT Map Book	Pages 20–21
Trails Illustrated Maps	Nos. 108, 109, 1202
Latitude 40° Map	Summit County Trails
Jurisdiction	Dillon Ranger District, White River National Forest

ACCESS FROM
DENVER END

ACCESS FROM
DURANGO END

AVAILABILITY
OF WATER

BICYCLING

ABOUT THIS SEGMENT: This segment of The Colorado Trail climbs 3,300 feet in 9 miles across 1.7 billion-year-old basement rocks to gain the crest of the Tenmile Range, then descends 2,700 feet in 4.5 miles through similar rocks to the narrow valley below. This is the first time the trail is above tree line between miles 7 and 11, rewarding trail users with great views of the surrounding mountains and communities below, but also requiring a close watch of the weather. Take note of the alpine wildflowers in the summer—the blooms can be magnificent. There can be snow along the high parts of this segment until mid-July, and

A well-deserved rest at the top. Photo by Pete and Lisa Turner

summer thunderstorms can move in quickly. There are good water sources throughout, but camping is limited due to the thick forests and steep watersheds. The best camping is near Miners Creek with some possibilities on the west side of the range at and below tree line.

Nearly all of this segment is located within the Tenmile Area of the recently created (2022) Camp Hale-Continental Divide National Monument, the only national monument the trail passes through. See sidebar on page 136 in Segment 8 for more detail on the monument.

TRAILHEAD/ACCESS POINTS

Gold Hill Trailhead: From the C-470–I-70 interchange on the west side of the Denver area, travel west on I-70 for about 57 miles to exit 203 (Frisco/Breckenridge). Proceed south on CO Highway 9 for about 5.7 miles. The trailhead is on the right side of the highway at the intersection with Gateway Drive.

Miners Creek Trailhead: The CT can be accessed via FS Road 1000.1/Miners Creek Road at Segment 6 **mile 5.3**. Miners Creek Road departs south of Peak One

> The hanging glacial valley at 11,000 feet in the Tenmile Range supports a huge colony of **pikas**. You are more likely to hear these tiny creatures of the rock slides before seeing them. The uninitiated may confuse their alarm calls with marmots, which are also numerous in this high cirque. Marmots make a high-pitched whistle, whereas the pika's call is a shrill bark.
>
> **TRAVEL TIP**

Atop the Tenmile Range at the end of June, when the snow has melted enough to pass over.
Photo by Bernard Wolf

Boulevard at the south edge of Frisco (just west of the Summit County government offices). The lower part of the 3.4-mile road is suitable for high-clearance vehicles, but the last 1.3 miles is not recommended without low-range 4WD and high clearance.

Copper Far East Lot Trail Access (also referred to as Corn Lot Trailhead): See Segment 8 on page 131.

TRAIL DESCRIPTION: Segment 7 begins at the Gold Hill Trailhead, **mile 0.0.** Leave the parking lot on single-track to the west and enter the Tenmile Area of the recently established Camp Hale-Continental Divide National Monument (see sidebar on page 136), then begin climbing where trees killed by pine beetles have been cut down. Turn left at **mile 0.5** on a realigned section where the closed and rehabbed trail continues straight. The trail climbs to **mile 1.4** where the trail intersects the Ophir Mountain Trail (non-motorized gravel road) and then leaves to the left. Cross a closed logging spur road at **mile 2.0**, passing an old clear-cut area that has been replanted. Curve sharply to the right at **mile 2.2**, where a social trail leaves to the left. Angle right across the Ophir Mountain Trail (well-defined road) at **mile 3.2** and into

BRECKENRIDGE AND FRISCO

SERVICES, SUPPLIES, AND ACCOMMODATIONS

Breckenridge is approximately 4 miles south of the Gold Hill Trailhead on Highway 9. Frisco has comparable services and is located approximately 5 miles northwest of the trailhead. The Summit Stage provides free bus service between the towns. There is a bus stop on Highway 9 about 0.2 mile south of the trailhead. Both towns are restored mining/railroad towns serving the popular Summit County ski resorts.

Distance from CT: 4 miles to Breckenridge
(5 miles to Frisco)
Elevation: 9,605 feet
Zip code: 80424 (Frisco 80443)
Area code: 970

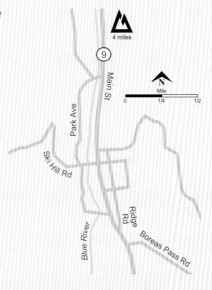

Bus
Summit Stage
(970) 668-0999

Gear (including fuel canisters)
Mountain Outfitters
112 S. Ridge St.
(970) 453-2201

Groceries
City Market
400 N. Park Ave.
(970) 453-0818

Info
Breckenridge Tourism Office
111 Ski Hill Road
(970) 453-2913

Laundry
Frisco's Washtub Coin Laundry
406 Main (Frisco)
(970) 668-3552

Lodging
Fireside Inn B&B and Hostel
114 N French St.
(970) 453-6456

The Bivvi Hostel
9511 Highway 9
(970) 423-6553

Medical
Breckenridge Medical Clinic
555 S. Park Ave.
(970) 453-1010

Post Office
Breckenridge Post Office
305 S. Ridge St.
(970) 547-0347

Frisco Post Office
35 W. Main St.
(970) 668-0610

Showers
Breckenridge Recreation Center
880 Airport Rd.
(970) 453-1734

Hikers on the ridge of the Tenmile Range. Photo by Jeff Sellenrick

a narrow strip of live trees. At **mile 3.7** the trail turns left and joins the Peaks Trail near some beaver ponds. There is water and good camping here.

At **mile 4.0**, turn right onto the Miners Creek Trail, leaving the Peaks Trail. Over the next mile, cross and recross a small tributary to Miners Creek several times on small bridges and pass through a recent burn area. There are good campsites in the vicinity of the crossings. At **mile 5.3**, reach the Miners Creek Trailhead, with good camping in the area.

Turn left after passing through the parking area to continue on the Miners Creek Trail. Cross two bridges over Miners Creek at **mile 5.4** with more camping potential just beyond. Cross the first of many avalanche paths on the CT at **mile 6.4**, evidence of the power of moving snow. Water is available at creek crossings at **mile 6.7** and **mile 6.9**. Camping can be found nearby.

The trail reaches tree line and continues in a southerly direction, climbing below Tenmile Peak and Peaks 3, 4, and 5, briefly leaving the National Monument before reaching the crest of the Tenmile Range at **mile 9.0** and the high point of the CT to this point (12,491'). The CT won't exceed this elevation again until Segment 20 (if traveling the CT Collegiate East route) or Segment CW01 (if traveling the CT Collegiate West route). The views on a clear day are magnificent. Along the way up, Lake Dillon and the town of Dillon are visible to the north, Breckenridge sits

TRAIL WORK COMPLETE

CTF trail crews, along with Forest Service staff and other partner organizations, have been working to complete a realignment between **mile 5.4** and **mile 6.7** to improve the sustainability of the trail. The trail construction was completed during the 2023 season; however, final trail data for this section of the segment was not available prior to publication and the segment description describes the old route. Check the CTF website (ColoradoTrail.org) for updated information on the new trail section.

TUNDRA PLANTS

VIEWING
OPPORTUNITY

In portions of Segments 6 and 7, the CT passes into the open realm of the tundra for the first time. In Colorado, this alpine zone varies from above an altitude of 10,500 feet in the northern part of the state to more than 12,000 feet near the border with New Mexico. Above tree line, a harsh environment exists—one where summer lasts a fleeting 30 to 40 frost-free days, and in winter, temperatures can fall to well below zero. In essence, the tundra is a cold desert with precipitation levels of 20 inches per year or less, mainly in the form of snow. How this snow is distributed by the wind dictates the distribution of hardy alpine plants.

Tiny blue alpine forget-me-nots.
Photo by Bill Manning

Compared with other alpine regions in the lower 48 states, Colorado's alpine tundra is particularly rich in plant numbers and species, putting on a spectacular display beginning with the first alpine forget-me-nots (*Eritrichium elongatum*) in June and lasting until arctic gentians (*Gentiana algida*) in early September signal the rapid approach of fall. Most species are "cushion" plants or miniature versions of species common at lower altitudes, a concession to the severe environment. Their growth rate is slow, with some plants taking up to a century to produce a mat only a foot or so in diameter, and this slow growth is all the more reason to stay on the trail to avoid damaging them.

As you progress westward on the CT, the display of wildflowers becomes even more striking in the deeper soils of the moister western ranges, reaching a climax in the high alpine basins of the San Juan Mountains.

Ross Avens are wonderfully colorful at high altitude. Photo by Bill Manning

far below to the east, and Copper Mountain lies 2,500 feet below to the west. After topping out, follow the ridge, passing just west of Peak 6.

The trail descends to the south, steeply at times, and reaches tree line, where there is camping potential shortly below, with water at **mile 11.0** and **mile 11.1**. The trail continues down then makes a sharp right turn and joins the Wheeler National Recreation Trail at **mile 11.4**. Traverse downhill to the northwest, crossing several small seasonal streams, some with bridges and puncheons (similar to boardwalks but not raised above the ground), as well as large avalanche paths and resulting debris, and exit the National Monument before reaching the valley floor. There is limited camping potential on this section because of the generally steep terrain, but some suitable sites can be found on small areas of flatter terrain.

As the trail curves to the left near the valley floor, join a paved path and then cross a large bridge over Tenmile Creek at **mile 13.4**. Shortly after, there is access to the Copper Far East Parking Lot (also referred to as the Corn Lot Trailhead), then leave the paved path to the left onto single-track at **mile 13.5**. There is good access to water and possible campsites before reaching CO Highway 91, where parking is prohibited, and the end of Segment 7 at **mile 13.8**. There is no camping within the first 4 miles of Segment 8 while on Copper Mountain Resort property.

AVALANCHE!

VIEWING OPPORTUNITY

Significant portions of the CT pass through prime avalanche terrain, typically consisting of high alpine peaks and ridges, steep slopes, and deep snow depths. When a large amount of snow falls over a relatively short period of time or weak layers develop in the snowpack, the snow can break loose either as an isolated layer or all the way to the ground and slide down the slope, forming an avalanche. In typical winters, many slopes avalanche but stay within the existing avalanche path. Avalanche paths are most obvious below tree line where they are characterized by a relatively open slope with many small to medium trees, frequently aspens, with a path defined by larger, more mature trees along each side. On occasion, a few mature trees that have withstood previous avalanches may remain as islands within the path. Avalanches also occur above tree line, but generally there is no visible defined path after the snow has melted.

2019 was a historic year for avalanches throughout Colorado and impacted the CT on several segments. The winter of 2018–2019 was a slightly better than average snow year for most of Colorado through the end of February. Early March brought a series of storms that added a significant amount of snow to the snowpack over a two-week period. The snowpack increased in many areas to as much as 170 percent of average. These storms added a significant weight of snow that the snowpack could not support, and a historic avalanche cycle ensued. In some cases, the avalanches exceeded their historical width and length, breaking or knocking down many large mature trees. In some locations, when the snow stopped, these trees and hardened snow came to rest on the CT. The greatest impact from avalanches to the CT occurred on Segments 7 (west side of the Tenmile Range), 13 (immediately south of the Avalanche Trailhead), and 24 (upper and lower Elk Creek valley). Several of the avalanches filled in the creeks in the bottom of the valleys, and the momentum of the snow caused it to continue uphill on the other side of the valley where the snow and trees finally came to rest. It took many days for CTF Adopters and trail crew volunteers, Forest Service staff, and other partner organizations to clear the trail so that it was passable, as well as rebuild several bridges damaged by the avalanches. The avalanche debris on Segment 24 was particularly challenging because of the remote location, wilderness regulations requiring all trees to be cut out using hand saws, and the depth of the debris, including piles of snow that didn't melt until the following year. Because of these challenges, Segment 24 did not get fully cleared until the 2022 field season. Take note of the piles of debris as you travel the trail and appreciate the power of natural forces and the amount of effort expended by many people to make the trail passable again.

Features

MILEAGE	COMMENTS	ELEVATION
0.0	Begin Segment 7 at Gold Hill TH	9,199'
0.5	Left (closed trail straight ahead)	9,426'
1.4	Left (Ophir Mountain Tr [gravel road] to right)	9,640'
2.0	Straight across closed road	9,987'
2.2	Sharp right (side trail to left)	10,092'
3.2	Angle right across Ophir Mountain Tr (non-motorized road)	10,170'
3.7	Left onto Peaks Tr	9,955'
4.0	Right onto Miners Creek Tr (Peaks Tr continues to left)	10,017'
4.1	Bridge over creek	10,026'
4.6	Bridge over creek	10,311'
5.3	Left on Miners Creek Tr at Miners Creek TH	10,555'
5.4	Bridges over Miners Creek	10,579'
6.7	Stream	11,116'
6.9	Stream	11,284'
9.0	High point of Tenmile Range crossing	12,491'
11.0	Small stream	11,502'
11.1	Seasonal stream	11,439'
11.4	Sharp right onto Wheeler Tr	11,243'
13.4	Left onto paved path and Tenmile Creek bridge	9,766'
13.5	Copper Far East Parking Lot access, then left onto single-track (paved path continues straight)	9,770'
13.8	End Segment 7 at Hwy 91	9,820'

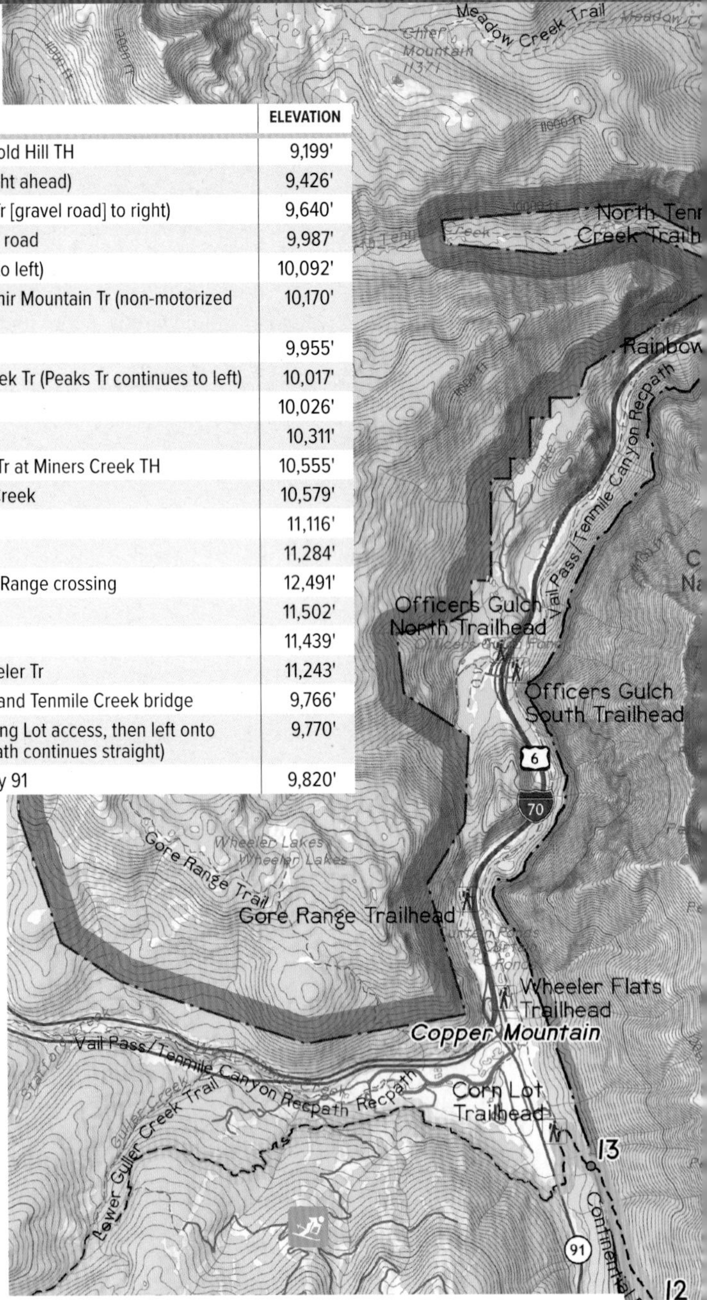

Legend:
- ▲ Peak
- 🚶 Trailhead
- ⚊ Campground
- 37 County Road
- 37 Forest Route
- ----- Trails
- FS 564.N Forest Road
- ⚊ Interstate
- ⚊ Highway
- ⚊ County Road
- Monument
- Wilderness Area
- National Forest
- BLM Public Land
- State Lands

Elevation and Distance

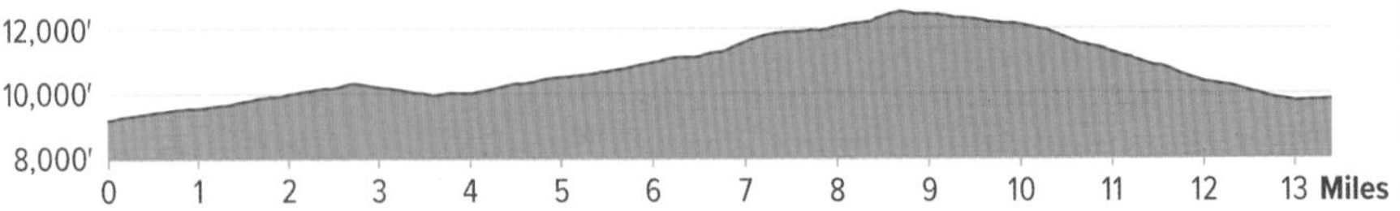

THE COLORADO TRAIL

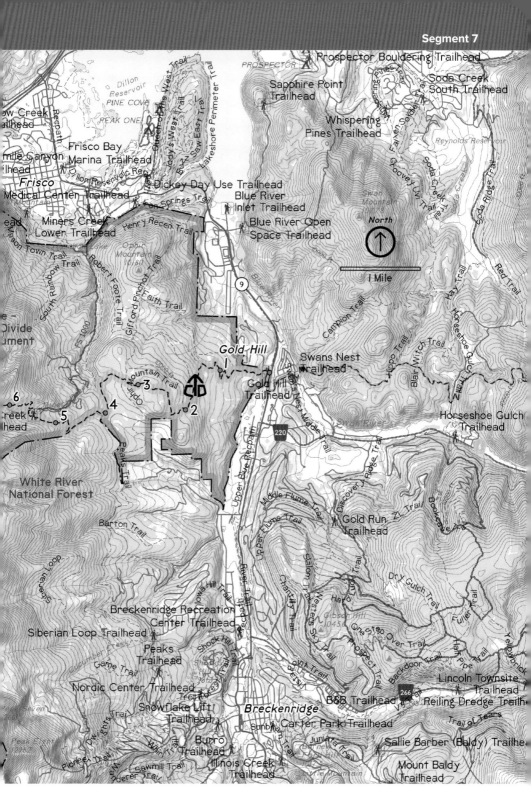

SEGMENT 8
Copper Mountain to Tennessee Pass

Forest Service workers pack in supplies for a volunteer crew.
Photo by Bill Bloomquist

Distance	25.0 miles
Elevation Gain	Approx. 4,417 feet
Elevation Loss	Approx. 3,810 feet
USFS Map	White River National Forest
The CT Databook, 8th Edition	Pages 26–27
The CT Map Book	Pages 21–24
Trails Illustrated Maps	No. 109, 1202
Latitude 40° Map	Summit County Trails
Jurisdiction	Holy Cross and Dillon Ranger Districts, White River National Forest

ACCESS FROM
DENVER END

ACCESS FROM
DURANGO END

AVAILABILITY
OF WATER

BICYCLING

ABOUT THIS SEGMENT: The beginning of Segment 8 is much different from the preceding segments. The trail passes through Copper Mountain Resort, traversing ski slopes, edging along a golf course, and skirting the Copper Mountain Village Center, where there are restaurants, outdoor shops, lodging, and limited grocery shopping. While convenient for resupply, this area can be pricier than other resupply spots. Camping is also prohibited for the first 4 miles of Segment 8, where the CT passes through the resort property.

Somewhere on the slopes of Copper Mountain the trail crosses the Gore fault, a major fault active during the uplift of the Ancestral Rockies. Rocks west of the fault were displaced downward 10,000 feet or more relative to basement rocks of the Tenmile Range. Both the fault and the bedrock on either side are concealed beneath glacial deposits, but west of the fault redbeds deposited during the rise of the Ancestral Rockies are exposed as the trail climbs toward Searle Pass. On the ridges near the pass, the redbeds are cut by irregular bodies and sheetlike layers of porphyry that were injected during the Laramide Orogeny.

The middle of this segment takes trail users back into the tundra after a long climb from the resort. Again, the views of the surrounding mountains are impressive. After crossing Searle Pass, there are many opportunities for side trips to nearby

Cataract Falls at the edge of the Camp Hale valley, next to the CT at **mile 17.2**. Photo by David Dolton

Copper Mountain to Tennessee Pass

Elk Ridge, the high point of Segment 8. Behind looms the Tenmile Range. Photo by Dan Milner

peaks. The descent to Eagle Park and Camp Hale provides an entirely different feel from Copper Mountain. This abandoned training ground for the 10th Mountain Division is steadily deteriorating under the extreme weather conditions but retains its rich military legacy. Much of the second half of this segment is located within the Camp Hale Area of the recently created Camp Hale-Continental Divide National Monument, the only national monument the trail passes through. See sidebar on page 136 for more detail on the monument.

The CT joins an old railroad bed and passes the ruins of several coking ovens just before reaching Tennessee Pass, capping a scenic walk through a variety of eras that have left their mark on this stretch of the trail.

Crossing Searle and Kokomo Passes exposes trail users to potential severe weather for more than 5 miles while above tree line, **mile 7.5** to **mile 13.0**.

Camp Hale recently became an official national monument, so be sure to enjoy it by stopping for a quick shower along Cataract Creek. There's even a resting bench. But take note of all the shell holes made during World War II training at Camp Hale in the Tennessee Pass area. They're potential "pitfalls" when walking at night or during an engrossing conversation.

TRAVEL TIP

COPPER MOUNTAIN

SERVICES, SUPPLIES,
AND ACCOMMODATIONS

The Colorado Trail passes near the Copper Mountain Resort in the first miles of this segment. Copper Mountain is not a town, but rather a large ski and summer resort. Overnight accommodations and restaurants may be pricey. There is a convenience store/gas station 0.5 mile north of the Copper Far East Lot accessible by either the rec path or CO Highway 91.

Distance from CT: 0 miles
Elevation: 9,600 feet
Zip code: 80443
Area code: 970

Bus
Summit Stage
(970) 668-0999

Groceries
McCoy's Mountain Market
Center Village
(970) 968-2182

Info
Copper Mountain Resort Association
Center Village
(970) 968-6477

Lodging
Copper Mountain Lodging Services
(800) 458-8386

Medical
Closest services in Frisco
(970) 668-3300

Post Office
West Lake Lodge
800 Copper Road
(970) 968-2318 ext. 41873 (Self-service only; full service available in Frisco)

TRAILHEAD/ACCESS POINTS: Access to the trail in this area is a bit unusual. Parking is prohibited on the wide shoulders of CO Highway 91 where Segment 8 begins. Nevertheless, there are convenient parking areas.

Copper Far East Lot Trail Access (also referred to as Corn Lot Trailhead): This large parking area is adjacent to Segment 7, **mile 13.5**, 0.3 mile of nearly flat trail from the beginning of Segment 8. From the C-470–I-70 interchange on the west side of the Denver area, travel west on I-70 for 64 miles and take exit 195 (Copper Mountain/Leadville/CO Highway 91). Drive beyond the stoplight and entrance to Copper Mountain (on the right) and, less than a half mile farther, turn left into the large Copper Far East Parking Lot where there are bathrooms, though at times they are locked. Mid-lot on the east edge, find the CT (and CDT) trailhead with sign. To reach the start of CT Segment 8, beyond the trailhead sign and paved rec path, follow the CT south 0.3 mile to where it crosses CO 91. Segment 8 begins on the west side of the highway. Use caution when crossing the highway; traffic comes very fast from both directions.

The CT crosses beneath the ski lifts at Copper Mountain Resort. Photo by Julie Vida and Mark Tabb

Tennessee Pass Trailhead: 🚗 See Segment 9 on page 141.

TRAIL DESCRIPTION: Begin Segment 8 on the west side of CO Highway 91 (no parking) at **mile 0.0**. Camping is prohibited for the next 4 miles. The trail enters the forest southwest and follows a few switchbacks uphill as it skirts the golf course, crosses a stream at **mile 0.5**, a bridge at **mile 0.8**, and passes under a power line. The CT then heads northwest and traverses ski runs, goes under a ski lift, and crosses a ski area two-track at **mile 1.2**. The trail turns left to follow a ski area road at **mile 1.4**, crosses a stream, and passes nearest the Copper Mountain Resort base facilities at **mile 1.5**. There are restaurants, sporting goods shops, and some grocery shopping available. The trail angles left and passes under another ski lift and then joins the uphill leg of another ski area road at **mile 1.6**. The trail passes under another ski lift, then the elevated alpine coaster track, and then another ski lift. At a road junction at **mile 2.0**, the CT angles left onto single-track then turns left at a trail junction at **mile 2.1**. The trail crosses a creek in Union Gulch on a bridge at **mile 2.5**, then passes several trail junctions at **mile 2.6** (turn left), **mile 2.7** (stay right), and another shortly after (continue straight). At **mile 3.2**, cross a boardwalk, under a ski lift, then the last of the ski runs to leave the resort.

MOUNT OF THE HOLY CROSS

VIEWING
OPPORTUNITY

From several vantage points on Segment 8, hikers have excellent views to the west of the photogenic Mount of the Holy Cross. Nearly a century ago, this was perhaps the most famous and revered mountain in America.

In the early 1800s, explorers brought back rumors of a great mountain in the West that displayed a giant cross on its side, but the exact location was shrouded in mystery. The search for the peak became one of the most

W. H. Jackson's famous image.

intriguing in the history of the West. F. V. Hayden made it his top priority in the 1873 field session of his topographic survey. Hayden's team determined that the peak lay somewhere north and west of Tennessee Pass. After several arduous days of travel, Hayden reached the summit on August 22. From Notch Mountain across the valley, famed photographer W. H. Jackson captured an image of the immense snowy cross.

It's hard to imagine today the sensation Jackson's photo caused around the country. Henry Wadsworth Longfellow was moved to write a poem after viewing the image, and well-known artists such as Thomas Moran journeyed to Colorado to paint the peak. Hundreds of people made pilgrimages up Notch Mountain to view the cross, faith healings were reported, and Congress established it as a national monument in 1929.

The mountain was used for mountaineering training by troops from nearby Camp Hale during World War II, including a first-ever winter ascent of the 1,200-foot-high cross in December 1943. But as time passed, religious interest faded and the mountain's monument status was rescinded shortly after the war.

A later USGS survey determined that the 14,005-foot peak just barely qualified as a fourteener (Hayden had listed it at 13,999 feet), and today, Mount of the Holy Cross is a favorite among peak-baggers.

A side trail merges from the left at **mile 4.2**, where the CT continues straight ahead. Cross Jacque Creek at **mile 4.5**, followed by a bridge over Guller Creek at **mile 4.6**. There is a campsite just up the hill between the two creeks. Continue upstream through the meadow along Guller Creek; look off-trail for camping with reasonable water access along the way. Reach tree line just before **mile 8** before staying above tree line for the next 5+ miles. At **mile 8.2**, continue straight at a side trail to Janet's Cabin (reservations required, huts.org).

Continue climbing to reach Searle Pass at **mile 9.1** where you will find spectacular views of the Tenmile Range to the east and the more distant Gore Range to

West of Kokomo Pass descending toward Camp Hale. Photo by Scott Ryberg

the north. In the next few miles, the trail undulates across tundra and crosses seasonal streams with exposed camping. The alpine flowers can be outstanding from this section down Cataract Creek in July and into August. Climb to the top of Elk Ridge at **mile 11.8** (12,284') and the high point of the segment, then enter the Camp Hale Area of the National Monument on the descent to Kokomo Pass, reached at **mile 12.3**. Mount of the Holy Cross (14,005') comes into view to the west across the upper Eagle Creek valley as the trail descends the headwaters of Cataract Creek. Reach the first crossing of Cataract Creek at **mile 13.0** and tree line shortly after. Continue descending on the north side of Cataract Creek where there are several areas with potential campsites with water access along the way.

The trail joins an old roadbed, diverting several times onto single-track realignments. At **mile 15.8**, rejoin the old roadbed and ford Cataract Creek. Continue straight at a junction with a closed road at **mile 16.0**, where there is camping nearby

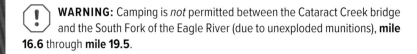

WARNING: Camping is *not* permitted between the Cataract Creek bridge and the South Fork of the Eagle River (due to unexploded munitions), **mile 16.6** through **mile 19.5**.

The CT begins a steady ascent to Searle Pass just past Copper Mountain. Photo by Mike Windsor

below the trail. The trail turns right at a junction with a short spur trail leading to the FS Road 714.1/East Fork Eagle Road, **mile 16.5**. Cataract Creek is crossed just below Cataract Falls on a beautiful bridge constructed in 2019 by Forest Service staff and CTF trail crew volunteers at **mile 16.6**. Camping is not allowed between this point and **mile 19.5** due to possible unexploded munitions within Camp Hale, and trail users should stay on the trail and roads at all times. At **mile 17.3**, the trail turns right onto FS Road 714.1, then leaves the road to the right onto single-track at **mile 17.5**. The trail turns left at **mile 18.1**, passes through the Camp Hale Trailhead, then immediately turns right onto FS Road 714.1. Turn left onto a gated road at **mile 18.3**. The road curves to the left at **mile 18.6** near the remains of Camp Hale concrete bunkers, where the CT angles left onto single-track, crosses a bridge over the East Fork Eagle River, and heads uphill. At **mile 19.5**, angle left across FS Road 726.1/Old Highway Road to regain the trail, which angles right and uphill.

The trail crosses a couple of streams and then crosses the two-track FS Road 798.1/Jones Gulch Way at **mile 20.7**, with potential camping in the area. Cross a bridge at Fiddler Creek, **mile 21.1**, then continue south, leaving the National Monument just before reaching US Highway 24 at **mile 21.6**.

CAMP HALE-CONTINENTAL DIVIDE NATIONAL MONUMENT

In 2022, the Camp Hale-Continental Divide National Monument was created under the provisions of the Antiquities Act of 1906. The National Forest Service cites the natural and cultural history as driving forces for the area's protection. The Ute tribe first used this area for hunting and foraging. Later, Camp Hale would house upwards of 15,000 soldiers, including the 10th Mountain Division, who trained for combat along the ridgelines in the 1940s.

The monument spans nearly 54,000 acres in two units, both of which share a significant footprint with the Colorado Trail. The first covers the Tenmile Range between Copper Mountain Ski Resort and Breckenridge, a fitting location since most consider this area the home of the American ski industry. Today, the Tenmile Range is known to CT hikers as one of the most beautiful yet exposed parts of the Colorado Trail.

The second unit encompasses the Camp Hale area, and trail users will recognize the ruins of army bunkers that serve as an important landmark for any thru-traveler. Fittingly, veterans from Camp Hale made significant contributions to conservation and outdoor education following their time in the service. Notably, David Brower went on to serve as the Sierra Club's first executive director, and Paul Petzoldt went on to found the National Outdoor Leadership School (NOLS).

Taken together, the two units represent a major victory for conservation and outdoor recreation advocates who fought for years to see this area receive the national monument designation. In the years to come, local, state, and national agencies will partner to care for this unique location.

Cross the highway, go around a closed gate and down a dirt road, then cross railroad tracks. At **mile 21.8**, cross a narrow bridge over the South Fork Eagle River at Piney Gulch. The CT turns to the southwest and follows the Mitchell Creek valley in a wide grassy meadow, which features several potential campsites. At **mile 23.1**, the trail angles left onto an old railroad grade then reaches the remains of old coke ovens at **mile 24.5**. Reach the Tennessee Pass Trailhead, adjacent to US 24, and the end of Segment 8 at **mile 25.0**. Camping is allowed more than 100 feet from the trail and parking lot.

THE SHORT LIFE AND
LONG LEGACY OF CAMP HALE

VIEWING
OPPORTUNITY

Camp Hale bunkers. Photo by Bernard Wolf

Now an official national monument, Camp Hale's storied history as part of the legacy of the US Army's 10th Mountain Division began in 1942. Nestled in a large valley north of Tennessee Pass along Highway 24 between Leadville and Minturn and surrounded by mountains at an altitude of 9,200 feet, it offered an ideal location to train troops for mountain and winter warfare during World War II.

In 1942, the valley was transformed in a matter of months into a military camp with more than 1,000 buildings, including barracks, administrative offices, stables, a hospital, movie theater, and field house, capable of accommodating some 15,000 troops. Little evidence of the buildings remains, but visitors to the site can still wander the streets that made up the main camp area—three major north-south roads labeled A, B and C, and 21 cross streets numbered 1st through 21st—and read scattered plaques containing historical information about the camp's construction and activities.

The first troops, members of the First Battalion of the 87th Mountain Infantry Regiment, began arriving at Camp Hale in November 1942. This all-volunteer unit consisted of recreational skiers, cowboys, trappers, forest rangers, and other outdoorsmen who began their training at Fort Lewis in Washington. In 1943, the 85th and 86th Infantry Regiments were activated at Camp Hale, joining the 87th in forming a unit that ultimately became the 10th Mountain Division in 1944. In addition to regular military training, the men of the 10th also became experts in winter survival, skiing, and rock climbing.

Attached to the 5th Army, the 10th fought bloody battles up the spine of Italy's Apennine Mountains in 1945, culminating in February of that year with the taking of the strategic Riva Ridge and Mount Belvedere. The division suffered nearly 25 percent casualties, one of the highest of any unit in the war. Among the wounded was Robert Dole, who went to become a longtime US senator from Kansas and Republican presidential candidate. The division was still fighting in Italy when German forces surrendered in May 1945, ending the war in Europe.

After the war, many veterans of the 10th, drawn by their experiences in Colorado, returned to the state and were instrumental in developing its ski industry. This group included founder of the nearby Vail Ski Resort in 1962, Pete Seibert.

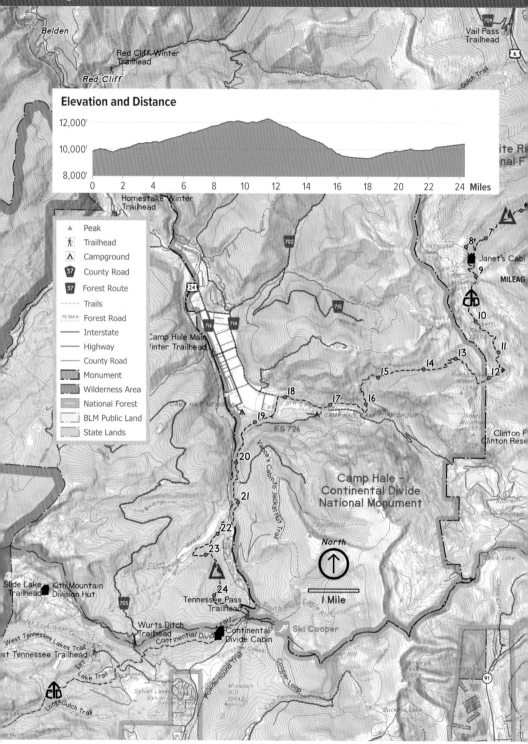

Elevation and Distance

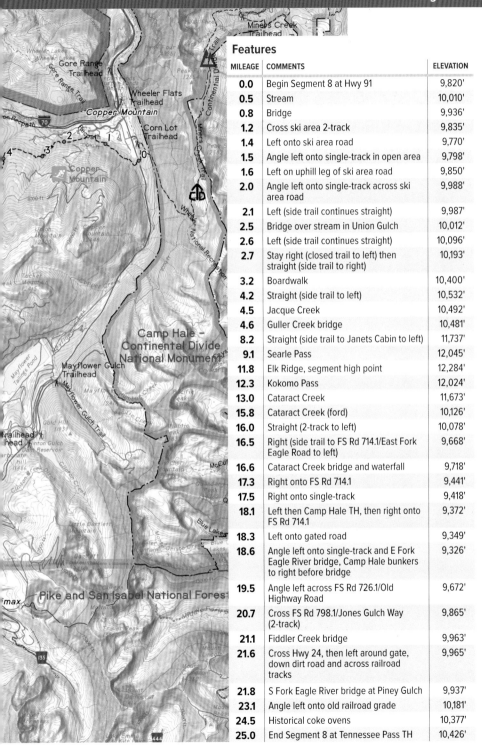

Features

MILEAGE	COMMENTS	ELEVATION
0.0	Begin Segment 8 at Hwy 91	9,820'
0.5	Stream	10,010'
0.8	Bridge	9,936'
1.2	Cross ski area 2-track	9,835'
1.4	Left onto ski area road	9,770'
1.5	Angle left onto single-track in open area	9,798'
1.6	Left on uphill leg of ski area road	9,850'
2.0	Angle left onto single-track across ski area road	9,988'
2.1	Left (side trail continues straight)	9,987'
2.5	Bridge over stream in Union Gulch	10,012'
2.6	Left (side trail continues straight)	10,096'
2.7	Stay right (closed trail to left) then straight (side trail to right)	10,193'
3.2	Boardwalk	10,400'
4.2	Straight (side trail to left)	10,532'
4.5	Jacque Creek	10,492'
4.6	Guller Creek bridge	10,481'
8.2	Straight (side trail to Janets Cabin to left)	11,737'
9.1	Searle Pass	12,045'
11.8	Elk Ridge, segment high point	12,284'
12.3	Kokomo Pass	12,024'
13.0	Cataract Creek	11,673'
15.8	Cataract Creek (ford)	10,126'
16.0	Straight (2-track to left)	10,078'
16.5	Right (side trail to FS Rd 714.1/East Fork Eagle Road to left)	9,668'
16.6	Cataract Creek bridge and waterfall	9,718'
17.3	Right onto FS Rd 714.1	9,441'
17.5	Right onto single-track	9,418'
18.1	Left then Camp Hale TH, then right onto FS Rd 714.1	9,372'
18.3	Left onto gated road	9,349'
18.6	Angle left onto single-track and E Fork Eagle River bridge, Camp Hale bunkers to right before bridge	9,326'
19.5	Angle left across FS Rd 726.1/Old Highway Road	9,672'
20.7	Cross FS Rd 798.1/Jones Gulch Way (2-track)	9,865'
21.1	Fiddler Creek bridge	9,963'
21.6	Cross Hwy 24, then left around gate, down dirt road and across railroad tracks	9,965'
21.8	S Fork Eagle River bridge at Piney Gulch	9,937'
23.1	Angle left onto old railroad grade	10,181'
24.5	Historical coke ovens	10,377'
25.0	End Segment 8 at Tennessee Pass TH	10,426'

SEGMENT 9

Tennessee Pass to
Timberline Lake Trailhead

Wetlands in the Holy Cross Wilderness. Photo by Roger Forman

Distance	13.6 miles
Elevation Gain	Approx. 2,627 feet
Elevation Loss	Approx. 3,004 feet
USFS Map	San Isabel National Forest
The CT Databook, 8th Edition	Pages 28–29
The CT Map Book	Pages 24–26
Trails Illustrated Maps	Nos. 109, 126, 1202
Latitude 40° Map	Summit County Trails
Jurisdiction	Leadville Ranger District, San Isabel National Forest

ACCESS FROM
DENVER END

ACCESS FROM
DURANGO END

AVAILABILITY
OF WATER

BICYCLING

See page 143

ABOUT THIS SEGMENT: In Segment 9, The Colorado Trail turns south, passing through gneiss and 1.4-billion-year-old granite that forms the eastern flank of the Sawatch Range. Alternating between ascents to passes and ridges and descents to creeks or rivers at the bottom of drainages, elevations in the segment range between 10,000 and 12,000 feet. Much of this section of the CT follows the path of the old Main Range Trail, which was built by the Civilian Conservation Corps in the 1930s for both recreation and fire protection. There are great views along the trail of the Arkansas River valley and the Mosquito Range to the east. This part of the Arkansas valley marks the northern end of the Rio Grande Rift. The Sawatch Range peaks to the west provide equally dramatic views. Toward the end of the segment, the CT passes through the southeast corner of the Holy Cross Wilderness Area. Here, there are some great views to the south of Mount Massive, the second-highest mountain in Colorado at 14,421 feet.

The Holy Cross/Mount Massive Wilderness Bike Detour begins at mile 2.7 of this segment and rejoins the CT at the Mount Massive Trailhead and the beginning of Segment 11. See page 143 for a description of the route.

TRAILHEAD/ACCESS POINTS

Tennessee Pass Trailhead: 🚗 From the intersection of Highways CO 9 and US 24 at the north end of Leadville, travel northwest on US Highway 24 for 8.7 miles to

A sign marks the wilderness boundary, Segment 9, mile 6.8. Photo by Bernie Krausse

Left: Sunrise at Porcupine Lakes. Photo by Aaron Locander **Right:** Southbound in the Holy Cross Wilderness, looking toward the Continental Divide. Photo by Bernard Wolf

the top of Tennessee Pass. The trailhead is located on the west side of the highway and includes vault toilets in a frequently busy parking area.

Wurts Ditch Road Trail Access: From the intersection of Highways CO 9 and US 24 at the north end of Leadville, travel northwest on US Highway 24 for 7.1 miles, then turn left onto County Road 19/Meadows Drive and continue for 0.9 mile. Turn right onto FS Road 100/Wurts Ditch Road. It's easy to identify by the old-fashioned yellow road grader parked beside the road. Proceed 0.5 mile to the CT crossing. Parking is limited.

Timberline Lake Trailhead: See Segment 10 on page 149.

SERVICES, SUPPLIES, AND ACCOMMODATIONS: These amenities are available in Leadville; see Segment 10 on page 151.

TRAIL DESCRIPTION: Segment 9 begins at the Tennessee Pass Trailhead, **mile 0.0.** The trail begins left of the two-track heading west from the trailhead parking area. At **mile 0.6**, stay left at a side trail to Point Breeze and Continental Divide Cabins (reservations required, 8-person minimum, huts.org). Enjoy the swing seat with a view of Mount Elbert, Colorado's highest summit at 14,433 feet. Another side trail to the cabins is passed at **mile 0.9**. At **mile 1.2**, continue straight at an intersection with the Treeline Trail on the right, and pass a seasonal spring with potential camping in the area 0.1 mile farther. At **mile 2.5**, cross Wurts Ditch and a creek (both often dry)

HOLY CROSS/MOUNT MASSIVE WILDERNESS BIKE DETOUR

MOUNTAIN BIKING

This detour bypasses both the Holy Cross and Mount Massive Wilderness Areas, beginning at **mile 2.5** of CT Segment 9 and rejoining the CT at the beginning of Segment 11.

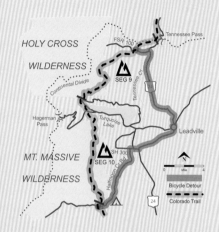

At **mile 0.0**, turn left (downhill) on FS Road 100/Wurts Ditch Road (gravel). At **mile 0.3**, turn left onto County Road 19/Meadows Drive (gravel). At **mile 1.2**, turn right (south) onto paved US Highway 24. Reach an intersection at **mile 8.3** and bear right onto CO Highway 91/ US Highway 24. At **mile 10.0**, reach downtown Leadville, a great place to stop and spend a night and resupply. The historic town has a post office, lodging, restaurants, Safeway grocery store, outdoor gear store, laundromat, and mining museum.

Leave Leadville south on US 24. At **mile 13.5**, turn right onto paved CO Highway 300. At **mile 14.3**, turn left onto County Road 11/Halfmoon Road (paved). At **mile 15.6**, turn right to continue on County Road 11 (paved, then gravel). Follow the road as it angles to the southwest where it becomes FS Road 110, then cycle past numerous campsites and Forest Service campgrounds. Rejoin the CT at the beginning of Segment 11 (**mile 21.1**) just before a bridge on Halfmoon Creek, where it takes off to the left.

Sign at north end of detour. Photo by Bill Manning

An alternate departure from Leadville follows lower-traffic roads and avoids the busy US 24 without a shoulder south of town. To follow this route, head west on 6th Street (paved). At **mile 0.8**, turn left onto County Road 4/ McWethy Drive (paved), then turn right at **mile 1.0** onto West 3rd Street (gravel) and turn right again shortly after onto County Road 36 (gravel). Follow County Road 36 west to **mile 2.5** and turn sharply left onto County Road 36A (dirt) shortly after a second crossing of closed railroad tracks. Follow County Road 36A as it parallels and then crosses the railroad tracks. At **mile 3.9** turn left onto County Road 39 (dirt) near a gas station and convenience store and reach US 24 at **mile 4.0**. Turn left and follow US 24 south for 0.2 mile to reach Highway 300, where the alternate route joins the standard mountain bike detour route at **mile 13.5**.

on two bridges, continuing straight at the junction with the Crane Park trail between the bridges. Cross FS Road 100/Wurts Ditch Road at **mile 2.7**. (the 10th Mountain Division Hut sits northwest 3 miles and 1,000 feet uphill, reservations required, huts.org.) There are good campsites in this area. **The Holy Cross/Mount Massive Wilderness Bike Detour begins here and rejoins the CT at the Mt. Massive Trailhead and the beginning of Segment 11.** See page 143 for a description of the route.

Cross FS Road 131/Lily Lake Road (signed with Lily Lake Loop) at **mile 3.5**, then cross a bridge over the North Fork West Tennessee Creek at **mile 3.6**. After crossing a closed road just beyond (also signed with Lily Lake Loop), cross the West Tennessee Creek bridge at **mile 3.8**, with camping potential nearby. At **mile 4.1**, the trail joins a very old roadbed.

After a gentle climb, continue straight at a rustic trail sign at **mile 4.9**. The trail enters the Holy Cross Wilderness at **mile 6.8** then crosses a small bridge over the stream in Longs Gulch at **mile 6.9**. Climb to Porcupine Lakes at **mile 7.8**, where there are potential campsites near tree line and great views of Galena Mountain along the Continental Divide. Descend and cross a log bridge over Porcupine Creek at **mile 8.1** and then a seasonal stream at **mile 8.3**. Climb above tree line and traverse a short section of tundra with expansive views, then drop back into the forest. Cross a small stream at **mile 9.6** with more camping potential. At **mile 10.0**, angle right at a junction with the trail to Bear Lake Trailhead and access to Uncle Bud's Hut (reservations required, huts.org). Cross a bridge over a small stream at **mile 10.3** and turn right at the junction with the side trail to Bear Lake at **mile 10.5**. Cross small bridges at outlets from unnamed lakes at **mile 10.7** and **mile 11.0**. There are more good campsites in the area.

Climb to a saddle at **mile 11.4** where dry camping is possible. The trail climbs above tree line briefly here, then descends steeply on a series of switchbacks, re-enters the trees, and passes two small seasonal streams. Leave the Holy Cross Wilderness at **mile 12.6**. Continue downhill then cross Mill Creek on a sturdy bridge at **mile 13.5** and reach the Timberline Lake Trailhead and the end of Segment 9 at **mile 13.6**.

The Holy Cross Wilderness is notorious for **mosquitos**, especially in the weeks after the initial snowmelt. Be sure to have a bug protection plan in place before starting this segment.

TRAVEL TIPS

There are several lakes and ponds ideal for **camping** situated just off the trail and glaciated headwalls of the Continental Divide, exemplified by Porcupine Lakes (**mile 7.8**), a beautiful spot for high-altitude camping.

10TH MOUNTAIN DIVISION HUT SYSTEM

For backcountry skiing, snowshoeing, and snowboarding enthusiasts, there are several winter access points to the CT, usually where the trail crosses a major pass at a regularly plowed highway. Undoubtedly, the best of these is the Tennessee Pass access at the start of Segment 9, which is smack in the middle of a network of mountain huts run by the 10th Mountain Division Hut Association.

Photo by Bill Manning

The hut association is a nonprofit founded in 1980 by a group of backcountry recreationalists, including several veterans of the US Army's famed 10th Mountain Division, which trained at nearby Camp Hale in the 1940s.

The hut system lies within a large triangle roughly formed by Vail, Breckenridge, and Aspen. In the style of traditional alpine hut-to-hut travel, thirty-four huts provide overnight shelter for backcountry skiers, snowboarders, snowshoers, mountain bikers, and backpackers. Six of the huts were built with donations from family and friends to honor individuals who died while serving in the 10th Mountain Division during World War II.

Janet's Cabin Photo by Bill Bloomquist

The huts are situated between 9,700 and 11,700 feet and are designed for experienced backcountry travelers. Most operate in the winter between late November and late April and then again for three months in the summer.

Accommodations are best described as comfortably rustic, with bunks sleeping about fifteen people in a communal setting. Huts are equipped with wood stoves for heat, propane for cooking, photovoltaic lighting, mattresses, and utensils. Guests bring their own sleeping bags, food, and clothing. Users melt snow for water in winter and collect it from streams in summer.

More than 300 miles of trails link the huts, and several are close to The Colorado Trail, including Janet's Cabin, 10th Mountain Division Hut, and Uncle Bud's Hut. Reservations are required. Contact the 10th Mountain Division Hut Association at (970) 925-5775 or visit its website at huts.org. Note that this website administers a system of huts, including those of the 10th as well as the Summit Huts Association, the Alfred A. Braun Huts, Grand Huts Association, Friends Huts, and privately owned huts.

Features

MILEAGE	COMMENTS	ELEVATION
0.0	Begin Segment 9 at Tennessee Pass TH	10,426'
0.6	Left (side trail straight ahead to cabins)	10,533'
0.9	Straight ahead (side trail to right to cabins)	10,498'
1.2	Straight ahead ("Treeline" Tr to right)	10,479'
2.5	Wurts Ditch and seasonal creek bridges (side trail to Crane Park to left)	10,433'
2.7	Straight across FS Rd 100/Wurts Ditch Road	10,488'
3.5	Straight across FS Rd 131/Lily Lake Road	10,392'
3.6	N Fork W Tennessee Creek bridge, then cross closed road	10,391'
3.8	W Tennessee Creek bridge	10,365'
4.1	Angle right onto old roadbed	10,487'
4.9	Straight at trail jct	10,722'
6.8	Enter Holy Cross Wilderness	10,913'
6.9	Longs Gulch bridge	10,917'
7.8	Porcupine Lakes	11,452'
8.1	Porcupine Creek bridge	11,252'
8.3	Seasonal stream	11,314'
9.6	Small stream	11,465'
10.0	Angle right (side trail to Bear Lake TH to left)	11,342'
10.3	Bridge over small stream	11,247'
10.5	Right (side trail to Bear Lake to left)	11,128'
10.7	Two bridges over small stream near shallow unnamed lake	11,122'
11.0	Bridge over small stream near unnamed lake	11,044'
11.4	Saddle	11,426'
12.6	Exit Holy Cross Wilderness	10,564'
13.5	Mill Creek bridge	10,085'
13.6	End Segment 9 at Timberline Lake TH	10,041'

North

↑

1 Mile

THE COLORADO TRAIL

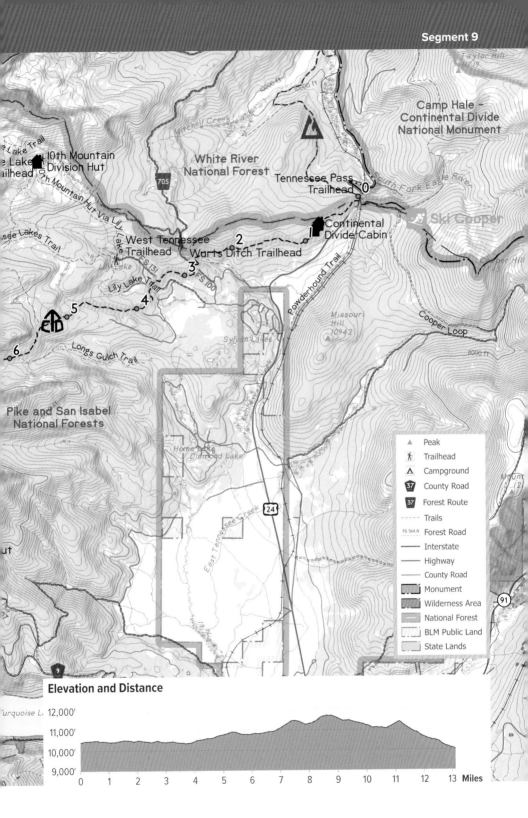

Camp Hale –
Continental Divide
National Monument

White River
National Forest

Tennessee Pass
Trailhead

10th Mountain
Division Hut

Ski Cooper

Continental
Divide Cabin

West Tennessee
Trailhead

Warts Ditch Trailhead

Lily Lake Trail

Longs Gulch Trail

Powderhound Trail

Missouri
Hill
10,943

Cooper Loop

Sylvan Lakes

Pike and San Isabel
National Forests

Home Lake
Diamond Lake

East Tennessee Creek

24

91

Legend

▲	Peak
🚶	Trailhead
△	Campground
37	County Road
37	Forest Route
-----	Trails
FS 564.N	Forest Road
——	Interstate
——	Highway
——	County Road
	Monument
	Wilderness Area
	National Forest
	BLM Public Land
	State Lands

Elevation and Distance

Tennessee Pass to Timberline Lake Trailhead   147

SEGMENT 10
Timberline Lake Trailhead to Mount Massive Trailhead

A stout bridge crosses Busk Creek near the start of Segment 10.
Photo by Pete Turner

Distance	13.3 miles
Elevation Gain	Approx. 2,690 feet
Elevation Loss	Approx. 2,676 feet
USFS Map	San Isabel National Forest
The CT Databook, 8th Edition	Pages 30–31
The CT Map Book	Pages 26–28
Trails Illustrated Maps	Nos. 126, 127, 1202
Latitude 40° Map	Summit County Trails
Jurisdiction	Leadville Ranger District, San Isabel National Forest

ACCESS FROM
DENVER END

ACCESS FROM
DURANGO END

AVAILABILITY
OF WATER

BICYCLING

See page 143

ABOUT THIS SEGMENT: Segment 10 takes trail users into the Mount Massive Wilderness and features multiple long climbs and descents. The segment begins at the Timberline Lake Trailhead, which has water sources and potential camping nearby but limited parking capacity. Around **mile 6.0**, the CT crosses into the Leadville National Fish Hatchery, one of the oldest hatcheries in the federal system. It was established by Congress in 1889 and is still active. The hatchery buildings are about 2 miles east of where the CT crosses Rock Creek. Slightly past **mile 10.0**, a side trail leads to the top of Mount Massive (14,421'), the second-highest mountain in Colorado. For those interested in the side trip, it is 3.5 miles each way, with about 3,350 feet of climbing. This segment ends soon after leaving the wilderness area and reaches the Mount Massive Trailhead.

A green carpet of groundcover surrounds the path. Photo by Roger Forman

During the last ice age, the Sawatch Range was arrayed with glaciers and ice-fields. Glaciers in the major valleys advanced beyond the mountain front and into the Arkansas valley, leaving massive lateral and terminal moraines composed of glacial debris that accumulated as the glaciers advanced down the valleys and the ice melted at their snouts. Turquoise Lake lies behind one of these terminal moraines. The valley of Halfmoon Creek was also occupied by a glacier that left prominent lateral moraines, which the trail descends and then climbs when traveling from Segment 10 to 11.

TRAILHEAD/ACCESS POINTS

Timberline Lake Trailhead: Timberline Lake Trailhead is at the western-most point of Turquoise Lake Road, which travels around Turquoise Lake. To get

Left: Looking north at peaks in the Holy Cross Wilderness Area. Photo by Carl Brown
Right: Airing out one's feet is delightful! Photo by Pete Turner

to the trailhead from US Highway 24/Harrison Avenue in the center of Leadville, turn west on West 6th Street and follow it to a T intersection with County Road 4/ McWethy Drive. Turn right onto County Road 4 and curve to the left after 0.1 mile where McWethy Drive angles right. Continue following County Road 4 at all intersections, which then is also Turquoise Lake Road as it crosses the Sugarloaf Dam that forms the reservoir. Follow the road along and above the south and west side of the reservoir, angling to the right onto County Road 9/Turquoise Lake Road at the intersection for FS Road 105/Hagerman Pass Road. Follow County Road 9 to its westernmost point and turn west onto the 100-yard access road to the trailhead. It is also possible to reach the trailhead via County Road 9 around the north side of the lake, but the southern route is a bit shorter from town.

Mt. Massive climbers diverge here.
Photo by Bill Manning

Mount Massive Trailhead: See Segment 11 on page 158.

TRAIL DESCRIPTION: Segment 10 begins at the Timberline Lake Trailhead at the head of Turquoise Lake, **mile 0.0**. Leave the trailhead to the west, crossing a small creek on a boardwalk, then cross the Lake Fork Arkansas River on a substantial bridge where there is camping nearby. At **mile 0.1**, go left at the Timberline

LEADVILLE

Leadville, a historic mining and railroad town, is about 8 miles east of the trail access points by way of Turquoise Lake Road.

Distance from CT: 8 miles
Elevation: 10,152 feet
Zip code: 80461
Area code: 719

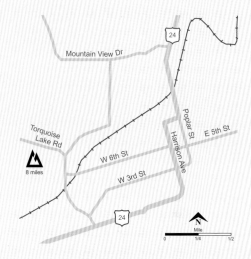

Dining
Several locations in town

Gear (including fuel canisters)
Leadville Outdoors
225 Harrison Ave.
(719) 293-2728

Groceries
Safeway
1900 N. Poplar Way
(719) 486-0795

Info
Chamber of Commerce
809 Harrison Ave.
(719) 486-3900

Laundry
Mountain Laundry
1707 Poplar Ave.
(719) 486-0551

Lodging (several)
Inn the Clouds Hostel & Inn
500 E. 7th St.
(719) 427-4888

Colorado Trail House
127 E. 8th St.
(305) 458-8540

Medical
St. Vincent General Hospital
822 W. 4th St.
(719) 486-0230

Post Office
Leadville Post Office
130 W. 5th St.
(719) 486-9397

Lake Trail junction, then cross a small creek. Cross Glacier Creek at **mile 0.4** on a bridge, then cross Busk Creek on another bridge at **mile 1.2**, with good camping nearby. Climb steadily to FS Road 105/Hagerman Pass Road at **mile 1.8** and angle left across the road, where there is a good, dry campsite. Continue climbing until reaching the Sugarloaf Mountain saddle at **mile 3.0**, where the trail crosses a two-track FS Road 105.A/Sugarloaf Mountain Road. Great views of Mount Elbert open up when the CT reaches the high point on the ridge. Enter the Mount Massive Wilderness at **mile 3.3**, with several small streams and good camping just ahead.

Kearney Park offers some welcome openness. Photo by Scott Ryberg

Pass under the summits of Bald Eagle Mountain to the west, crossing several small streams, then descend after reaching a saddle. Angle right at the junction with the Kearney Park Trail, signed to the Fish Hatchery, at **mile 5.5**. There is a good, dry campsite here. Shortly after, at **mile 5.6**, turn left at the junction with the Swamp Lake Trail. At **mile 6.3**, cross the Rock Creek Trail, a closed two-track, then a bridge over Rock Creek. At **mile 6.7,** cross South Rock Creek, then cross the Highline Trail at **mile 8.0**.

At **mile 8.8**, cross a bridge over North Willow Creek, with potential camping in the area. Climb to the top of a ridge at **mile 9.4**, where there is an exposed, dry campsite. Head downhill to **mile 10.2**, where the CT passes the Mount Massive Trail (signed Main Massive Trail). Shortly after, ford Willow Creek at **mile 10.3** and continue descending, then ford South Willow Creek at **mile 10.9**. Leave the Mount Massive Wilderness at **mile 13.1** and reach the Mount Massive Trailhead near Halfmoon Creek and the end of Segment 10 at **mile 13.3**. Elbert Creek Campground, a highly popular campground (fee) for Mount Elbert and Mount Massive climbers, sits just east on FS Road 110/Halfmoon Road.

Rock Creek in the Mount Massive Wilderness Area. Photo by Bill Manning

THE FOURTEENERS AND CLIMBING
MOUNT ELBERT AND MOUNT MASSIVE

HIKING
TIPS

Of the 58 peaks in Colorado that rise above 14,000 feet, nearly two-thirds are within 20 miles of The Colorado Trail. They are a common and inspiring sight from many a ridgetop along the trail. The CT's closest encounter with a fourteener, however, comes when it passes San Luis Peak (14,014') in Segment 20.

All of Colorado's fourteeners lie within a radius of 120 miles, centered in the Sawatch Range near Buena Vista. None of the other Rocky Mountain states has even one fourteener, despite their related geologic history. The reason why may rest with two geological features unique to Colorado: the Colorado Mineral Belt and the Rio Grande Rift. The Colorado Mineral Belt is a northeast-southwest band of igneous rock that follows roughly the same line as the CT. The Rio Grande Rift is a narrow rift valley that includes the San Luis and Arkansas valleys. Both of these features tend to push overlaying rock upward. All but one or two of the fourteeners are along these two features, and the highest and most numerous lie at the intersection of the two.

It is thought that although the entire Rocky Mountain region, including Colorado, Wyoming, and New Mexico, went through a broad uniform uplift, the fourteeners appear to be the result of an additional localized growth spurt involving these two geological features.

Mount Elbert and Mount Massive are the two highest peaks in the state and offer tempting side trips on this stretch of the CT. No technical skills are required for either climb. Nevertheless, one must regard these as serious undertakings due to potentially adverse weather conditions and the strenuous high-altitude hiking. Be prepared—start early; carry warm clothing, rain gear, and plenty of water; and turn back if you encounter bad weather or experience symptoms of altitude sickness.

The Hayden Survey named Mount Massive (14,421') in the 1870s, and despite several subsequent attempts to rename it after various individuals, the descriptive appellation has stuck. Mount Elbert (14,433') was not so lucky. Like so many other mountains in Colorado, it was named for a politician, Samuel H. Elbert, who was appointed by President Abraham Lincoln in 1862 as secretary of the new Colorado Territory. After a succession of posts, Elbert became a Supreme Court justice when Colorado achieved statehood. Elbert the mountain is the highest peak in Colorado and second highest in the contiguous United States. Mount Whitney in California tops it by only 72 feet.

Each summit is about a 7-mile round trip hike from the CT and both can be reached from the Mount Massive Trailhead on Halfmoon Road (the end of Segment 10 and start of Segment 11). The Mount Massive Trail begins just over 3 miles from the end of Segment 10, proceeding west and then north about 3.5 miles to the summit. To climb Mount Elbert, go south on Segment 11 for 1.4 miles, then take the North Mount Elbert Trail another 3.5 miles west to the top.

Features

MILEAGE	COMMENTS	ELEVATION
0.0	Begin Segment 10 at Timberline Lake TH, cross boardwalk, then Lake Fork Arkansas River bridge	10,041'
0.1	Left (Timberline Lake Tr to right)	10,093'
0.4	Glacier Creek bridge	10,124'
1.2	Busk Creek bridge	10,038'
1.8	Angle left across FS Rd 105/Hagerman Pass Road	10,334'
3.0	Angle left across 2-track FS Rd 105.A/ Sugarloaf Mountain Road	11,095'
3.3	Enter Mount Massive Wilderness	11,069'
5.5	Angle right (Kearney Park Tr to left (old roadbed, signed to Fish Hatchery)	10,644'
5.6	Left (Swamp Lakes Tr straight ahead)	10,660'
6.3	Straight (Rock Creek Tr (2-track) to left (signed to Fish Hatchery), then Rock Creek bridge	10,285'
6.7	S Rock Creek	10,348'
8.0	Cross Highline Tr	11,009'
8.8	N Willow Creek bridge	11,087'
9.4	Top of ridge	11,309'
10.2	Straight (Mt. Massive Tr [signed Main Massive Tr] to right)	11,062'
10.3	Willow Creek (ford)	11,036'
10.9	S Willow Creek (ford)	10,816'
13.1	Exit Mount Massive Wilderness	10,067'
13.3	End Segment 10 at Mount Massive TH	10,066'

▲ Peak	----- Trails	▓ Monument	
🚶 Trailhead	FS 564 N Forest Road	▓ Wilderness Area	
Λ Campground	—— Interstate	▓ National Forest	
37 County Road	—— Highway	BLM Public Land	
37 Forest Route	—— County Road	State Lands	

Elevation and Distance

Holy Cross Wilderness

Uncle Bud's Hut

St. Kevin's Lake Trail

Timberline Trail

Timberline Lake Trailhead

0

1 MAY QUEEN

104

2

Turquoise Lake Trail

TABOR

BABY DOE

9

BELLE OF COLORADO

Turquoise Lake

PRINTERBOY GROUP

MATCHLESS

Leadville Junction
Trailhead

SILVER DOLLAR

38

Colorado Midland
Centennial Trailhead

3

Sugarloaf
Mountain

Sugarloaf Dam
Trailhead

Windsor Lake Trailhead

4

Native Lake
Trailhead

4

5

Mt. Massive Golf Course Winter Trailhead

Ice Palace Park Trailhead

4

Lake County
Park Trailhead

Leadville

Swamp Lake Trail

Twin Mounds

Dutch Henry Trailhead

Colorado Mountain College Winter Trailhead

Swamp Lakes

6

Kearney Park Trail

Rock Creek Trail

300

7

160

Leadville National
Fish Hatchery

8

Continental Divide Trail

Mount Massive
Wilderness

9

Willow
Trailhead

Mt. Massive Trail

North

10

24

110

140

North Halfmoon Lakes Trail

11

South Willow Creek Trail

1 Mile

12

East Willow Creek

Arkansas River

13

HALFMOON WEST

HALFMOON EAST

North Halfmoon
Trailhead

Mount Massive
Trailhead

Mt. Elbert
Trailhead

24

Pike and San Isabel
National Forests

North Mt. Elbert Trail

Arkansas River Ranch Trail

Union Creek

Elbert Creek

South Mt. Elbert Trail

Herrington Creek

Corske Creek

SEGMENT 11

Mount Massive Trailhead to Clear Creek Road

Sunset over Twin Lakes. Photo by Jeff Sellenrick

Distance	21.6 miles
Elevation Gain	Approx. 2,910 feet
Elevation Loss	Approx. 4,042 feet
USFS Map	San Isabel National Forest
The CT Databook, 8th Edition	Pages 32–33
The CT Map Book	Pages 28–30
Trails Illustrated Maps	Nos. 110, 127, 1202
Jurisdiction	Leadville Ranger District, San Isabel National Forest

ACCESS FROM
DENVER END

ACCESS FROM
DURANGO END

AVAILABILITY
OF WATER

BICYCLING

ABOUT THIS SEGMENT: Segment 11 starts with a steep climb up the lateral moraine left by the Halfmoon Creek glacier to two climbers' trails that lead to the summit of Mount Elbert (14,433'), the highest mountain in Colorado. The CT skirts the eastern flank of the peak then descends past several creeks and beautiful displays of summer wildflowers and fall aspen colors on the route to Twin Lakes, which lie behind another conspicuous terminal moraine. The Twin Lakes Reservoir, which is part of the Fry-Ark Project, diverts water from the Arkansas River to Colorado's Front Range cities via tunnels.

The trail wraps around the eastern lake and crosses the dam. Along the lake's southern edge, users encounter the decision point and must choose whether to take the CT Collegiate West or the CT Collegiate East. Each route is roughly 80 miles long. Turn left to continue Segment 11 and the Collegiate East, or continue straight for Segment CW01, the start of the Collegiate West. The western route continues along the co-located CDT, as the CT has been from just above Georgia Pass in Segment 6.

Segment 11 travelers may want to take a one-mile (one-way) side trip at this junction to the historic Interlaken to see restored resort buildings of days gone by. After Segment 11 climbs away from the reservoir, there are a lot of intersections. Be sure to keep an eye out for confidence markers and signs at trail junctions.

Cyclists along the south shore of Twin Lakes. Photo by Dan Milnar

Cache Creek in Lost Canyon, 4 miles west of the CT. Photo by Dale Zoetewey

Be advised that the approximately 4 miles traversing around Twin Lakes and the 1½-mile descent to the Clear Creek valley bottom at the end of the segment are exposed to strong sun and severe weather.

TRAILHEAD/ACCESS POINTS

Mount Massive Trailhead: Drive south from Leadville on US Highway 24 for about 3.5 miles. Turn right (west) onto CO Highway 300. Drive 0.8 mile, turn left (south) onto County Road 11/Halfmoon Road, and continue 1.2 miles to an intersection. Take the right-hand road to continue on County Road 11, which becomes FS Road 110. Continue 5.5 miles to the trailhead on the right-hand side of the road, just after crossing Halfmoon Creek.

Twin Lakes Trail Access: Drive south from Leadville on US 24 for approximately 15 miles to CO Highway 82, or north from Buena Vista 19.5 miles. Turn west onto Highway 82 and drive 0.6 mile. Turn left onto graveled County Road 25 and proceed about 1 mile, staying left at all intersections. Reach a small trailhead with limited parking where the road is gated; additional parking is available at two parking areas below and to the west.

TWIN LAKES VILLAGE

SERVICES, SUPPLIES,
AND ACCOMMODATIONS

Twin Lakes Village, an old mining town and perhaps Colorado's oldest resort town, is 1.5 miles south of The Colorado Trail via the Twin Lakes Trail and FS Road 124. The Twin Lakes General Store is delightfully historic and provides many supplies for trail users.

Distance from CT: 1.5 miles
Elevation: 9,210 feet
Zip code: 81251
Area code: 719

Dining
Punky's Smokehouse BBQ Trailer
CO Highway 82 just west of General Store

The Twin Lakes Inn
6435 E. State Highway 82
(719) 486-7965

Gear and Groceries
Twin Lakes General Store
6451 E. State Highway 82
(719) 486-2196

Lodging
The Twin Lakes Inn
6435 E. State Highway 82
(719) 486-7965

Windspirit Cottage & Cabins
6559 E. State Highway 82
(719) 486-8138

Twin Lakes Roadhouse Lodge
6411 E. State Highway 82
(888) 486-4744

Medical
Nearest facilities in Leadville

Clear Creek Road Trail Access: See Segment 12 on page 168.

TRAIL DESCRIPTION: Segment 11 starts at the Mount Massive Trailhead next to Halfmoon Creek, **mile 0.0**. Mountain bikers rejoin the trail here after detouring around the Holy Cross and Mount Massive Wilderness Areas. Turn left onto FS Road 110/Halfmoon Road to cross Halfmoon Creek then turn right onto single-track at **mile 0.1**. Continue straight at a junction with the Mount Elbert Cutoff Trail at **mile 0.3**, then cross Elbert Creek on a bridge. Pass by the remains of an old log cabin and begin climbing a series of switchbacks. At **mile 1.4**, the North Mount Elbert Trail angles to the right while the CT continues straight.

Cross several streams over the next mile, including Box Creek (ford) at **mile 1.9** and Mill Creek at **mile 2.2**. There are good campsites near some of these streams.

The walk around the **Twin Lakes** is flat but very exposed, so many hikers choose to take an afternoon break in town before tackling the six miles around the shore.

TRAVEL
TIP

Segment 11, near its south end, descends toward the Clear Creek Reservoir. Photo by Bernie Krausse

The CT begins following an old roadbed at the last of these stream crossings, **mile 2.5**. Cross Herrington Creek at **mile 3.4** and continue south. Continue straight at **mile 4.8** where the South Mount Elbert Trail angles back sharply to the right. Switchback right at **mile 4.9**, where a side trail goes straight to Lily Pond. At **mile 5.1**, angle right at a junction with another side trail to Lily Pond. At **mile 5.2**, cross a large bridge over Corske Creek and angle to the right. The Upper South Elbert Trailhead is down the trail a few hundred feet and to the left.

Cross FS Road 125.C at **mile 5.3**, then cross a small stream at **mile 5.5**. Continue straight at **mile 6.1** at the junction with the Twin Lakes Trail that leads to Twin Lakes Village (via FS Road 124). Cross two small bridges at **mile 6.2**, then a larger bridge over the fast-moving Bartlett Gulch Creek at **mile 6.3**.

Follow the CT in an easterly direction to an intersection with the trail to the South Elbert Trailhead at **mile 7.2**. Bear right and then straight ahead and follow

WHEN EAST MEETS WEST

Collegiate East or Collegiate West?

It's a question every thru-hiker, biker, or rider faces on the way to or from Durango. Some have a plan going in after carefully considering the virtues of each. Others let inspiration guide them and make a decision only after reaching Twin Lakes in the north or the Fooses Creek turnoff in the south. Still others gather opinions from those they meet along the trail and make their decision en route.

Whatever you decide, there is no right or wrong answer. Neither option is a "short-cut." Lengthwise, they differ by slightly less than 7 miles, the western route being longer. As for elevation gain and loss, Collegiate East gains roughly 17,800 and loses 15,100 feet. For Collegiate West, it's 19,800 and 17,100 feet, not a major difference over an 80-mile stretch.

Here, however, are some factors that may sway your decision one way or the other:

1. Collegiate East is the "classic" route. It has been part of The Colorado Trail since 1987, the year the Trail from Denver to Durango was officially linked. Collegiate West is the "new" route. Though long a part of the Continental Divide National Scenic Trail, it was added to The Colorado Trail only in 2012. Furthermore, Segment CW03 as it currently exists wasn't completed until 2014.

2. East is a bit more "civilized," with higher foot and rider traffic and good access to three major resupply points: Buena Vista, about 10 miles on a well-traveled road; Mount Princeton Hot Springs, right on the trail; and Salida, 13 miles from the trail crossing on US Highway 50. West is wilder and resupply is trickier, with less convenient access to a full range of services until reaching Monarch Pass and access to Salida 22 miles to the east or Gunnison 42 miles to the west, both on US 50.

3. Thunderstorm activity can be a factor. The East is lower in average elevation, more distant from the Continental Divide ridge line, generally less exposed due to fewer and shorter sections above tree line, and may offer better safety when there's lightning. The West is higher overall, closely tracks the Continental Divide, and has much more above-tree line exposure where the storms are most intense.

4. Want to climb a fourteener? Take your pick. East provides relatively close and straightforward access to Mounts Yale, Princeton, Antero, and Shavano, and Tabeguache Peak. From the West, you don't have to go far off trail to access good climbing routes to Mounts Oxford and Belford, Missouri Mountain, and La Plata and Huron Peaks.

5. Mountain bikers take the East route because it offers the only practical detour around extensive portions where bicycles are prohibited, including the Collegiate Peaks Wilderness (Segment CW02), as well as Segment CW03 (not located in wilderness, but Forest Service rules prohibit mountain bike use on the segment).

Aspens in the area of North Willow Creek. Photo by Roger Forman

the trail along the southwestern edge of Lake View Campground, crossing closed two-tracks at **mile 7.4** and **mile 7.6**. The trail then descends a long radius switchback to **mile 7.8**, where it crosses under CO Highway 82 via a large concrete box culvert. This culvert has the distinction of being the only pedestrian underpass on The Colorado Trail. This is another location where many CT users will diverge to Twin Lakes Village, 1.5 miles west along CO 82. The trail beyond here is the beginning of a long—and potentially hot—hike along the shoreline of Twin Lakes.

The trail passes through a grove of large ponderosa pines on the south side of CO 82 and passes the Mount Elbert Pumped-Storage Power Plant at **mile 8.4**. Cross several roads in the next 3 miles, with posts and markers delineating the route. The CT then turns to the right at **mile 11.5** and crosses Twin Lakes Dam. After leaving the dam, continue following the road as it angles right at **mile 12.0**. Continue straight at several road intersections then angle left onto a two-track at **mile 12.1**. Following the two-track leads to a small parking lot and a gate across the two-track at **mile 12.3**. Pass around the gate and continue on the two-track a couple hundred feet, then leave the two-track to the right onto single-track. Follow the trail west above the south shore of Twin Lakes. Reach the junction where the CT Collegiate East and CT Collegiate West routes diverge at **mile 13.8**. Segment 11, the beginning of the CT Collegiate East, turns sharply to the left and climbs away from the lake, while the CT Collegiate West continues straight along with the CDT. For CT Collegiate West directions, skip to page 302 of the *Guidebook*.

Segment 11 continues climbing to reach a ridge, then descends and angles right onto a two-track at **mile 14.7**. At **mile 15.1**, the CT leaves the two-track onto single-track. Cross a seasonal stream with potential campsites, then a small stream at **mile 16.1** where there is good camping. Angle left across FS Road 399/Flume Gulch Road at **mile 16.7**, then enter a spectacular aspen forest. After crossing another small stream, turn left onto the well-used FS Road 398/Lost Canyon Road at **mile 17.6**.

For northbound hikers, it is especially important to note this junction because it is easy to overlook. At **mile 17.7**, continue straight where the road curves to the left, following posts and markers, first on a two-track for a short distance then angling left onto single-track. There is plentiful dry camping potential in this area.

Cross an irrigation ditch that sometimes has water at **mile 18.2**. At **mile 18.4**, reach a two-track and turn right, with a seasonal stream just beyond. At a 4-way intersection at **mile 18.9**, turn right and follow a powerline road. Angle right at an intersection at **mile 19.0** then continue straight, leaving the powerline road at **mile 19.4**. Turn left at an intersection marked with a post at **mile 19.8** and continue climbing to **mile 19.9**, where the CT bears to the right onto single-track, gaining the top of the lateral moraine left by the Clear Creek glacier several hundred feet later. Begin a big-view descent down the moraine into the Clear Creek drainage, staying close to the powerline road before crossing it at **mile 20.3**. The trail continues the long descent before reaching County Road 390/Clear Creek Road. Cross the road to reach the end of Segment 11 at **mile 21.6**, where there is room for a few vehicles to park.

The Collegiate Peaks Wilderness Bike Detour begins here and mountain bikers rejoin the CT on Cottonwood Pass Road at **mile 6.7** of Segment 13, just south of the Avalanche Trailhead. See page 171 for a description of the route.

Features

MILEAGE	COMMENTS	ELEVATION
0.0	Begin Segment 11 at Mount Massive TH	10,066'
0.1	Cross Halfmoon Creek and FS Rd 110/Halfmoon Road, right onto single-track	10,065'
0.3	Straight (Mt Elbert Cutoff Tr to left), then Elbert Creek bridge	10,134'
1.4	Straight (N Mt Elbert Tr to right)	10,588'
1.9	Box Creek (ford)	10,456'
2.2	Mill Creek	10,350'
2.5	Join old roadbed near stream	10,278'
3.4	Herrington Creek	10,316'
4.8	Straight (S Mt Elbert Tr to right)	10,520'
4.9	Sharp right and uphill (side trail to Lily Pond straight ahead)	10,521'
5.1	Angle right (side trail to Lily Pond to left)	10,532'
5.2	Corske Creek bridge, then angle right; Upper S Elbert TH to left	10,518'
5.3	Cross FS Rd 125.C	10,478'
6.1	Straight (Twin Lakes Tr to right)	10,025'
6.3	Bridge over Bartlett Gulch creek	10,041'
7.2	Straight (side trail to S Elbert TH to left)	9,603'
7.4	Straight at abandoned 2-track/ditch	9,474'
7.6	Cross side trail/abandoned 2-track	9,398'
7.8	Hwy 82 underpass	9,322'
8.4	Cross Mt. Elbert Pumped Storage Power Plant driveway, then cross several recreation site access roads	9,296'
11.5	Angle right to cross Twin Lakes Dam	9,220'
12.0	Angle right on road at end of dam	9,212'
12.1	Angle left onto 2-track	9,229'
12.3	Straight around gate after parking area, then right onto single-track	9,243'
13.8	Turn sharply left (CDT/CT Collegiate West continues straight)	9,212'
14.7	Angle right onto 2-track	9,707'
15.1	Straight onto single-track (2-track angles right)	9,839'
16.1	Small stream	9,844'
16.7	Angle left across FS Rd 399/Flume Gulch Road	9,878'
17.6	Left onto FS Rd 398/Lost Canyon Road	9,810'
17.7	Straight ahead onto 2-track, then single-track	9,788'
18.2	Irrigation ditch	9,527'
18.4	Right onto 2-track, then cross seasonal stream	9,426'
18.9	Right onto powerline road	9,372'
19.0	Angle right at intersection	9,396'
19.4	Straight ahead leaving powerline road	9,501'
19.8	Left at intersection	9,730'
19.9	Angle right onto single-track	9,847'
20.3	Cross powerline road	9,492'
21.6	End Segment 11 at County Road 390/Clear Creek Road	8,937'

Elevation and Distance

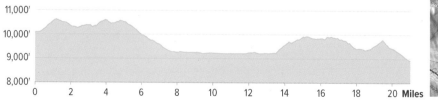

THE COLORADO TRAIL

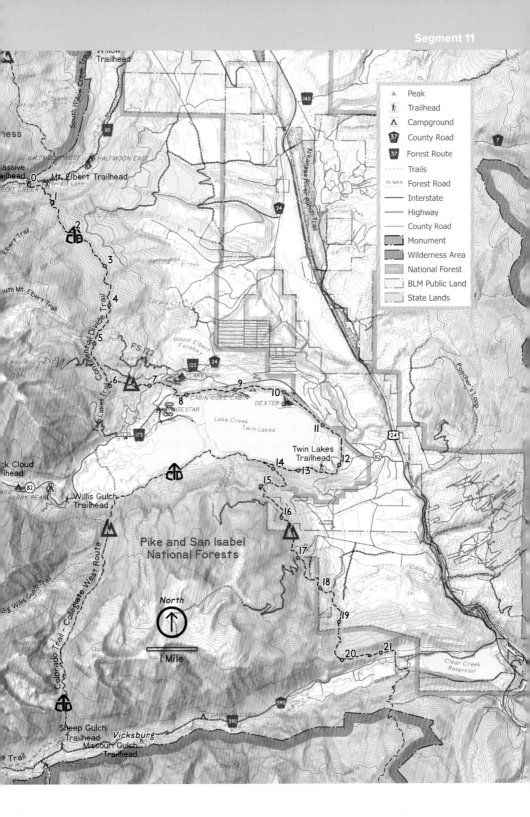

Peak
Trailhead
Campground
37 County Road
37 Forest Route
Trails
FS 564.N Forest Road
Interstate
Highway
County Road
Monument
Wilderness Area
National Forest
BLM Public Land
State Lands

North

! Mile

Pike and San Isabel
National Forests

Twin Lakes
Trailhead

Willis Gulch
Trailhead

Sheep Gulch
Trailhead
Vicksburg
Missouri Gulch
Trailhead

Clear Creek
Reservoir

SEGMENT 12
Clear Creek Road to Silver Creek Trailhead

Beginning of Segment 12 along Clear Creek Road. Photo by David Dolton

Distance	18.7 miles
Elevation Gain	Approx. 4,866 feet
Elevation Loss	Approx. 4,364 feet
USFS Map	San Isabel National Forest
The CT Databook, 8th Edition	Pages 34–35
The CT Map Book	Pages 30–32
Trails Illustrated Maps	Nos. 110, 129, 1202
Jurisdiction	Leadville Ranger District, San Isabel National Forest

ACCESS FROM
DENVER END

ACCESS FROM
DURANGO END

AVAILABILITY
OF WATER

BICYCLING

See page 171

ABOUT THIS SEGMENT: Segment 12 and the first portion of Segment 13 travel through the Collegiate Peaks Wilderness where mountain bikes are not permitted. Mountain bikers begin the wilderness detour at the end of Segment 11 and rejoin the CT on Cottonwood Pass Road at **mile 6.7** of Segment 13. See page 171 for a description of the route.

Clear Creek Reservoir is cradled within the massive terminal moraine of the Clear Creek glacier. At its maximum extent, this glacier advanced far enough to dam the Arkansas River, forming a large temporary lake.

Segment 12 travels through the Collegiate Peaks Wilderness, climbing then descending several times into valleys draining multiple fourteeners and other high peaks to the west. Three fourteeners (Mounts Oxford, Harvard, and Columbia) are located within 3 miles of the trail through this segment. With a little planning, it is possible to climb all three of these peaks in a relatively short period of time. Two other fourteeners (Mounts Belford and Missouri) are also accessible from the CT but require more significant time and effort. There are many great campsites throughout this segment and plenty of water sources.

A major winter blowdown from 2012 in wilderness was cleared with hand saws by CTF volunteers. Photo by Tom Parchman

Clear Creek Road to Silver Creek Trailhead

CTF volunteers installed the eighty-foot steel bridge over Clear Creek in 2007. Photo by Keith Evans

TRAILHEAD/ACCESS POINTS

Clear Creek Road Trail Access: Drive north from Buena Vista approximately 17 miles. Turn left on County Road 390/Clear Creek Road. Drive 2.1 miles to a small, rough parking area just west of the Colorado Division of Wildlife Campground. Three large boulders on the south side of the road mark this trailhead. There are Colorado Trail markers on both sides of the road.

Silver Creek Trailhead: See Segment 13 on page 176.

SERVICES, SUPPLIES, AND ACCOMMODATIONS: These amenities are available in Buena Vista; see Segment 13 on page 179.

TRAIL DESCRIPTION: Segment 12 begins at the very small parking pullout where the CT crosses County Road 390/Clear Creek Road, **mile 0.0**. Follow marker posts south (SWA pass or fishing/hunting license required; see sidebar page 169), then angle left at **mile 0.2** and continue to the east toward the SWA campground (fee required for camping within the SWA). Follow marker posts through the campground then south toward Clear Creek. At **mile 0.5**, cross the steel bridge over Clear

CLEAR CREEK RESERVOIR STATE WILDLIFE AREA FEE

The first one-half mile of Segment 12 passes through the Clear Creek Reservoir State Wildlife Area (SWA). Colorado Parks and Wildlife (CPW) requires an SWA pass (or hunting or fishing license) to access the portion of the CT passing through the SWA. Trail users not possessing a valid hunting or fishing license are required to purchase an SWA pass. Annual passes are available, as are day passes. Passes may be purchased at some local businesses (verify ahead of time) or may be purchased online at cpwshop.com/, select "State Wildlife Area Pass," then "Land & Trails." Online purchases require a Reserve America or CPW account; if you don't have an account, you will need to create one. If purchasing a day pass, trail users must plan carefully as they are only valid for the single date shown on the pass. Neither a State Parks Pass nor a CORSAR card satisfy this requirement.

Creek, constructed with assistance from CTF volunteer trail crews. Begin a steady climb, crossing a closed two-track in Columbia Gulch at **mile 1.9**. At **mile 2.0**, the trail enters the Collegiate Peaks Wilderness. There are several small seasonal streams in the next few miles.

Gain the ridge off Waverly Mountain at **mile 4.9** in a stand of bristlecone pines mixed with firs, where camping is possible not too far beyond the last water. Descend via a series of steep switchbacks. In the valley bottom, the Pine Creek Trail joins the CT from the right at **mile 6.4**. (Diverge here for a major side trip possible to Missouri Basin and/or to climb fourteeners Oxford, Belford, and Missouri.) Continue left and cross a bridge over Pine Creek at **mile 6.6**, then a junction with the Pine Creek Trail heading down-valley to the left just beyond the bridge.

> **(!) WARNING:** Hikers need a one-day pass to cross the Clear Creek Reservoir State Wildlife Area (the first half mile of the segment). These can be bought inexpensively online.

If you have the time, a hike up **Pine Creek into Missouri Basin** is a rewarding side trip. In this emerald-clad basin, you are seemingly in the very heart of the sky-touching Collegiates, surrounded by four fourteeners: Harvard, Missouri, Belford, and Oxford. This long day trip into Missouri Basin, one of the largest alpine basins in the Sawatch Range, is about 5.5 miles each way.

TRAVEL TIP

There is plentiful camping potential in the upper Pine Creek valley. Follow the CT as it bears right and climbs away from Pine Creek. Climb several steep switchbacks before coming to the Rainbow Lake Trail junction at **mile 8.2**. Continue straight ahead, then follow the trail as it travels through scattered open meadows. At **mile 9.1**, gain a ridge off Mount Harvard.

Descend and ford Morrison Creek at **mile 9.9**. At **mile 10.6**, the trail continues straight at a junction with the Wapaca Trail, which leads to the old Lienhart Mine and road. Head downhill and cross Frenchman Creek on a sturdy log bridge at **mile 12.0**. There is a large campsite to the right and uphill on the south side of the creek. At **mile 12.1**, pass junctions with the Frenchman Creek Trail, first to the right and then to the left, continuing straight at each junction.

Gain a ridge below Mount Columbia then descend to **mile 14.4**, where the CT passes an old mine and road, now known as Bunny's Trail. Cross Three Elk Creek and exit the Collegiate Peaks Wilderness at **mile 15.3**, then continue straight where Three Elk Trail crosses the trail at **mile 15.4**. There is potential camping between here and the Harvard Lakes at **mile 15.6**.

The trail continues to descend, crossing Powell Creek at **mile 16.1**, then passing a side trail to the A/U Ranches at **mile 16.7**. At **mile 18.0**, pass another side trail to the A/U Ranches. Reach FS Road 365/North Cottonwood Road at **mile 18.5**. Turn right on the road and reach the Silver Creek Trailhead and the end of Segment 12 at **mile 18.7**. There is a large parking lot with interpretive signs and a vault toilet here.

BLOWDOWN!

VIEWING OPPORTUNITY

Evidence remains of a massive blowdown south of Morrison Creek to Frenchman Creek (**mile 9.9 to mile 12.0**). The trees fell during a 2011–12 winter or spring storm and completely obstructed the trail at many spots along this section. The CTF put a call out for volunteers, who rose to the occasion. Because the blowdown was within the Collegiate Peaks Wilderness, all trees had to be cut using crosscut and other hand saws. The cut ends of downed trees are still visible along the trail as you pass through this section. After nearly 500 hours by over 40 volunteers, including the CTF Adopters of the section, the trail was clear by early July for the 2012 trail season!

COLLEGIATE PEAKS WILDERNESS BIKE DETOUR

MOUNTAIN
BIKING

This mandatory detour bypasses the Collegiate Peaks Wilderness Area. Cyclists will enjoy majestic views of the Collegiate Peaks to the west. Although riders can stay on US Highway 24, which has a reasonably good shoulder, it is more pleasant to turn onto the side roads for the 10-mile pedal into Buena Vista.

Start this detour at the end of Segment 11, **mile 0.0**, and ride east on the graveled County Road 390 past Clear Creek Reservoir. At **mile 2.1**, turn right (south) onto US Highway 24. Continue along the highway to **mile 7.9** then turn left onto the graveled County Rd 371 and cross over the Arkansas River. At **mile 8.1**, curve south onto an abandoned railroad bed of the Colorado Midland Railway, still County Road 371, that follows the Arkansas River and passes through old railroad tunnels as it heads toward Buena Vista, then crosses back over the Arkansas River. The road becomes North Colorado Avenue upon entering neighborhoods at **mile 17.2**.

At **mile 17.4**, turn right (west) onto Main Street and ride through downtown Buena Vista. At **mile 17.6**, Main Street crosses US 24. Continue cycling west on Main Street as it becomes County Road 306/Cottonwood Pass Road. At **mile 26.8**, reach the CT where it crosses County Road 306 just south of the Avalanche Trailhead (vault toilets). Cyclists rejoin the CT here at **mile 6.7** of Segment 13.

Features

MILEAGE	COMMENTS	ELEVATION
0.0	Begin Segment 12 at County Road 390/Clear Creek Road	8,937'
0.2	Angle left toward campground	8,932'
0.5	Clear Creek bridge	8,917'
1.9	Cross closed 2-track	9,656'
2.0	Enter Collegiate Peaks Wilderness	9,730'
4.4	Spring	11,330'
4.9	Ridge off Waverly Mountain	11,654'
6.4	Angle left (Pine Creek Tr to right)	10,437'
6.6	Pine Creek bridge, then angle right (Pine Creek Tr to left)	10,429'
8.2	Straight (Rainbow Lake Tr to right)	11,556'
9.1	Ridge off Mount Harvard	11,850'
9.9	Morrison Creek (ford)	11,575'
10.6	Straight (Wapaca Tr to left)	11,526'
12.0	Frenchman Creek bridge	11,031'
12.1	Cross Frenchman Creek Tr	10,968'
14.4	Straight (Bunny's Tr to left)	10,644'
15.3	Three Elk Creek and exit Collegiate Peaks Wilderness	10,284'
15.4	Cross Three Elk Tr	10,278'
15.6	Harvard Lakes	10,241'
16.1	Powell Creek	10,048'
16.7	Pass side trail to A/U Ranch	9,958'
18.0	Pass 2nd side trail to A/U Ranch	9,865'
18.5	Right onto FS Rd 365/North Cottonwood Road	9,421'
18.7	End Segment 12 at Silver Creek TH	9,435'

Elevation and Distance

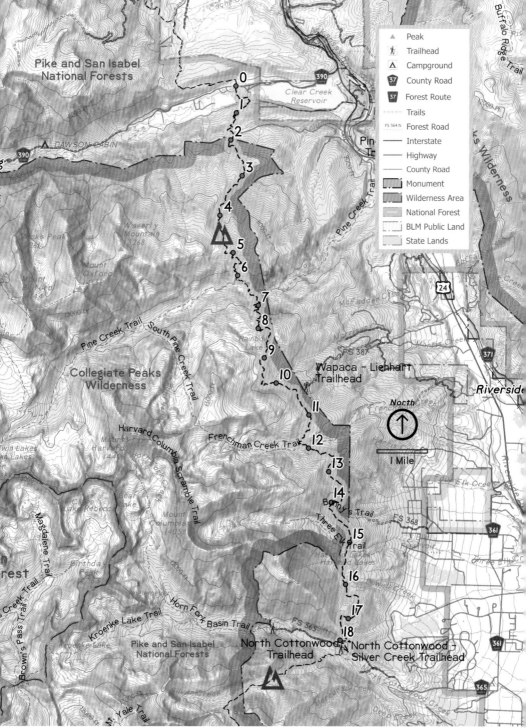

Legend

- ▲ Peak
- 🚶 Trailhead
- ⛺ Campground
- 🛢 37 County Road
- 🛢 37 Forest Route
- - - - - Trails
- FS 564.N Forest Road
- Interstate
- Highway
- County Road
- Monument
- Wilderness Area
- National Forest
- BLM Public Land
- State Lands

Pike and San Isabel
National Forests

Clear Creek
Reservoir

DAWSON CABIN

Collegiate Peaks
Wilderness

Pine Creek Trail

South Pine Creek Trail

Harvard Columbia Scramble Trail

Frenchman Creek Trail

Wapaca - Lienhart
Trailhead

North
↑
I Mile

Benny's Trail

Three Elk Trail

FS 368

Riverside

Horn Fork Basin Trail

Kroenke Lake Trail

Magdalene Trail

Brown's Pass Trail

Mt. Yale Trail

Pike and San Isabel
National Forests

North Cottonwood
Trailhead

North Cottonwood -
Silver Creek Trailhead

SEGMENT 13
Silver Creek Trailhead
to Chalk Creek Trailhead

Mount Princeton from Mount Yale. Photo by Jeff Sellenrick

Distance	22.4 miles
Elevation Gain	Approx. 4,296 feet
Elevation Loss	Approx. 5,343 feet
USFS Map	San Isabel National Forest
The CT Databook, 8th Edition	Pages 36–37
The CT Map Book	Pages 32–34
Trails Illustrated Maps	No. 129, 1202
Jurisdiction	Salida Ranger District, San Isabel National Forest

ACCESS FROM
DENVER END

ACCESS FROM
DURANGO END

AVAILABILITY
OF WATER

BICYCLING

See page 171

ABOUT THIS SEGMENT: Segment 13 begins at the Silver Creek Trailhead with a long climb up the Silver Creek valley, passes into the Collegiate Peaks Wilderness, then tops out on a saddle on the east ridge of Mount Yale (14,196'). The views from here are outstanding, and a short jaunt up the knoll to the east of the saddle brings the Arkansas valley into view. (It is possible and straightforward to climb Mount Yale via the east ridge, although the faint trail disappears and it's necessary to do some scrambling. Allow about four hours for the round trip and don't be discouraged by the false summits along the route.) The descent to the Avalanche Trailhead has some very steep sections and trekking poles come in handy on the descent.

The CT leaves the wilderness area just before reaching the Avalanche Trailhead, where mountain bikers can rejoin the trail. Eventually, the trail contours around the base of Mount Princeton (14,200'). As it approaches Chalk Creek, the CT descends along a lateral moraine left by the Chalk Creek Glacier—the terminal moraine of the glacier and the broad aprons of gravel spread by its melt water are conspicuous in the valley below. The CT begins a 5.7-mile road walk where it joins County Road 322 to bypass private land. The Colorado Trail Foundation has been searching for a way to realign this onto trail for years but has not had any luck yet. A soak at the Mount Princeton Hot Springs Resort can help ease the monotony of road walking, though. West of the resort, the road route skirts the base of the Chalk Cliffs, which are not chalk at all but 65-million-year-old granite largely altered to white clay by water from the hot springs. Staying on the route in this area can be tricky due to the numerous road intersections, so be alert and consult your *Guidebook, Databook, Map Book,* or phone app to ensure you stay on route.

West along one of the county roads near Segment 13's end with part of Mt. Princeton behind.
Photo by Jeff Sellenrick

Silver Creek Trailhead to Chalk Creek Trailhead

Chalk Cliffs from near Mount Princeton Hot Springs. Photo by Julie Vida and Mark Tabb

TRAILHEAD/ACCESS POINTS

Silver Creek Trailhead: From US Highway 24 at the north end of Buena Vista, 7 blocks north of Main Street, turn west on Crossman Avenue, also known as County Road 350. Follow it for 2 miles to its end where it intersects County Road 361. Turn right (north), proceed 0.9 mile, and make a sharp left turn (south) onto County Road 365, a gravel road. The road soon turns west and continues for 3.5 miles (sometimes rough and rutted) to the northbound CT trailhead. A trail register and sign identify it and there is a small informal parking area on the south side of the road. Continue 0.1 mile to the Silver Creek Trailhead on the south side of the road, the end of Segment 12 and beginning of Segment 13. There is a large gravel parking lot, interpretive signs, and a vault toilet here. On the north side of the road, there is an even larger parking lot suitable for horse trailers.

Avalanche Trailhead: From US Highway 24 in Buena Vista, turn west at a traffic light onto West Main Street, which becomes County Road 306/Cottonwood Pass Road at the edge of town. Drive 9.1 miles to the Avalanche Trailhead on the north side of the highway. You may spot Colorado Trail markers on both sides of the highway about 0.2 mile before the trailhead entrance sign on the right-hand side. The CT crosses through the parking area, with marker posts on either side.

South Cottonwood Trailhead: 🚗 From the traffic light at US Highway 24 and Main Street in Buena Vista, proceed west on Main Street, becoming County Road 306/Cottonwood Pass Road for nearly 7 miles. Turn left onto County Road 344/Cottonwood Lake Road. After about 0.3 mile, the CT crosses the road. There is a small primitive parking area at the South Cottonwood Trailhead on the left-hand side of the road.

Chalk Creek Trailhead: 🚗 See Segment 14 on page 185.

TRAIL DESCRIPTION: Segment 13 begins at the Silver Creek Trailhead, **mile 0.0.** Begin south beyond the signs and cross a bridge over North Cottonwood Creek at **mile 0.1.** Pass a trail register then climb through a mixed spruce and fir forest. There are some potential campsites with accessible water in the first couple of miles, although the best camping with good water access is in the upper Silver Creek valley near **mile 2.2.** Continue following Silver Creek to **mile 2.4,** where the trail crosses the creek on a small bridge. Enter the Collegiate Peaks Wilderness at **mile 2.7** and climb to the saddle on the east ridge of Mount Yale at **mile 3.4.** There is dry camping potential in the area. A short uphill trail east leads to an expansive view. A faint trail west leads to Mount Yale (14,196'). Descend from the pass through a forest of bristlecone pine just below the saddle, transitioning to spruce and fir lower in Avalanche Gulch. There is potential camping west of the trail with reasonable access to water in Hughes Creek at **mile 4.7.** Leave the Collegiate Peaks Wilderness at **mile 6.4** and cross two small streams with good camping in the area. Arrive at the Avalanche Trailhead (vault toilets and huge paved parking lot) at **mile 6.6.**

Angle right across the parking lot to single-track, marked by a post, where the trail winds through debris from the 2019 Sheep Mountain avalanche. The avalanche traveled down the peak, across Middle Cottonwood Creek, across Cottonwood Pass Road, and came to rest on the CT just below the trailhead parking area. Cross County Road 306/Cottonwood Pass Road and then pass through a small dirt parking area at **mile 6.7.** Mountain bikers rejoin the CT here at the end of the Collegiate Peaks Wilderness detour. Turn left onto single-track and cross Middle Cottonwood Creek on a bridge at **mile 6.8,** where you can see the debris from a second 2019 Sheep Mountain avalanche that crossed the trail and Middle Cottonwood Creek, and only narrowly missed the bridge over the creek.

> ⚠ **WARNING:** There is no feasible camping for nearly all of the last 6.3 miles of the segment beyond Dry Creek (**mile 15.5**) due to the trail passing through private property.

Trekking through a grove of mature aspen. Photo by Keith Evans

The trail climbs alongside Middle Cottonwood Creek then turns to the south-east and follows along private property and above Rainbow Lake. Trail users are asked to stay on the trail and respect the private property. After crossing a small stream at **mile 7.7**, continue straight where a side trail leaves to the left at **mile 8.3**. Reach County Road 344/Cottonwood Lake Road and cross the road to reach the South Cottonwood Trailhead (limited parking) at **mile 8.9**.

The trail leaves the trailhead to the right and crosses a bridge over South Cottonwood Creek, the last reliable water source for the next 4 miles, at **mile 9.1**. There are a lot of good campsites in this area. The trail follows the creek for about 0.5 mile, gradually rising, then angles left across County Road 343 at **mile 9.6**. The trail climbs a series of switchbacks, then gains views of the Arkansas valley as it crosses open slopes. Cross Silver Prince Creek at **mile 13.3** and Maxwell Creek at **mile 13.9**. There is a good campsite 300 feet south of Maxwell Creek. Cross Dry Creek (not typically dry) on a bridge at **mile 15.5**. The trail enters signed private property at **mile 16.1**, then reaches FS Road 322 at **mile 16.7**. The Mount Princeton climbers' route diverges uphill to the right, while the CT follows the road to the left and downhill. This begins a 5.7-mile section located on roads due to steep terrain on public land and the prevalence of private land. This long section of road is narrow and without shoulders. Please use caution. Stay on the main road at all trail and other road intersections through the end of this segment.

The trail exits signed private property at **mile 17.0**, although it continues to travel through unsigned private property. Pass through a large trailhead parking

BUENA VISTA

Buena Vista, as might be gathered from its Spanish name, is a beautiful place to visit because of its striking location in the Arkansas valley between the mineralized Mosquito Range and the towering Sawatch Range. The town, just short of halfway between Denver and Durango on The Colorado Trail, is an ideal resupply point for long-distance travelers. The most direct way to reach Buena Vista from the CT is to follow County Road 306. The town is just over 9 miles east of the Avalanche Trailhead.

Distance from CT: 9.1 miles
Elevation: 7,954 feet
Zip code: 81211
Area code: 719

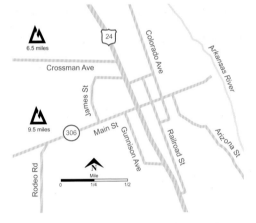

Dining
Several locations in town

Gear (including fuel canisters)
The Trailhead
402 E. Main St.
(719) 395-8001

Groceries
City Market
438 US Highway 24 N.
(719) 395-2431

LaGree's
415 Highway 24 N.
(719) 966-5291

Info
Chamber of Commerce
111 E. Main St.
(719) 395-6612

Laundry and Showers
Wally Lala's Laundromat & Shower
211 US Highway 24 N.
(719) 395-2989

Missing Sock Laundromat
522 Antero Circle #1
(719) 285-7663

Public Showers
(near BV Community Center, fee)
715 W. Main St.

Lodging (several)
Lakeside Motel
112 W. Lake St.
(719) 395-2994

Medical
Heart of the Rockies
Regional Medical Center
28374 County Rd. 317
(719) 395-9048

Post Office
Buena Vista Post Office
110 Brookdale Ave.
(719) 395-2445

Left: Approach to climb Mt. Yale from the CT. Photo by Jeff Sellenrick **Right:** End of Segment 13 follows roads, like this County Road 162 that passes Mount Princeton Hot Springs. Photo by Jeff Sellenrick

area, then under a large entry gate at **mile 17.8** and past private camp facilities. Continue on paved County Road 322, following it to the east and as it curves to the left at **mile 18.4**. Follow a curve to the right and then turn right onto County Road 321 at **mile 18.7**. Continue following the road, bending to the east, then turning hard to the southwest. The road descends the lateral moraine left by the Chalk Creek glacier, then follows a curve to the left then back to the right.

At **mile 20.0**, turn right onto County Road 162 across from Mount Princeton Hot Springs Resort. At **mile 20.6**, cross a major wash that drains the Chalk Cliffs. Significant thunderstorms in the area can wash massive amounts of gravely debris down this wash, closing the road until the runoff has passed and the county road department clears the gravel from the wash crossing. At **mile 21.3**, continue straight onto gravel County Rd 291 (Bunny Lane) as County Rd 162 curves to the right. This road goes through a residential area to the end of Segment 13 at the Chalk Creek Trailhead on the left, **mile 22.4**.

Be respectful of the long stretch of **private property** as the trail descends into the Chalk Creek valley.

Although CT travel here is primarily on public corridors, there is **no public camping** available on the surrounding private land.

TRAVEL TIPS

MOUNT PRINCETON HOT SPRINGS RESORT

VIEWING OPPORTUNITY

This spot was long frequented by Native Americans before being taken over and developed by settlers, beginning in 1860. The fortunes of the Mount Princeton Hot Springs Hotel rose and fell with the fortunes of area mines and the coming of the railroad and its subsequent departure in 1926. The elaborate hotel on the site was demolished for scrap lumber in 1950. The resort has been rebuilt and promises to "melt your cares away." Pools are a delight and open every day of the year (admission fee required). The resort store (maildrop and modest resupply) and the lodging may also be of interest to CT travelers.

THE COLLEGIATE PEAKS

This impressive collection of skyscraping four-teeners, with names such as Harvard, Columbia, Yale, and Princeton, are collectively known as the Collegiate Peaks, a subset of the greater Sawatch Range. These peaks were first surveyed by a team led by Harvard Professor Josiah Dwight Whitney (for whom California's Mount Whitney is named). They started the tradition of naming the fourteeners in this area for universities after climbing Mount Harvard

Collegiate Wilderness boundary sign. The CT passes through six wilderness areas. Photo by Aaron Locander

(14,420') in 1869. Mount Yale (14,196') was named after Whitney's alma mater. Later climbers continued the practice, adding Princeton, Oxford, and Columbia.

Despite their proximity, some of the Collegiate fourteeners don't lend themselves to a day climb from The Colorado Trail. Possibly the best opportunity comes with Mount Yale in Segment 13. At **mile 3.4** of that segment, the CT gains the long east ridge of Yale, offering a moderate—though without well-defined trail—route to the summit with a bit of rock hopping and a few false summits along the way.

Another fourteener, Mount Princeton (14,196'), also offers relatively direct access from the CT, but the round-trip is a challenging 12 miles with 4,700 feet of elevation gain above the trail. At **mile 16.7** of Segment 13, diverge from the CT and hike 3 miles uphill on a dirt road open to vehicles. (It might be feasible to trim your hiking miles by soliciting a ride from one of the many peak-baggers, especially easy very early on a weekend morning.) Hike 3 more miles beyond where vehicles must park on good trail to the summit.

Features

MILEAGE	COMMENTS	ELEVATION
0.0	Begin Segment 13 at Silver Creek TH	9,435'
0.1	N Cottonwood Creek bridge	9,361'
2.2	Old cabin, camping, and Silver Creek access	11,058'
2.4	Silver Creek bridge	11,100'
2.7	Enter Collegiate Peaks Wilderness	11,267'
3.4	Saddle on E ridge Mount Yale, high point on segment	11,884'
4.7	Camping potential	10,709'
6.4	Exit Collegiate Peaks Wilderness	9,496'
6.6	Cross Avalanche TH parking area	9,384'
6.7	Cross County Road 306/Cottonwood Pass Road onto gravel drive then left onto single-track	9,365'
6.8	Middle Cottonwood Creek bridge	9,332'
7.7	Stream	9,295'
8.3	Straight (side trail to left)	9,087'
8.9	Straight across County Road 344/Cottonwood Lake Road to S Cottonwood TH, then right on single-track	8,965'
9.1	S Cottonwood Creek bridge	8,922'
9.6	Angle left across County Road 343	8,868'
13.3	Silver Prince Creek	9,931'
13.9	Maxwell Creek	10,000'
15.5	Dry Creek (typically not dry) bridge	9,524'
16.1	Enter signed private property	9,648'
16.7	Join road left and downhill on County Road 322/Mt Princeton Road	9,495'
17.0	Leave signed private property	9,356'
17.8	Pass through large trailhead parking area and under gate and onto paved County Road 322	8,923'
18.4	Follow road curve to the left	8,681'
18.7	Follow curve to the right then turn right onto paved County Road 321	8,629'
20.0	Turn right onto paved County Road 162 (Mount Princeton Hot Springs Resort across road)	8,201'
20.6	Cross major wash	8,306'
21.3	Straight onto gravel County Road 291/Bunny Lane	8,304'
22.4	End Segment 13 at Chalk Creek TH	8,389'

Elevation and Distance

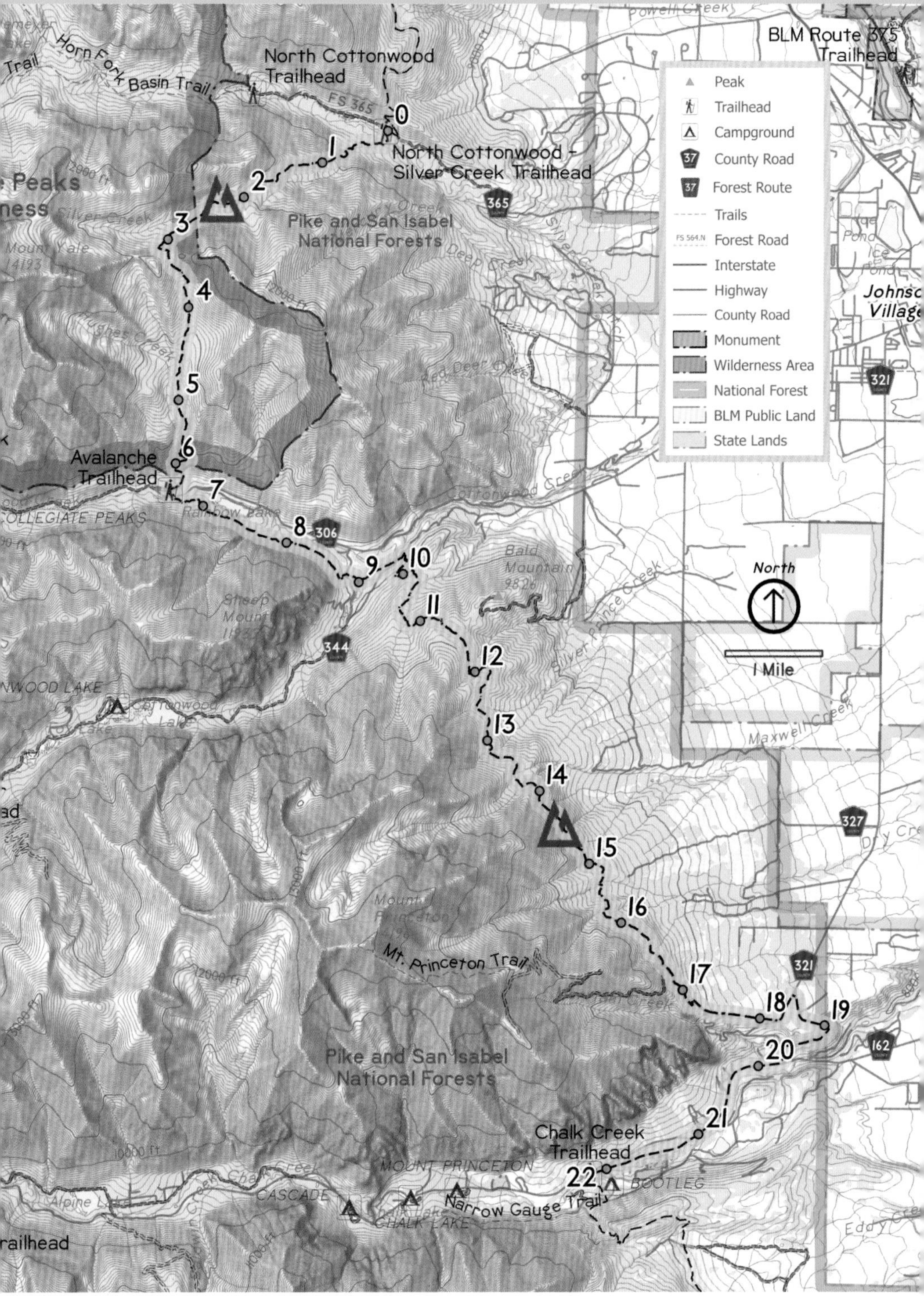

BLM Route 375
Trailhead

North Cottonwood
Trailhead

North Cottonwood -
Silver Creek Trailhead

Pike and San Isabel
National Forests

Peaks
ness

Mount Yale
14193

Avalanche
Trailhead

COLLEGIATE PEAKS

Bald
Mountain
9826

Sheep
Mount
10

COTTONWOOD LAKE

Mt. Princeton Trail

Pike and San Isabel
National Forests

Chalk Creek
Trailhead

MOUNT PRINCETON

CASCADE
CHALK LAKE

Narrow Gauge
Trail

BOOTLEG

Johnson
Village

	Peak
	Trailhead
	Campground
37	County Road
37	Forest Route
	Trails
FS 564.N	Forest Road
	Interstate
	Highway
	County Road
	Monument
	Wilderness Area
	National Forest
	BLM Public Land
	State Lands

North

1 Mile

Silver Creek Trailhead to Chalk Creek Trailhead

SEGMENT 14
Chalk Creek Trailhead to US Highway 50

Chalk Cliffs north of Segment 14. Photo by Carl Brown

Distance	20.8 miles
Elevation Gain	Approx. 4,007 feet
Elevation Loss	Approx. 3,531 feet
USFS Map	San Isabel National Forest
The CT Databook, 8th Edition	Pages 38–39
The CT Map Book	Pages 34–37
Trails Illustrated Maps	No. 130, 1202
Latitude 40° Maps	Salida-Buena Vista Trails
Jurisdiction	Salida Ranger District, San Isabel National Forest

ACCESS FROM
DENVER END

ACCESS FROM
DURANGO END

AVAILABILITY
OF WATER

BICYCLING

Segment 14 travels through the southern end of the Sawatch Range, passing Mounts Antero and Shavano and Tabeguache Peak, all fourteeners. The trail climbs steeply at the start of the section, but soon levels off and travels through open forest before reaching Little Browns Creek, the first reliable water source since Chalk Creek, a distance of 6.7 miles. After this, there are several water sources and good camping as the northern part of the Sangre de Cristo Range comes into view ahead. The descent at the end of the segment finishes at US Highway 50.

TRAILHEAD/ACCESS POINTS

Chalk Creek Trailhead: Drive south from Buena Vista on US Highway 285 to Nathrop. Turn right (west) onto County Rd 162 for nearly 7 miles. The trailhead is on the left side of the road, slightly below road level.

Waterfall on Browns Creek 1.5 miles west of the CT. Photo by Dale Zoetewey

Browns Creek Trailhead: Drive south from Nathrop on US Highway 285 for 3.6 miles. Turn right (west) on County Road 270 for 1.5 miles to where it turns north. Continue straight ahead onto County Road 272 (which becomes FS Road 272/Browns Creek Road) for 2 miles to where it turns left (south) at an intersection. Continue south on FS Road 272 for 1.6 more miles to the Browns Creek Trailhead, where there is a large parking area and a vault toilet. Walk west on the Browns Creek Trail for 1.4 miles to intersect the CT.

Angel of Shavano Trailhead: From the northern intersection of US Highway 285 and US Highway 50 at Poncha Springs, drive west on US 50 for about 6 miles. Turn right (north) onto County Road 240. Proceed on County Road 240 for 3.8 miles to the trailhead parking area opposite the Angel of Shavano Campground.

US Highway 50 Trail Access: See Segment 15 on page 193.

Chalk Creek Trailhead to US Highway 50

Northbound hikers in Segment 14. Mount Princeton is in the background. Photo by Keith Evans

TRAIL DESCRIPTION: Segment 14 begins at the Chalk Creek Trailhead, **mile 0.0.** Chalk Creek is the last reliable water until Little Browns Creek, 6.7 miles ahead. Go south across the Chalk Creek bridge and begin hiking uphill. Pass a side trail to the left to Bootleg Campground at **mile 0.1**. This fee campground with a vault toilet is open for a limited season and located about 100 yards from the CT. At **mile 0.4,** angle right across County Road 290. Ascend several steep switchbacks, turn left at a bare sandy area, then reach a high point on the lateral moraine left by the Chalk Creek Glacier at **mile 1.4.** After heading downhill to the east, turn to the right at a junction with a side trail at **mile 2.1** and head down a steep, rocky hillside, crossing Eddy Creek (typically dry) at **mile 2.3.** Shortly after, cross FS Road 274/Eddy Creek Road at **mile 2.5.**

Contour through a mix of ponderosa pine forest and open meadows, eventually crossing FS Road 273/Raspberry Gulch Road at **mile 4.0,** with dry camping in the area. The trail passes through a gate at **mile 5.0,** then climbs more steeply and turns left at the junction with the Little Browns Creek Trail, **mile 6.1.** At another trail junction at **mile 6.4,** the trail turns right to join the Browns Creek Trail. There

SALIDA/PONCHA SPRINGS

SERVICES, SUPPLIES, AND ACCOMMODATIONS

Salida, an old railroad town and now a commercial center for the Arkansas valley, is about 13 miles east of the CT crossing at US Highway 50. Poncha Springs, 8 miles east of the crossing, has a grocery store, outdoor store, and several small restaurants. Monarch Spur RV Park, about a mile east of the CT Collegiate East on US 50, has camping, a small store, and laundry and showers.

Distance from CT: 13 miles
Elevation: 7,036 feet
Zip code: 81201
Area code: 719

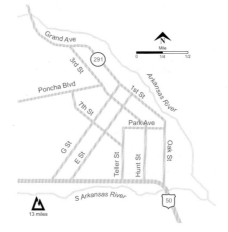

Bus
Chaffee Shuttle
54 Jones Ave.
(719) 530-8980

Dining
Several locations in town

Gear (including fuel canisters)
Salida Mountain Sports
110 N. F St.
(719) 539-4400

The Outpost
(Poncha Springs)
10955 County Rd. 128
(719) 539-1295

**Groceries
(several including)**
Walmart Supercenter
7865 W. US Highway 50
(719) 539-3566

Safeway
232 G St.
(719) 539-3513

Natural Grocers
200 F St.
(719) 239-7161

LaGree's Food Store
(Poncha Springs)
10100 US Highway 50
(719) 207-4564

Info
Chamber of Commerce
406 W. Rainbow Blvd.
(719) 539-2068

Laundry
Salida Laundromat
1410 E St.
(719) 433-8069

Monarch Spur Campground
18989 W. US Highway 50
(719) 530-0341

Lodging
The Simple Lodge & Hostel
224 E. First St.
(719) 650-7381

The Salida Inn and Hostel
225 W. CO Highway 291
(719) 530-1116

Medical
Heart of the Rockies
Regional Medical Center
1000 Rush Dr.
(719) 530-2200

Post Office
Poncha Springs Post Office
6500 US Highway 285
(719) 539-2117

Salida Post Office
310 D St.
(719) 539-2548

Showers
Salida Hot Springs
Aquatic Center
410 W. US Highway 50
(719) 539-6738

Monarch Spur Campground
18989 W. US Highway 50
(719) 530-0341

Bridge over Chalk Creek at the Segment 14 trailhead. Photo by Keith Evans

is potential camping with water nearby over the next 0.4 mile. After crossing a bridge over a small creek, the CT turns left at **mile 6.6**, leaving the Browns Creek Trail. Cross Little Browns Creek on a narrow bridge at **mile 6.7**, then cross Browns Creek on a larger bridge at **mile 6.8**.

Continue straight at a junction with the Wagon Loop Trail at **mile 7.0** and head in a generally southerly direction until reaching Fourmile Creek at **mile 8.8**. Cross Sand Creek on a very small bridge and then pass through a gate at **mile 10.1**. Cross the renamed Tabeguache Creek on a bridge at **mile 12.3**. Both creeks offer camping possibilities nearby. The trail passes an intersection with the Mount Shavano Trail at **mile 12.9**. Cross a cattleguard (gate option for stock) and arrive in an open meadow with a buck-and-rail log fence adjacent to the trail. Angle right at a spur trail to the Mount Shavano and Tabeguache Peak Trailhead (signed as Blanks Trailhead) at **mile 13.1**. Cross the two-track FS Road 254 at **mile 13.3**, continuing southwest. Reach Lipe Meadow at **mile 13.7**, with streams and camping potential nearby. Descend the lateral moraine above the North Fork South Arkansas River and reach the Angel of Shavano Trailhead at **mile 15.1**. The trail crosses County Road 240 at **mile 15.2** and continues to a stout bridge over the North Fork South Arkansas River at **mile 15.4**. Camping with drinking water and vault toilets is available at the nearby Angel of Shavano Campground for a fee, although there is also dispersed camping potential in the area.

The short (5-mile), but often overlooked, stretch between Angel of Shavano Campground and US Highway 50 wanders through **lovely aspen** and lodgepole pine forests.

TRAVEL TIPS

Trail users should note that **Cree Creek** at **mile 19.6** is the last decent camping spot north of the highway.

MOUNT SHAVANO AND TABEGUACHE PEAK

Want to climb a fourteener (or two) as part of your Colorado Trail trek? This side trip opportunity is very straightforward. The Mount Shavano Trail, which intersects the CT at **mile 12.9**, is the Colorado Fourteeners Initiative's recommended route. Follow the Mount Shavano Trail west about 4 miles, first to a saddle and then along the ridge to top of Mount Shavano (14,229'). If you're still feeling strong and the weather is favorable when you reach the top of Shavano, travel northwest along the connecting ridge to Tabeguache Peak's summit (14,155'), less than a mile and 500 feet of climbing away. Return via the same route. Although technically easy, don't underestimate the difficulty. Get an early start and be prepared for 5,000 feet of elevation gain and an arduous 10-mile round trip.

Begin a climb up several switchbacks, eventually reaching the top of the lateral moraine at **mile 16.8**. From here, the CT skirts the edge of an old logging area that has been replanted. There is a spring-fed, seasonal pond with campsites at about **mile 17.5**. At **mile 18.2**, the trail crosses Lost Creek then angles right across a closed two-track. Angle right across the end of FS Road 228.A next to a large meadow at **mile 19.0**, then angle left across FS Road 228/Taylor Mountain Road just past the meadow at **mile 19.3**. At **mile 19.6**, cross a bridge over Cree Creek, passing the last good camping area until about a mile into Segment 15. Go under a power line at **mile 19.9**, then follow the power line maintenance road until turning sharply left onto single-track at **mile 20.3**. Turn sharply left again to cross an old railroad grade at **mile 20.5**. Reach US Highway 50 and the end of Segment 14 at **mile 20.8**.

Features

MILEAGE	COMMENTS	ELEVATION
0.0	Begin Segment 14 at Chalk Creek TH, cross Chalk Creek bridge	8,389'
0.1	Straight (side trail on left to Bootleg Campground [fee])	8,428'
0.4	Angle right across County Road 290	8,504'
1.4	Left in bare sandy area then reach top of Chalk Creek glacier lateral moraine	9,309'
2.1	Sharply right (side trail straight ahead)	9,022'
2.3	Cross Eddy Creek (typically dry)	8,928'
2.5	Cross FS Rd 274/Eddy Creek Road	8,903'
4.0	Cross FS Rd 273/Raspberry Gulch Road	8,907'
5.0	Gate	9,081'
6.1	Left (Little Browns Creek Tr straight ahead)	9,667'
6.4	Right onto Browns Creek Tr	9,549'
6.6	Left (Browns Creek Tr straight ahead)	9,614'
6.7	Little Browns Creek bridge	9,598'
6.8	Browns Creek bridge	9,592'
7.0	Straight (Wagon Loop Tr to left)	9,612'
8.8	Fourmile Creek	9,768'
10.1	Sand Creek bridge then gate	9,622'
12.3	Tabeguache Creek (new name) bridge	9,853'
12.9	Straight (Mount Shavano Tr to right)	9,884'
13.1	Cattleguard, then angle right (trail to Mount Shavano/Tabeguache Peak TH (signed Blanks TH) to left)	9,813'
13.3	Straight across FS Rd 254	9,833'
13.7	Lipe Meadow, then stream	9,803'
15.1	Angel of Shavano TH	9,208'
15.2	Cross County Rd 240	9,190'
15.4	N Fork S Arkansas River bridge	9,134'
16.8	Top of lateral moraine	9,739'
17.5	Seasonal pond with campsites	9,575'
18.2	Lost Creek, then angle right across old roadbed	9,468'
19.0	Angle right across end of FS Rd 228.A	9,355'
19.3	Angle left across FS Rd 228/Taylor Mountain Road	9,344'
19.6	Cree Creek bridge	9,209'
19.9	Straight ahead following power line maintenance road	9,323'
20.3	Sharply left onto single-track	9,231'
20.5	Sharply left across old railroad grade	8,961'
20.8	End Segment 14 at US Hwy 50	8,872'

Elevation and Distance

Chalk Creek Trailhead to US Highway 50

SEGMENT 15
US Highway 50 to Marshall Pass

On the Continental Divide above South Fooses Creek, Segment 15.
Photo by Ben Kraushaar

Distance	14.5 miles
Elevation Gain	Approx. 3,576 feet
Elevation Loss	Approx. 1,608 feet
USFS Maps	San Isabel and Gunnison National Forests
The CT Databook, 8th Edition	Pages 40–41
The CT Map Book	Pages 37–39
Trails Illustrated Maps	Nos. 130, 139, 1201
Latitude 40° Maps	Salida-Buena Vista Trails
Jurisdiction	Salida and Gunnison Ranger Districts, San Isabel and Gunnison National Forests

ACCESS FROM
DENVER END

ACCESS FROM
DURANGO END

AVAILABILITY
OF WATER

BICYCLING

ABOUT THIS SEGMENT: After leaving US Highway 50 and beginning this segment, there are no convenient resupply points for the next 100 miles until the town of Creede. The first few miles climb gently southwest on a dirt road passing campsites. The route becomes single-track and turns south, crossing North Fooses Creek and then South Fooses Creek several times before climbing the head of the valley to reach the Continental Divide. This is the south junction of the CT Collegiate East and the CDT/CT Collegiate West. It is also part of the Monarch Crest Trail, popular with a variety of trail users that include motorcyclists, and can be particularly busy with mountain bikers, especially on weekends. (See the sidebar in Segment 16 on page 203). Be on the alert for mountain bikers, who frequently make little noise, approaching from behind.

From here, the trail follows the Continental Divide closely until the end of the segment at Marshall Pass and beyond. Just before Marshall Pass the trail passes out of basement rocks and into gray volcanic rocks, part of the San Juan volcanic field that covers almost 10,000 square miles and includes at least 10,000 cubic miles of volcanic rocks.

TRAILHEAD/ACCESS POINTS

US Highway 50 Trail Access: From the intersection of US Highway 285 and US Highway 50 at Poncha Springs, drive west on US 50 for approximately 10 miles to County Road 225/Fooses Creek Road. There is a wide shoulder on the south side of US 50 that provides limited parking. This is the official beginning of Segment 15.

Fooses Creek Trailhead: The Fooses Creek Trailhead can be reached by following the directions above, then turn left and follow County Road 225 for 2.8 miles (left at junctions) to the Fooses Creek Trailhead and limited parking. The road to the trailhead is rather primitive, but most vehicles can make it.

Marshall Pass: See Segment 16 on page 201.

Once up on the Divide, you'll have **unobstructed views** in every direction. Three of our mightiest mountain ranges—the Sawatch, the San Juan, and the Sangre de Cristo—reach for the sky.

TRAVEL TIPS

The Divide is lofty and remote. There are no towns close by for convenient resupply, and cell phones are unlikely to work in an emergency. The next 100 miles is the least-traveled portion of the CT.

Mountain bikers on the famous Monarch Crest Trail. Photo by Anthony Sloan

SERVICES, SUPPLIES, AND ACCOMMODATIONS: These amenities are available in Salida; see Segment 14 on page 187.

TRAIL DESCRIPTION: Segment 15 begins at the intersection of US Highway 50 and County Road 225, **mile 0.0**. Follow the gravel road through private property, where camping is prohibited, staying on the main road at all driveway and minor road intersections for the next 0.8 mile. After crossing the South Arkansas River at a sharp left turn, **mile 0.1**, cross Fooses Creek at **mile 0.3**. The road curves to the west at an intersection with Puma Path, a residential road, **mile 0.4**. Pass by the former site of Fooses Lake at **mile 0.8**, a small reservoir that was removed in 2023. Camping is allowed beyond this point and several good sites exist.

Stay on this main road, now dirt, until reaching an intersection at **mile 2.8**. Turn left onto FS Road 225.C and shortly reach the end of the road and the small Fooses Creek Trailhead at **mile 2.9**. There are campsites with access to water near the trailhead.

Continue on single-track, crossing North Fooses Creek on a bridge at **mile 3.0**. The trail heads up the South Fooses Creek valley, staying generally close to the creek and many potential campsites for the next 4 miles. At **mile 3.3**, the trail crosses the creek on the first of three sturdy bridges built by CTF Trail Crew volunteers and US Forest Service staff. The final crossing of South Fooses Creek comes at **mile 5.0**, although several smaller streams are crossed over the next 3 miles. Just before reaching the head of the South Fooses Creek valley, begin a climb that ascends a steep, rutted section of trail that ascends at a 20 percent grade, one of the steepest grades on the entire CT.

Gain the crest of the Continental Divide at **mile 8.6** and reach the southern junction of the CT Collegiate East and CT Collegiate West (along with the CDT). The CT resumes traveling the co-located CDT and joins the famed Monarch Crest Trail at this point. Expect southbound bicycles, especially on weekends. This also begins a section of the trail that allows motorcycles, through the midpoint of Segment 19.

Continue left in a generally southeasterly direction. At the junction with the Greens Creek Trail at **mile 10.3**, the CT continues straight and heads south. The very rustic Greens Creek Shelter is just east of and visible from the trail junction, with water available 0.3 mile north and below along the Greens Creek Trail. Pass the faint Little Cochetopa Creek Trail on the left and the well-used Agate Creek Trail on the right at **mile 11.4**. (The summit of Mount Ouray, a high thirteener at 13,971', is to the east and can be climbed by following the Little Cochetopa Creek Trail to the Divide and traversing the ridge to the peak.) Cross a seasonal stream at **mile 12.6**, then continue ahead until joining a dirt road at **mile 12.8**. There is a piped spring that flows reliably at **mile 13.0**. Cross the Larkspur Ditch at **mile 14.0**, where water may be available. Reach FS Road 200/Marshall Pass Road, located on

TRAIL WORK AHEAD

CTF trail crews, along with Forest Service staff, professional trail crews, and other partner organizations, are completing a realignment between **mile 7.3** and the Continental Divide (**mile 8.6**) to improve the sustainability of the trail. The trail construction is expected to be completed in 2023 or 2024. Final trail data was not available prior to publication and the segment description below describes the old route. Check the CTF website (ColoradoTrail.org) for updated information on the new trail section.

an old railroad grade, at **mile 14.2** and turn right onto the road. The Marshall Pass Trailhead with vault toilets and parking sits just across the road. Water from Poncha Creek is available in a large swampy area 0.25 mile east of the restrooms—either follow the road to the east or just head downhill past the restrooms. If you don't mind a little road traffic, Marshall Pass is good for camping given the toilets and water. In dry periods, this may be the last water available for the next 10 or 12 miles.

WORKING TOWARD A NON-MOTORIZED TRAIL HIKING TIPS

The CT was established by linking existing trails and roads, closed roads, and building new trail where connecting sections were necessary to develop a continuous route. Some of these trails (and all of the open roads) allowed motorized use prior to establishing the CT and that use has continued in most cases to this day. Over time, some of the trail has been moved off motorized routes and onto non-motorized trail. These changes require Forest Service guidance and approvals, as well as the efforts of CTF and other partner organization volunteers, Forest Service staff, and sometimes paid trail contractors.

Since its inception, the CTF's goal has been an entirely non-motorized route, but impacts to wildlife habitat, private property issues, terrain limitations, and general reluctance to develop parallel motorized and non-motorized trails sometimes makes it challenging to develop successful non-motorized trail proposals. However, there have been many successes over the years since the trail was completed, including on Segments 6, 11, 24, CW02, CW03, CW04, and CW05, where new trail was constructed to remove the CT (and frequently CDT) from roads. In addition, a new section of non-motorized trail that will move the CT/CDT off the motorized Timberline Trail on Segment CW02 will likely have been completed by the time of publication.

The most continuous and extensive motorized section remaining on the CT is from Monarch Pass to Cochetopa Creek, including all or portions of Segments 15 through 19 and CW05, totaling 66.5 miles allowing motorized use. Motorcycles are allowed on all of this section, but only 13.8 miles are on roads open to all other motorized vehicles. The Forest Service has been considering a proposed new section of non-motorized trail that would move the CT (and CDT) off 23.1 miles of the motorized roads and trail on all or portions of Segments 17 through 19, including all of the road sections, but it will likely be many years before the new trail is approved and constructed. The CTF supports this and other efforts to move the trail off of motorized sections but understands that there will likely always be some portions of the CT where that will not be possible.

SPRUCE BEETLES

Near the headwaters of South Fooses Creek in Segment 15, trail users may note that the branches on many large Engelmann spruce trees are bare of needles while most of the smaller spruce trees are green and healthy. The dead mature trees are the result of spruce beetles (*Dendroctonus rufipennis*), the native bark beetles that inhabit high elevation spruce forests in Colorado. Colorado State Forest Service data shows observable spruce beetle impact beginning in 2000 and peaking in 2014, affecting nearly 2 million acres of Colorado forest as of 2022. Although the spruce beetle impact peaked in 2014, some outbreaks in the central and south-western portions of the state continue to expand.

The spruce beetle is only about the size of a grain of rice, with a typical two-year life cycle in spruce trees growing above 9,000 feet. Adult beetles are usually dark brown to black with reddish-brown or black wing covers. At endemic or low population levels naturally present in the forest, spruce beetles generally infest only downed trees. However, epidemic events can occur where conditions are suitable and the beetles may infest live standing trees, as well as downed trees. These conditions include spruce-dominated forest with large (16 inches in diameter or greater), mature and overmature spruce trees, where tree growth has slowed.

The results of the current spruce beetle epidemic along the CT can be observed from Segment 15 to 24 and on Segments CW04 and CW05. Although it will take many decades for these forests to recover, the preference of the spruce beetle for large, mature trees leaves many smaller trees to begin the forest recovery.

More information on the spruce beetle is available at csfs.colostate.edu/forest -management/common-forest-insects-diseases/spruce-bark-beetle/.

Continue following Marshall Pass Road uphill to **mile 14.3**, then angle left onto FS Road 203/Poncha Creek Road as FS Road 200 curves to the right through the deep railroad grade cut. Continue generally straight and slightly uphill on a rough road at the 4-way intersection, **mile 14.4**, using the unmarked two-track. Continue left and slightly uphill on another unmarked two-track to a large wood sign and the beginning of a single-track section marking the end of Segment 15.

Features

MILEAGE	COMMENTS	ELEVATION
0.0	Begin Segment 15 at US Hwy 50, south on County Road 225	8,861'
0.1	S Arkansas River bridge	8,828'
0.3	Fooses Creek bridge	8,802'
0.4	Right (Puma Path [road] on left)	8,827'
0.8	Former Fooses Lake site, continue on FS Rd 225/Fooses Creek Road	8,956'
2.8	Left on FS Rd 225.C (FS Rd 225 continues straight)	9,555'
2.9	End of FS Rd 225.C at Fooses Creek TH, begin single-track	9,553'
3.0	N Fooses Creek bridge	9,561'
3.3	First S Fooses Creek bridge	9,667'
4.3	Second S Fooses Creek bridge	9,896'
5.0	Third S Fooses Creek bridge	10,170'
8.6	Left, rejoining CDT (CDT/CT Collegiate West to right)	11,904'
10.3	Straight (Greens Creek Tr and shelter to left)	11,501'
11.4	Straight (Little Cochetopa Creek Tr to left, then Agate Creek Tr to right)	11,812'
12.6	Seasonal stream	11,395'
12.8	Straight onto dirt road	11,364'
13.0	Piped spring	11,278'
14.0	Larkspur ditch	10,865'
14.2	Right onto FS Rd 200/Marshall Pass Road, pass Marshall Pass TH to left	10,821'
14.3	Left on FS Rd 203/Poncha Creek Road (FS Rd 200 continues to right)	10,833'
14.4	Straight on 2-track (FS Rd 203 to left, FS Rd 243 to right)	10,862'
14.5	End Segment 15 at start of single-track above Marshall Pass	10,893'

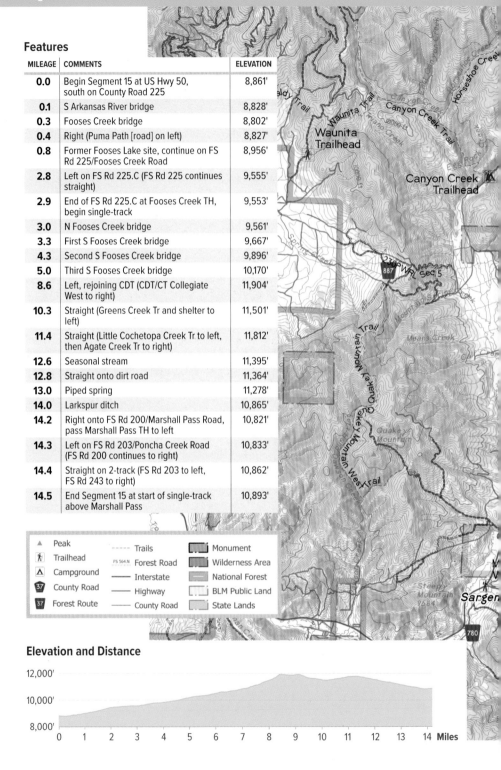

Legend:
- ▲ Peak
- 🚶 Trailhead
- ⚠ Campground
- 37 County Road
- 37 Forest Route
- ----- Trails
- FS 564.N Forest Road
- —— Interstate
- —— Highway
- —— County Road
- Monument
- Wilderness Area
- National Forest
- BLM Public Land
- State Lands

Elevation and Distance

Boss Lake
Trailhead

Garfield

Collegiate West Route

Contact
Hill
11585

Boss Lake
Reservoir

West Point Hill
10650

Waterdog
Lakes
11572

Waterdog Lakes Trail

GUNNISON RD

Colorado Trail

Waterdog Lakes
Trailhead

Fooses Creek
Trailhead

Monarch

MONARCH PARK

50

237

Basin View Trail

Monarch Pass
Trailhead

Continental Divide Trail

Gunnison
National Forest

Agate Creek Trail

Buck's Trail

North

1 Mile

Adventure Creek

Lime Ridge Trail

Lime Creek Trail

Agate Creek Trail

Agate
Trailhead

Brush Creek

ead

243

243

Chester

Pike and San Isabel
National Forests

Greens Creek Trail

Pahlone
Peak

Beel Point
11742

Little Cochetopa Tr

Pass Creek Trail

Monarch Crest Trail

Summit Trail

Marshall Pass
Trailhead

Starvation Creek Tr

243

200

0
1
2
3
4
5
6
7
8
9
10
11
12
13
14

50

236

SEGMENT 16
Marshall Pass to Sargents Mesa

Jerry Brown in camp warming up for another long day of surveying the CT. Photo by Carl Brown

Distance	14.6 miles
Elevation Gain	Approx. 3,184 feet
Elevation Loss	Approx. 2,405 feet
USFS Maps	San Isabel, Gunnison, and Rio Grande National Forests
The CT Databook, 8th Edition	Pages 42–43
The CT Map Book	Pages 39–41
Trails Illustrated Maps	No. 139, 1201
Jurisdiction	Salida, Gunnison, and Saguache Ranger Districts, San Isabel, Gunnison, and Rio Grande National Forests

ACCESS FROM
DENVER END

ACCESS FROM
DURANGO END

AVAILABILITY
OF WATER

BICYCLING

THE COLORADO TRAIL

ABOUT THIS SEGMENT: The trail stays very close to the Continental Divide through most of this segment, which means reliable water sources are few and scattered. There is water at Silver Creek about a quarter mile below the trail, 3.5 miles from the start of Segment 16. About 11 miles in, you will cross Tank Seven Creek, which is also a reliable source of water. In the meadow approaching Sargents Mesa near the end of Segment 16 is a metal stock tank where water can usually be found. Just beyond is Soldierstone, an interesting backcountry memorial to fallen soldiers in Indochina, including Vietnam.

TRAILHEAD/ACCESS POINTS

Marshall Pass Trail Access: Drive about 6 miles south of Poncha Springs on US Highway 285 and turn right (west) at the Marshall Pass and O'Haver Lake Campground turnoff. The road starts out as County Road 200 and toward the top of the pass becomes FS Road 200. It is about 13 miles from the highway to the summit of Marshall Pass. The Marshall Pass Trailhead is just 0.2 mile before the pass, with a parking area for about a dozen cars with a toilet. There is also limited parking at the top of the pass itself. Segment 16 starts at the top of the hill south of Marshall Pass, where a large wood sign and the beginning of single-track marks the beginning of Segment 16.

Sargents Mesa Trail Access: See Segment 17 on page 207.

SERVICES, SUPPLIES, AND ACCOMMODATIONS: There is no convenient resupply point for this segment.

TRAIL DESCRIPTION: Begin Segment 16 at the small parking area above Marshall Pass, **mile 0.0**, where a large wood sign marks the beginning of a non-motorized single-track section. Follow the trail south, turning sharply to the right at a junction with the Starvation Creek Trail at **mile 1.1**. At **mile 2.4**, the CT angles left and merges with the Summit Trail, initially two-track, where motorcycles are again allowed.

At **mile 3.5**, the Silver Creek Trail departs to the left. About a quarter mile down this trail is water and potential camping. Monarch Crest mountain bikers will diverge here if they haven't at other side trails along the way. Continue straight on the CT where the two-track narrows to single-track at **mile 4.1**.

Elk keep an eye on trail users. Photo by Pete Turner

Hikers use trekking poles to keep balance and momentum on trail. Photo by Bill Manning

Cross a seasonal stream at **mile 4.3**, but note that grazing cattle in the area sometimes impact the water quality. Pass through a gate at **mile 4.6**, then descend to an open saddle. The trail continues in a westerly direction where it traverses the south flanks of Windy Peak, reaches the segment's high point at 11,742', **mile 5.2,** and then begins a steep and sustained descent. Cross a dirt road at **mile 6.6**, then continue straight at the junction with the Middle Creek Trail at **mile 8.0**. A pipeline, with markers either side, crosses the trail at **mile 8.3**.

After several miles of remaining on or close to the Continental Divide, the trail reaches the junction with the faint Tank Seven Trail at **mile 10.5**, then angles right to descend into the Tank Seven Creek valley. Reach campsites, Tank Seven Creek, and a junction with the Tank Seven Creek Trail at **mile 11.0**, the last reliable water source until Baldy Lake 11 miles ahead. After crossing the creek, turn left and begin climbing into Cameron Park, where there is more camping and sometimes water still in the creek. Cross FS Road 578/Milk Creek Road at **mile 12.3**, where there are remains of crumbled buildings. Continue climbing to **mile 13.2** and cross FS Road 578.2A/ Sargents Mesa Road, with possible water south of the trail at **mile 13.3**. Angle left and follow an old two-track at **mile 13.6** and continue straight at a junction with the Big Bend Creek Trail at **mile 14.1**. Approximately 800 feet off the trail to the left at **mile 14.3** is a metal stock tank (possible water). A 10-foot granite monument named Soldierstone rests about 400 feet beyond amongst sparse trees. Diverge from the CT for this interesting backcountry memorial to fallen soldiers in Indochina, including Vietnam. Segment 16 ends on Sargents Mesa at **mile 14.6** at the junction of faint FS Road 850/Houghland Gulch Road and FS Road 855/Ward Gulch Road.

For over 50 miles beyond Marshall Pass, backpackers need to sharpen their focus on **water sources**, carry enough, and stay hydrated. Sargents Mesa and the rolling uplands along this section of the Continental Divide are known as the **Cochetopa Hills**. The area receives less snow than other ranges and water sources are widely scattered. Still, CT travelers who plan and are careful typically don't go dry.

TRAVEL TIP

MONARCH CREST TRAIL

MOUNTAIN BIKING

The Monarch Crest Trail has been rated by *Bicycling* magazine as one of the top five mountain bike rides in the country. It descends an epic 6,200 feet from tundra to sagebrush desert, although also requiring 2,600 feet of climbing, while covering nearly 30 miles of mostly single-track trail (including the connecting Silver Creek and Rainbow Trails).

Mountain bikers roll along the famous Monarch Crest. Photo by George Neserke

Riders begin atop Monarch Pass, many having taken a commercial shuttle from Poncha Springs. They pedal parts of CT Segments CW05, Segment 15, and Segment 16 (all part of the CDT), totaling 14.3 miles, before diverging on the Silver Creek and Rainbow Trail system to reach US Highway 285 far below. A swift 5-mile ride down the highway returns riders to Poncha Springs. There are several other side trails that can be descended off of the Crest, but the described route is the longest and one of the most popular.

THE LEGACY OF MARSHALL PASS

VIEWING OPPORTUNITY

In 1873, troubled by a toothache and in a big hurry to get to a dentist in Denver, Army Lieutenant William Marshall "discovered" this shortcut. For centuries, of course, bands of Ute Indians had been using the several gaps in this relatively low section of the Continental Divide to travel between the intermountain parks on the east side of the Divide and their lands to the west. Famed road and rail builder Otto Mears constructed the first wagon road over the pass, following existing paths, then sold it to the Denver & Rio Grande Western railroad, which laid rails over it in 1881.

General William Palmer's D&RGW was in a battle with John Evans' Denver, South Park & Pacific Railroad to be the first to reach Gunnison and tap the mineral-rich San Juans. While the DSP&P took the shorter route by tunneling under the Sawatch Range, Palmer chose the relatively low pass with modest grades for his route. The D&RGW won the race, pulling into Gunnison to an exuberant crowd on August 8, 1881. The DSP&P, meanwhile, labored for another year on its ill-fated Alpine Tunnel.

The rails are long gone today, but County Road 200 and FS Road 200 follow the old trackbed.

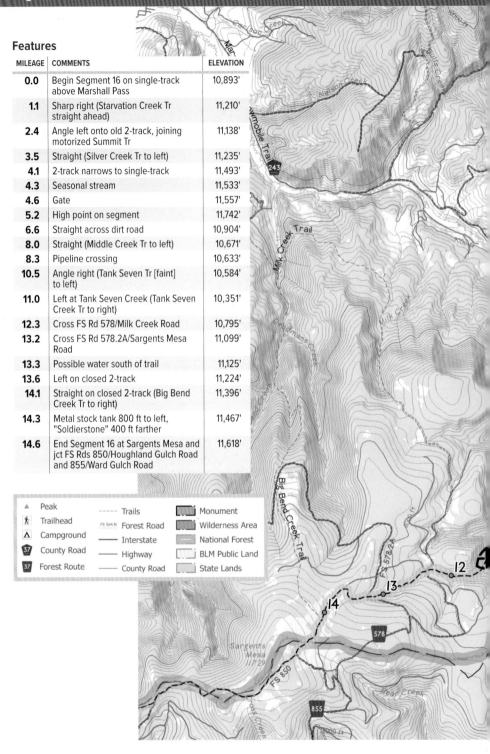

Features

MILEAGE	COMMENTS	ELEVATION
0.0	Begin Segment 16 on single-track above Marshall Pass	10,893'
1.1	Sharp right (Starvation Creek Tr straight ahead)	11,210'
2.4	Angle left onto old 2-track, joining motorized Summit Tr	11,138'
3.5	Straight (Silver Creek Tr to left)	11,235'
4.1	2-track narrows to single-track	11,493'
4.3	Seasonal stream	11,533'
4.6	Gate	11,557'
5.2	High point on segment	11,742'
6.6	Straight across dirt road	10,904'
8.0	Straight (Middle Creek Tr to left)	10,671'
8.3	Pipeline crossing	10,633'
10.5	Angle right (Tank Seven Tr [faint] to left)	10,584'
11.0	Left at Tank Seven Creek (Tank Seven Creek Tr to right)	10,351'
12.3	Cross FS Rd 578/Milk Creek Road	10,795'
13.2	Cross FS Rd 578.2A/Sargents Mesa Road	11,099'
13.3	Possible water south of trail	11,125'
13.6	Left on closed 2-track	11,224'
14.1	Straight on closed 2-track (Big Bend Creek Tr to right)	11,396'
14.3	Metal stock tank 800 ft to left, "Soldierstone" 400 ft farther	11,467'
14.6	End Segment 16 at Sargents Mesa and jct FS Rds 850/Houghland Gulch Road and 855/Ward Gulch Road	11,618'

▲	Peak	----- Trails	▓	Monument
🚶	Trailhead	FS 564.N Forest Road	▓	Wilderness Area
Ⓐ	Campground	—— Interstate	▓	National Forest
37	County Road	—— Highway	▢	BLM Public Land
37	Forest Route	—— County Road	▓	State Lands

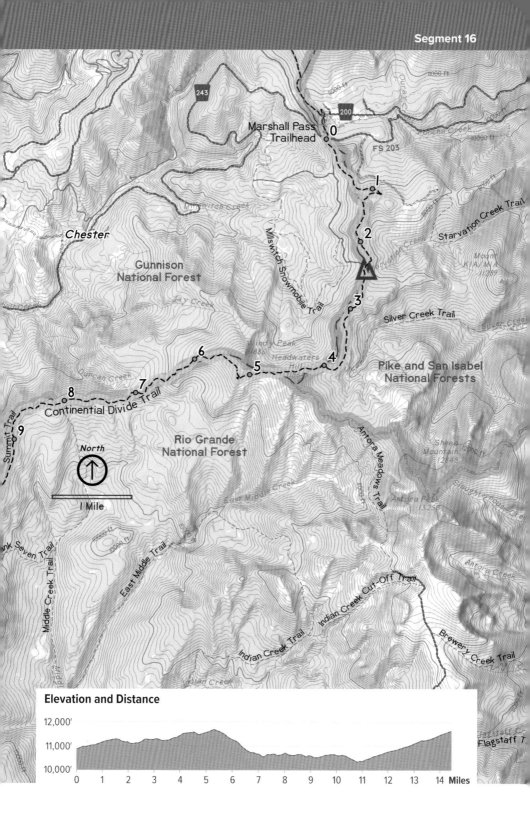

243

200

Marshall Pass
Trailhead

0

FS 203

Poncha Creek

10000 ft

11000 ft

Ouray

1

2

Starvation Creek Trail

Mount
KIAWA
11289

Chester

Gunnison
National Forest

Millswitch Creek

Millswitch Snowmobile Trail

3

Silver Creek Trail

Silver Creek

Jay Creek

6

Windy Peak
11886

Headwaters
Hill

4

Pike and San Isabel
National Forests

Duncan Creek

5

7

8

Continential Divide Trail

9

Summit Trail

Rio Grande
National Forest

Antora Meadows Trail

Sheep
Mountain
12801

Antora Peak
13258

Slaughterhouse Creek

East Middle Creek

North

↑

1 Mile

11000 ft

East Middle Trail

Middle Creek Trail

nk Seven Trail

Antora Creek

Indian Creek Cut-Off Trail

Indian Creek Trail

Brewery Creek Trail

Indian Creek

Flagstaff T

Elevation and Distance

12,000'

11,000'

10,000'

0 1 2 3 4 5 6 7 8 9 10 11 12 13 14 **Miles**

Marshall Pass to Sargents Mesa

205

SEGMENT 17
Sargents Mesa to CO Highway 114

Baldy Lake. Photo by Julie Vida and Mark Tabb

ACCESS FROM
DENVER END

ACCESS FROM
DURANGO END

AVAILABILITY
OF WATER

BICYCLING

Distance	20.6 miles
Elevation Gain	Approx. 2,810 feet
Elevation Loss	Approx. 4,810 feet
USFS Maps	Rio Grande and Gunnison National Forests
The CT Databook, 8th Edition	Pages 44–45
The CT Map Book	Pages 41–43
Trails Illustrated Maps	No. 139, 1201
Jurisdiction	Saguache and Gunnison Ranger Districts, Rio Grande and Gunnison National Forests

ABOUT THIS SEGMENT: In Segment 17, the CT continues to travel along the Continental Divide, relatively low in elevation and gentle through here. As in the previous segment, water sources can be scarce. Baldy Lake, north of **mile 6.9**, is the only reliable water source and it is well worth the short side trip. Early in the year or during particularly wet years, travelers may also find water in Razor or Lujan Creek, although grazing cattle may impact the water quality at these sources.

Backpackers admire the broad expanse of Sargents Mesa. Photo by Pete Turner

An expansive view can be enjoyed from Long Branch Baldy (11,974'), the highest peak for miles around and a great vantage point to identify distant mountains. At **mile 7.4,** diverge off trail, north and gently up a half mile along the rim towering above Baldy Lake until you reach the top.

TRAILHEAD/ACCESS POINTS

Sargents Mesa Trail Access: From the small town of Saguache on US Highway 285 in the San Luis Valley, proceed northwest on CO Highway 114 for 10.5 miles. Take the right-hand branch of the Y intersection here onto County Road EE38. Proceed 0.8 mile to the next Y and take the left branch, continuing on County Road EE38. Continue up Jacks Creek valley for 5 miles and turn right on County Road 32JJ which becomes FS Road 855. From the right turn, proceed 9.5 miles to an intersection and bear left at a sign for Sargents Mesa. Continue another 0.5 mile to a Y intersection. Park here and walk west 0.4 mile farther to the signed division between CT Segments 16 and 17.

Lujan Pass Trailhead: From Saguache drive west on CO Highway 114 for approximately 30 miles to North Pass. Continue 1.2 miles down from the pass to FS Road 785/Lujan Road (may be signed County Road 31CC) on your right. Follow this

---

Baldy Lake after Sargents Mesa is worth the half-mile detour; it's a haven along a dry segment of the trail.

TRAVEL TIPS

You'll need to plan your **camping and water** needs carefully for this segment. The only reliable water source is at Baldy Lake, north of **mile 6.9**. Livestock in this area is a reminder to purify all your water with a filter and/or chemicals. Camping is very limited at Baldy Lake, so plan to camp elsewhere.

Sargents Mesa to CO Highway 114

Left: Trekkers enjoy easy hiking and big views on Sargents Mesa. Photo courtesy of Colorado Mountain Expeditions **Right:** Cattle graze in the Cochetopa Hills. Photo by Julie Vida and Mark Tabb

narrow road for 2 miles up the Lujan Creek valley, where it makes an abrupt right turn at a switchback near the top; follow the main road at all intersections. Continue 0.1 mile and cross a cattle guard at Lujan Pass, where the road becomes FS Road 484/ Upper Spanish Creek Road. Continue on the main road for 0.1 mile to a small parking area on the left and the undeveloped Lujan Pass Trailhead.

CO Highway 114 Trail Access: See Segment 18 on page 213.

SERVICES, SUPPLIES, AND ACCOMMODATIONS: There is no convenient resupply point for this segment.

TRAIL DESCRIPTION: Segment 17 begins on the remote Sargents Mesa at the junction of faint FS Roads 850/Houghland Gulch Road and 855/Ward Gulch Road, **mile 0.0.** The trail follows FS Road 850 south and west to **mile 2.3,** where the CT angles to the right onto single-track. Pass the junction with the Long Branch Trail at **mile 2.4** and continue climbing and descending along the Continental Divide. Reach the junction of the Baldy Lake Trail (right) and the East Sheep Creek Trail (left) at **mile 6.9.** A good place to camp and the only reliable water on Segment 17, Baldy Lake is a moderate 0.4 mile north and 250 feet below the CT on a well-traveled trail.

Reach the high point of Segment 17 at **mile 7.4** (11,768'), then descend to a saddle then climb again to reach the summit of Middle Baldy Peak at **mile 9.2.** Turn left and begin descending the headwaters of Razor Creek at the junction with the Dutchman Creek Trail at **mile 9.9.** Reach a crossing of seasonal Razor Creek at **mile 10.7.** The creek is frequently dry at the crossing but small flows may sometimes be found upstream or downstream of the trail. After following along the creek bed, turn left at **mile 10.8** just after the intersection with the Razor Creek Trail.

Continue straight at the junction with the faint West Sheep Creek Trail on the left at **mile 11.2**. Regain the Divide then continue straight at the spur trail to the Razor Park Trailhead at **mile 11.7**. Bear left at the intersection with the Upper Razor Spur Trail at **mile 12.5**. The next section of trail ascends and then descends numerous minor summits, with potential dry camping along the way. Pass by the end of a little-used road at **mile 16.5** near the high point of the last minor summit of the segment. Shortly after, begin descending through several switchbacks to the Lujan Pass Trailhead and FS Road 784 at **mile 18.0**. This is also the end of the Summit Trail that the CT followed for nearly 30 miles.

Turn right and follow the road and cross a cattle guard, where the road becomes FS Road 785. Continue on the road as it curves sharply left at an intersection with FS Road 785.1A at **mile 18.2**. Cross Lujan Creek, where there is camping nearby and potentially water at **mile 18.6**, although the water quality may be impacted by cattle grazing in the area. Follow the road as it descends the valley, where there may be more flow in the creek and potential camping nearby. Reach CO Highway 114 at **mile 20.2** and turn right, following the highway shoulder. On the left at **mile 20.6** is a wide parking area on the south side of the highway, where Segment 17 ends at a fence gate.

POCKET GOPHERS

VIEWING
OPPORTUNITY

The long, sinuous casts packed with dirt that you see scattered over the grasslands and meadows of this and other segments of The Colorado Trail are evidence of pocket gophers at work.

This small, thickset, and mostly nocturnal animal is a regular biological excavation service, with burrow systems that may be more than 500 feet long, requiring the removal of nearly three tons of soil. Excess soil is thrown out in characteristic loose mounds. But it is the conspicuous

Pocket gopher at work.
Photo courtesy of Jim Herd

winter casts that attract the attention of curious hikers. These are actually tunnels made during the winter through the snow and along the surface of the ground and packed with dirt brought up from below. Sometimes the endless burrowing activities of pocket gophers can undermine an area to such an extent that a passing hiker can be surprised when the ground suddenly gives way under foot.

In Colorado, pocket gophers are found well up into the meager soils of the alpine zone and are a major factor in the soil-building process in mountain areas.

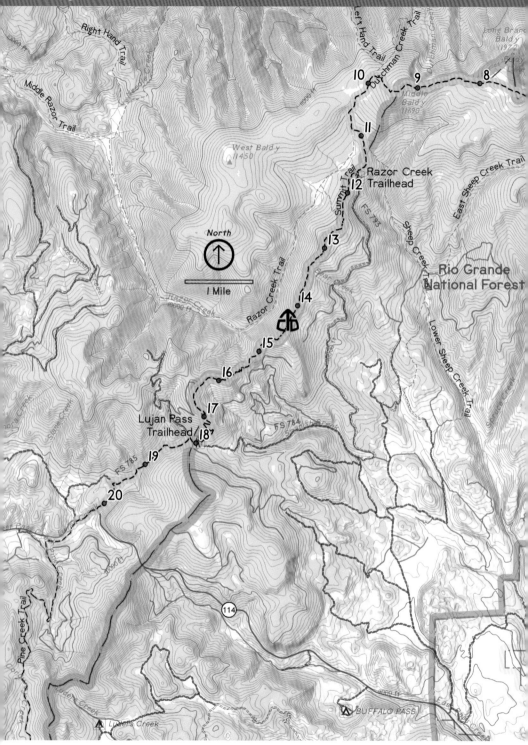

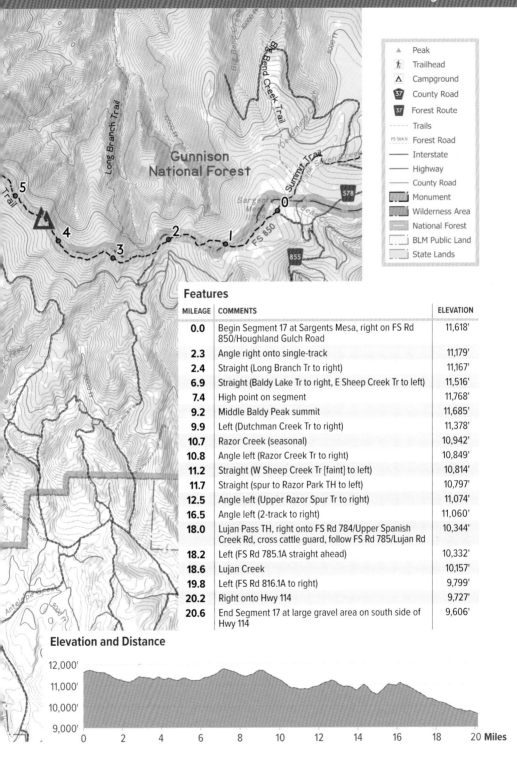

Features

MILEAGE	COMMENTS	ELEVATION
0.0	Begin Segment 17 at Sargents Mesa, right on FS Rd 850/Houghland Gulch Road	11,618'
2.3	Angle right onto single-track	11,179'
2.4	Straight (Long Branch Tr to right)	11,167'
6.9	Straight (Baldy Lake Tr to right, E Sheep Creek Tr to left)	11,516'
7.4	High point on segment	11,768'
9.2	Middle Baldy Peak summit	11,685'
9.9	Left (Dutchman Creek Tr to right)	11,378'
10.7	Razor Creek (seasonal)	10,942'
10.8	Angle left (Razor Creek Tr to right)	10,849'
11.2	Straight (W Sheep Creek Tr [faint] to left)	10,814'
11.7	Straight (spur to Razor Park TH to left)	10,797'
12.5	Angle left (Upper Razor Spur Tr to right)	11,074'
16.5	Angle left (2-track to right)	11,060'
18.0	Lujan Pass TH, right onto FS Rd 784/Upper Spanish Creek Rd, cross cattle guard, follow FS Rd 785/Lujan Rd	10,344'
18.2	Left (FS Rd 785.1A straight ahead)	10,332'
18.6	Lujan Creek	10,157'
19.8	Left (FS Rd 816.1A to right)	9,799'
20.2	Right onto Hwy 114	9,727'
20.6	End Segment 17 at large gravel area on south side of Hwy 114	9,606'

Elevation and Distance

SEGMENT 18
CO Highway 114 to Saguache Park Road

Vast pastureland characterizes this part of the CT. Photo by Carl Brown

Distance	13.7 miles	
Elevation Gain	Approx. 1,447 feet	
Elevation Loss	Approx. 1,534 feet	
USFS Map	Gunnison National Forest	
The CT Databook, 8th Edition	Pages 46–47	
The CT Map Book	Pages 43–45	
Trails Illustrated Maps	No. 139, 1201	
Jurisdiction	Gunnison Ranger District, Gunnison National Forest	

ACCESS FROM
DENVER END

ACCESS FROM
DURANGO END

AVAILABILITY
OF WATER

BICYCLING

See page 217

ABOUT THIS SEGMENT: Segment 18 travels through the relatively gentle Cochetopa Hills where early summer wildflowers and easy walking can make it very enjoyable. This is ranch and cattle country; the views are expansive and have an entirely different feel from the forested ridges above. Visible to the north, Cochetopa Dome and the surrounding valley remain largely unchanged from a century before. The only on-trail water source that flows often is Los Creek. After that, the next reliable water source is Cochetopa Creek, accessible just off the trail 11 miles beyond Los Creek. Be prepared for this, especially when temperatures are high. Much of the terrain in this segment is directly exposed to the sun, as well as thunderstorms.

A thru-hiker along Highway 114 hoping to resupply in Gunnison, 39 miles distant. Having a hiker sign often helps to secure a ride. Photo by Lane Early

Although the CT doesn't enter the La Garita Wilderness until midway through Segment 19, the most practical point for bikes to begin the bypass is at **mile 12.1** on Segment 18. The La Garita Wilderness Bike Detour rejoins the CT at Spring Creek Pass and the start of Segment 22. See page 217 for the route description.

TRAILHEAD/ACCESS POINTS

CO Highway 114 Trail Access: From Saguache on US Highway 285 in the San Luis Valley, drive west on CO Highway 114 for approximately 30 miles to North Pass. Continue 1.5 miles down the pass to a wide shoulder on the south side of the highway. This is the beginning of Segment 18 and the end of 17. Overnight parking here on the highway right-of-way has generated two tips from authorities: 1) place a visible "Do Not Tow. Using The Colorado Trail" so it's evident that the car is not abandoned, and 2) if parking for an extended time, longer than 72 hours, communicate the license plate number and plan to Montrose State Patrol at (970) 249-4392.

County Road NN14 Trail Access: From Saguache on US Highway 285, go west on CO Highway 114 for approximately 21 miles and take County Road NN14 to the left. Follow County Road NN14, becoming FS Road 750/Cochetopa Road, for nearly 9 miles to Luders Creek Campground, which has a continuously flowing spring in the back (north end). Continue 1.9 miles to Cochetopa Pass, where the road becomes County Road NN14 again. Continue another 1.3 miles to a gated road

The CT follows old ranching roads through this segment. Photo by Julia Taylor

on the right where the CT intersects and joins County Road NN14 from the north. From this point, the CT follows County Road NN14 for 0.6 mile down two switchbacks and then leaves the road, heading south on FS Road 864.2A/Archuleta Creek Road. This crossing point is considered the trail access point. There is no formal parking area here, but there's little traffic and the gated road at the top of the switchbacks where the CT joins County Road NN14 also offers room to park a few cars.

Alternate County Rd NN14 Trail Access: From west of Monarch Pass on US Highway 50, turn left (south) on CO Highway 114 just west of Parlin. Travel nearly 26 miles on CO 114 and turn right onto County Road 17GG. Follow County Road 17GG for slightly over 5 miles to a T intersection with County Road NN14. Turn left and follow County Road NN14 for 5.6 miles to reach FS Road 864.2A/Archuleta Road on the right, just before the road starts to switchback away from Archuleta Creek. The trail can be accessed at this point or at the top of a second switchback at a gated road. Both have limited room for parking, but little traffic.

Saguache Park Road Trail Access: See Segment 19 on page 221.

SERVICES, SUPPLIES, AND ACCOMMODATIONS: There is no convenient resupply point for this segment.

TRAIL DESCRIPTION: Begin Segment 18 on the south side of CO Highway 114 where there is a large, wide shoulder and potential parking, **mile 0.0**. Pass through the gate onto single-track and cross often-dry Lujan Creek on a small bridge at **mile 0.1**. Follow the CT to a junction with a faint side trail at **mile 0.6** where the CT turns left and follows Pine Creek, also often dry. At **mile 0.9**, the trail begins following an old roadbed where the Corduroy Connector Trail joins from the right. Continue straight where another old roadbed curves to the left at **mile 1.0** and cross Pine Creek at **mile 1.7**. Go right at the fork at **mile 1.8**, following a broad curve and head uphill into trees. The CT turns back to the south through a broad curve to the left and then leaves the old roadbed at **mile 3.6** and heads steeply uphill to the right on single-track.

Reach a saddle at **mile 3.9** and pass through a gate. Turn left onto an old road-bed at **mile 4.1**. Follow this roadbed until coming to another gate at **mile 6.4**. Pass around a third gate at **mile 6.6**, then reach County Rd NN14 at **mile 6.7**. This begins an almost 14-mile section of travel on lightly traveled dirt roads that ends midway on Segment 19 near Cochetopa Creek. (Reliable water, camping, and vault toilets are available at Luders Creek Campground (fee), just over 3 miles east on County Rd NN14, becoming FS Road 750/Cochetopa Road, where flowing spring water is available in the back of the campground).

Continuing on from **mile 6.7**, turn right onto County Road NN14 and head west and downhill on two long switchbacks until coming to FS Road 864.2A/Archuleta Road at **mile 7.3**. Take a sharp left here onto the two-track and cross Archuleta Creek, where water might be found in deep grass 50 feet upstream of the crossing. Follow FS Road 864.2A as it wraps around the base of a hill, continuing straight at a junction with a two-track angling to the right at **mile 7.6**. Continue straight at **mile 8.3** and just beyond, where the two-track FS Road 823.1A/Archuleta BR Road angles left and heads up the Los Creek drainage.

Travel along Los Creek to **mile 9.0**, where the two-track turns sharply left and crosses the creek. Water is likely here or possibly 0.1 mile downstream. Continue

Cows often share water sources with hikers through this segment, so travelers will want to stock up on clear water from the intermittent streams if available.

Los Creek often flows and **Lujan, Pine,** and **Archuleta Creeks** may have small flows at times, but are unreliable in dry years and later in the summer.

A thru-hiker heading west through the expanse of Segment 18. Photo by Mary Parlange

uphill to **mile 9.1** and turn right onto FS Road 864/Los Creek Road, which also continues straight ahead. There are good campsites farther uphill. After passing through a treed section, the trail turns downhill to reach a junction with FS Road 787.2A/Saguache Park BR 1 Road at **mile 9.7**, where you are again near Los Creek and possible last-chance water until Cochetopa Creek, 11 miles ahead. Turn left onto FS Road 787.2A and climb a gentle valley away from Los Creek.

Begin a gentle descent to reach a long, straight fence and angle left to follow the fence line. Ignore several two-tracks that leave FS Road 787.2A to either side as it angles slightly away from the fence. Reach another fence at **mile 11.9**, pass through a gate, and curve to the right at the intersection just beyond the gate. Take a sharp left onto the graded FS Road 787/Saguache Park Road where County Road 17FF continues to the right at **mile 12.1. (Mountain bikers divert here for the La Garita Wilderness Bike Detour.)** Ignore the two-tracks to either side, and cross Monchego Creek at **mile 12.7**. Continue on FS Road 787 as it wraps around a sparsely treed ridge, passing two two-track junctions on the left (FS Road 787.2B/Monchego Park Road) at **mile 13.1**. Cross a cattle guard at **mile 13.3**, wrap around another drainage, then reach the end of Segment 18 at the intersection of FS Road 787/Saguache Park Road and FS Road 787.2D/Quemedo Road at **mile 13.7**.

LA GARITA WILDERNESS BICYCLE DETOUR

MOUNTAIN
BIKING

This long, mandatory detour avoids the La Garita Wilderness. It is pleasant, passing through a remote part of Colorado, heavily timbered with aspen trees and spectacular in the fall. Part of the route was the planned itinerary of the infamous Alferd Packer, convicted for eating his snowbound companions in 1874. The detour passes the old Ute Indian Agency, which was Packer's destination.

The route begins where The Colorado Trail intersects the gravel FS Road 787/Saguache Park Road (left) and County Road 17FF (right) **mile 0.0**, CT Segment 18 **mile 12.1**. Ride north on County Road 17FF to a T intersection with the gravel County Road NN14, **mile 2.2**, where you turn left (west).

Pass an intersection with County Road 17GG, first on the left and then on the right, at **mile 3.2**. Before Dome Lakes, pass an intersection with County Road 15GG on the left at **mile 4.6**. Camping is allowed around the lakes. Continue following County Road NN14 in a more northerly direction past the lakes to **mile 8.2** and an intersection with County Road KK14 (may also be signed as George Bush Drive and BLM Rd 3084), also gravel. Turn left (southwest) and follow the road to **mile 14.3**, the old Ute Indian Agency location, now a Forest Service facility, where the road becomes FS Rd 788/Los Pinos-Cebolla Road. Continue to an intersection with FS Road 790/Big Meadows Road at **mile 17.1** and stay right, continuing on the main road. Ignore the second intersection with FS Road 790 on the left at **mile 25.9**, and continue following FS Road 788. Reach Los Pinos Pass at **mile 26.9**. Continue on FS Road 788 (also County Road 45) angling to the right at **mile 31.6**. The Cathedral Ranch Cabins—left on County Road 52 less than a mile—offers travelers a resupply store, mail drops, showers, laundry, and cabins (cathedralcabins.com).

Head downhill to **mile 32.8** and turn left at a T intersection to stay on the graveled FS Road 788 (also County Road 50) and begin following Cebolla Creek upstream. There's a Forest Service cattle guard at **mile 37.7** and, 1 to 3 miles beyond, are three Forest Service campgrounds along Cebolla Creek. After a prolonged climb, just beyond another FS campground, arrive at an intersection with the paved CO Highway 149, **mile 47.8**. It is near this point where Packer and his party became snowbound. If visiting Lake City, turn right onto CO 149 for the 9.5-mile downhill.

To continue on the CT, turn left (east) onto CO 149 and ride over Slumgullion Summit to **mile 55.5** at the top of Spring Creek Pass, the end of Segment 21 and the start of Segment 22.

Features

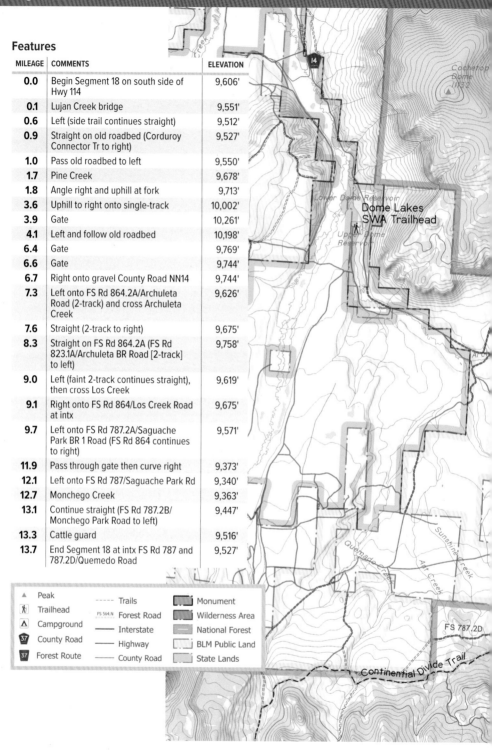

MILEAGE	COMMENTS	ELEVATION
0.0	Begin Segment 18 on south side of Hwy 114	9,606'
0.1	Lujan Creek bridge	9,551'
0.6	Left (side trail continues straight)	9,512'
0.9	Straight on old roadbed (Corduroy Connector Tr to right)	9,527'
1.0	Pass old roadbed to left	9,550'
1.7	Pine Creek	9,678'
1.8	Angle right and uphill at fork	9,713'
3.6	Uphill to right onto single-track	10,002'
3.9	Gate	10,261'
4.1	Left and follow old roadbed	10,198'
6.4	Gate	9,769'
6.6	Gate	9,744'
6.7	Right onto gravel County Road NN14	9,744'
7.3	Left onto FS Rd 864.2A/Archuleta Road (2-track) and cross Archuleta Creek	9,626'
7.6	Straight (2-track to right)	9,675'
8.3	Straight on FS Rd 864.2A (FS Rd 823.1A/Archuleta BR Road [2-track] to left)	9,758'
9.0	Left (faint 2-track continues straight), then cross Los Creek	9,619'
9.1	Right onto FS Rd 864/Los Creek Road at intx	9,675'
9.7	Left onto FS Rd 787.2A/Saguache Park BR 1 Road (FS Rd 864 continues to right)	9,571'
11.9	Pass through gate then curve right	9,373'
12.1	Left onto FS Rd 787/Saguache Park Rd	9,340'
12.7	Monchego Creek	9,363'
13.1	Continue straight (FS Rd 787.2B/ Monchego Park Road to left)	9,447'
13.3	Cattle guard	9,516'
13.7	End Segment 18 at intx FS Rd 787 and 787.2D/Quemedo Road	9,527'

Legend:
- ▲ Peak
- 🚶 Trailhead
- ⚠ Campground
- 37 County Road
- 37 Forest Route
- ----- Trails
- FS 564.N Forest Road
- —— Interstate
- —— Highway
- —— County Road
- Monument
- Wilderness Area
- National Forest
- BLM Public Land
- State Lands

Elevation and Distance

SEGMENT 19
Saguache Park Road to Eddiesville Trailhead

Southbound on Van Tassel Gulch Road. Photo by Luci Stremme

ACCESS FROM
DENVER END

ACCESS FROM
DURANGO END

AVAILABILITY
OF WATER

BICYCLING

See page 217

Distance	13.7 miles
Elevation Gain	Approx. 2,239 feet
Elevation Loss	Approx. 1,442 feet
USFS Map	Gunnison National Forest
The CT Databook, 8th Edition	Pages 48–49
The CT Map Book	Pages 45–47
Trails Illustrated Maps	No. 139, 1201
Jurisdiction	Gunnison Ranger District, Gunnison National Forest

ABOUT THIS SEGMENT: This segment rolls through cattle country, passing fields of summer wildflowers including paintbrush, larkspur, and various types of sunflowers. When the blooms peak, flatter areas around the trail appear like carpets of flowers. The segment is very dry until reaching Cochetopa Creek, one of the bigger waterways and a favorite of anglers. You'll find grassy meadows along the east side of the creek. The trail continues in a southwesterly direction until it crosses the creek where you'll need to ford. Upstream along the west side, you'll enter the La Garita Wilderness and one of the most remote parts of the CT before reaching the end of the segment at the Eddiesville Trailhead. Similar to Segment 18, much of the terrain in this segment is directly exposed to the sun, as well as thunderstorms.

TRAILHEAD/ACCESS POINTS

Saguache Park Road Trail Access: From Saguache, go west on CO Highway 114 for approximately 35 miles. Turn left onto County Road 17GG. Alternatively, from west of Monarch Pass on US Highway 50, turn left (south) on CO 114 just west of Parlin. Follow CO 114 for nearly 26 miles and turn right onto County Road 17GG.

From either direction, continue slightly over 5 miles to a T intersection with County Road NN14. Turn left (east) on County Road NN14 and drive 1 mile. Then turn right (south) on County Road 17FF, which becomes FS Road 787/Saguache Park Road, for 3.8 miles. Watch for the two-track FS Road 787.2D/Quemado Road

At the old log bridge site, a hiker readies their footwear to ford Cochetopa Creek. Photo by Matt Pierce

Old log fence. Photo by Luci Stremme

branching off to the right (southwest). This intersection is the end of Segment 18 and the beginning of Segment 19. There is no formal parking area at this trail access, but there is room to park on the side of the road.

Eddiesville Trailhead: See Segment 20 on page 229.

SERVICES, SUPPLIES, AND ACCOMMODATIONS: There is no convenient resupply point for this segment.

TRAIL DESCRIPTION: Segment 19 begins at the intersection of FS Road 787/ Saguache Park Road and FS Road 787.2D/Quemado Road, **mile 0.0**. Leave FS Road 787, angling to the right onto the two-track FS Road 787.2D, then continue straight onto the two-track Trail #9646 at **mile 0.1**. Cross seasonal Ant Creek, then pass through a gate at **mile 1.2**. Continue straight at **mile 1.5**, where a two-track joins the CT from the left. Cross the two-track FS Road 597/Van Tassel Road at **mile 2.2**, then continue on Trail #9646 as it curves to the right and parallels Quemado Creek. Turn

> ⚠ **WARNING:** Many hikers have reported overlooking the intersection of the Saguache Park Road with FS Road 787.2D. Pay close attention.

Beaver dam on Cochetopa Creek. Photo by Luci Stremme

left onto FS Road 597/Van Tassel Road and cross seasonal Quemado Creek at **mile 2.4**, then continue straight past on the right. Pass a two-track to the left and continue through a fence at **mile 3.2**. Reach Van Tassel Gulch at **mile 3.5** at a seasonal spring protected by fencing.

At **mile 3.8**, angle left and head uphill to continue on FS Road 597 (FS Road 597.1C departs to the north and then FS Road 597.1D angles to the left shortly after). Reach an open area at a high point and intersection at **mile 5.4**, where the CT bears to the right onto FS Road 597.1A/Van Tassel BR Road, FS Road 597 departing to the left. Pass through a gate at **mile 5.7** and descend to **mile 6.6**, where the CT curves sharply left at an intersection with a two-track on the right. Curve to the left again at **mile 6.8** to pass large boulders marking closure to vehicles. This ends the almost 14 miles of road travel that began midway on Segment 18 and the nearly 48

The remoteness of the **La Garita Wilderness** offers great opportunities for solitude. Those camping near Cochetopa Creek should get an early start if they plan to summit San Luis Peak the following day.

If you seek **solitude**, this is one of the least-traveled segments of the CT. The trailheads are remote and can be difficult to reach in wet weather. Don't expect your cell phone to work out here.

TRAVEL TIPS

Van Tassel Gulch Road. Photo by Luci Stremme

miles allowing motorcycles from the head of South Fooses Creek on Segment 15. The remainder of the trail to Durango is almost all on single-track and non-motorized, with minor exceptions.

Follow the trail on the closed two-track past a stock pond then onto the single-track Skyline Trail, crossing a closed two-track at **mile 7.1** and continuing up the Cochetopa Creek valley. At **mile 7.5**, take the lower trail at a junction, although the upper trail rejoins the lower trail in 0.1 mile. Numerous side trails lead to Cochetopa Creek, a reliable water source and fishery, with camping potential in the area. During the next 2.5 miles, the trail gradually climbs higher above the creek and then descends to it.

Reach Cochetopa Creek at **mile 9.8** (9,890') and ford the creek upstream of typically submerged old log bridges. Use caution when high water is present. In spring, flows can be lower in the morning, making crossing safer than later in the day. Climb steeply up the west bank to **mile 9.9** and turn left at a junction with a side trail. At **mile 10.9**, drop into the Nutras Creek drainage. A faint track leads left to a crossing of the creek on stepping stones or continue straight to ford the creek. Enter the La Garita Wilderness on the climb out of the drainage. Potential camping can be found on either side of Nutras Creek.

Pass through a gate at **mile 12.1** and cross a small stream with possible water at **mile 12.5**. Bear right at **mile 13.2** where a faint track leads to the left. Leave the La Garita Wilderness at **mile 13.6** and reach the end of the segment at the Eddiesville Trailhead at **mile 13.7**; vault toilet available here. There is camping nearby and water available from Stewart Creek just beyond the trailhead.

TREKKING WITH LLAMAS

Llamas have been used for centuries in South America as pack animals, as well as for their fiber and meat. Increasingly, hikers enjoy the advantages of these unique personal porters on long-distance trails such as the CT.

Llamas may be used for short hikes or may be fully loaded for traveling through the mountains on multi-day outings. An adult animal (3 years or more) can carry about 20 percent of its body weight in rough terrain, or about 70 pounds. Llamas have two-toed padded feet, which do much less damage to the terrain because they do not tear up the ground the way hooves do. Llamas are browsers, not grazers, which limits overgrazing of delicate backcountry meadows.

Using llamas to haul camping gear is a great way to go. Photo courtesy of Diane Gansauer

Highly social animals, llamas travel well in a string and are easy to train. Most importantly, they are calm and trusting with people. The common stigma, that llamas spit, is true in the sense that they use this behavior to gain advantage in their social structure. Just don't get stuck between two angry llamas.

With their panniers fully loaded, llamas can be expected to go 5 to 9 miles per day in the mountains. Smaller and far more maneuverable than other pack animals, their pace is perfectly suited for comfortable hiking. Being herd animals, llamas like to travel with companions and become anxious when separated from them. A good pack llama will follow its human leader willingly (nearly) anywhere, including areas where it might get hurt; so, the animal's welfare should be your primary concern at all times.

Several Colorado outfitters offer trekking services on the CT using llamas. As the price of pack stock continues to drop dramatically, they also are coming into use by individuals as well as by the Forest Service. Check with land management agencies in the segments you wish to travel about any restrictions regarding pack animals. The Colorado Trail Foundation's website (ColoradoTrail.org) also has a lot of good information about using llamas for pack stock.

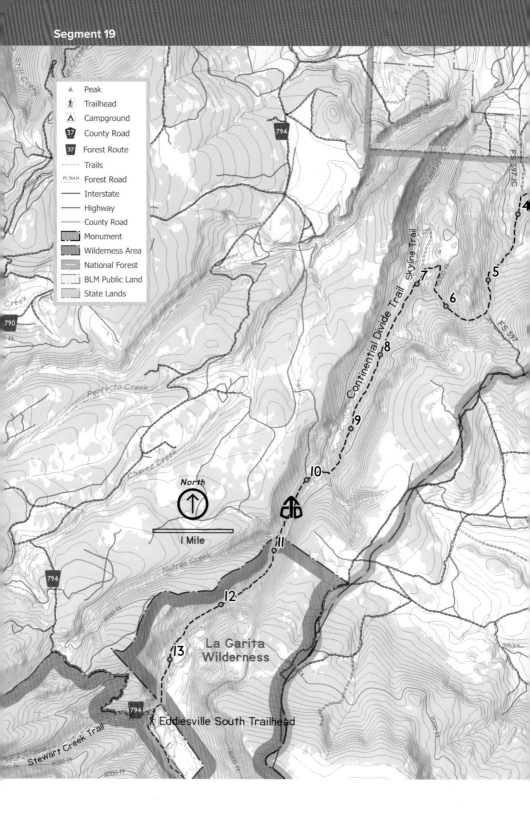

- ▲ Peak
- 🚶 Trailhead
- ⛺ Campground
- 37 County Road
- 37 Forest Route
- Trails
- FS 564.N Forest Road
- Interstate
- Highway
- County Road
- Monument
- Wilderness Area
- National Forest
- BLM Public Land
- State Lands

North

1 Mile

La Garita
Wilderness

Eddiesville South Trailhead

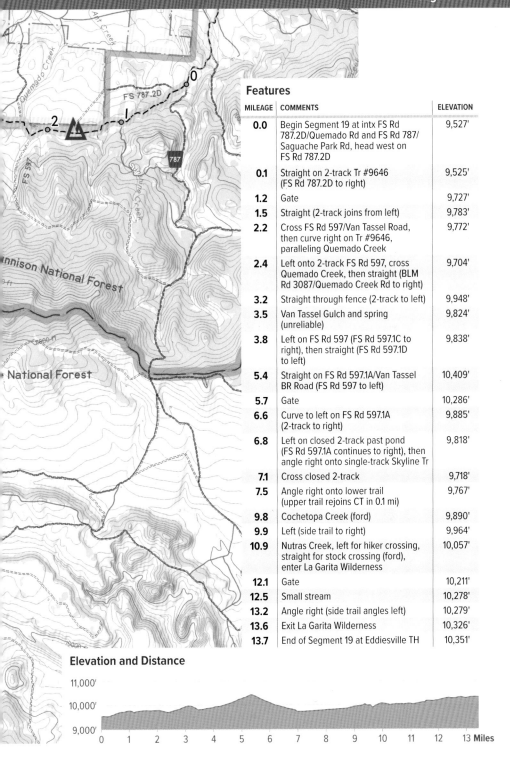

Features

MILEAGE	COMMENTS	ELEVATION
0.0	Begin Segment 19 at intx FS Rd 787.2D/Quemado Rd and FS Rd 787/ Saguache Park Rd, head west on FS Rd 787.2D	9,527'
0.1	Straight on 2-track Tr #9646 (FS Rd 787.2D to right)	9,525'
1.2	Gate	9,727'
1.5	Straight (2-track joins from left)	9,783'
2.2	Cross FS Rd 597/Van Tassel Road, then curve right on Tr #9646, paralleling Quemado Creek	9,772'
2.4	Left onto 2-track FS Rd 597, cross Quemado Creek, then straight (BLM Rd 3087/Quemado Creek Rd to right)	9,704'
3.2	Straight through fence (2-track to left)	9,948'
3.5	Van Tassel Gulch and spring (unreliable)	9,824'
3.8	Left on FS Rd 597 (FS Rd 597.1C to right), then straight (FS Rd 597.1D to left)	9,838'
5.4	Straight on FS Rd 597.1A/Van Tassel BR Road (FS Rd 597 to left)	10,409'
5.7	Gate	10,286'
6.6	Curve to left on FS Rd 597.1A (2-track to right)	9,885'
6.8	Left on closed 2-track past pond (FS Rd 597.1A continues to right), then angle right onto single-track Skyline Tr	9,818'
7.1	Cross closed 2-track	9,718'
7.5	Angle right onto lower trail (upper trail rejoins CT in 0.1 mi)	9,767'
9.8	Cochetopa Creek (ford)	9,890'
9.9	Left (side trail to right)	9,964'
10.9	Nutras Creek, left for hiker crossing, straight for stock crossing (ford), enter La Garita Wilderness	10,057'
12.1	Gate	10,211'
12.5	Small stream	10,278'
13.2	Angle right (side trail angles left)	10,279'
13.6	Exit La Garita Wilderness	10,326'
13.7	End of Segment 19 at Eddiesville TH	10,351'

Elevation and Distance

SEGMENT 20

Eddiesville Trailhead to San Luis Pass

Hoodoos carved from layers of volcanic ash, remnants of volcanic activity 27 million years ago. Photo by Elliot Forsyth

Distance	12.6 miles
Elevation Gain	Approx. 3,104 feet
Elevation Loss	Approx. 1,478 feet
USFS Maps	Gunnison and Rio Grande National Forests
The CT Databook, 8th Edition	Pages 50–51
The CT Map Book	Pages 47–49
Trails Illustrated Maps	No. 139, 1201
Jurisdiction	Gunnison Ranger District, Gunnison National Forest

ACCESS FROM
DENVER END

ACCESS FROM
DURANGO END

AVAILABILITY
OF WATER

BICYCLING

See page 217

ABOUT THIS SEGMENT: Segment 20 soon re-enters the La Garita Wilderness and detours around private property. The trail slowly bends westward as it climbs up the Cochetopa Creek watershed, eventually reaching a saddle below San Luis Peak (14,014') to the north. It is a relatively short side trip to the top of the peak, consisting of a 1,400-foot climb in 1.4 miles, where climbers enjoy great views of the surrounding area. From the saddle, the CT descends and ascends two more saddles before reaching the end of the segment at San Luis Pass. The trail is relatively steep throughout, but the views and summer wildflowers are terrific. After leaving tree line just above Cochetopa Creek, trail users are exposed to potential severe weather for many miles as the trail crosses tundra well into Segment 24, with limited protected sections below tree line.

A hiker takes a break along the saddle beneath San Luis Peak.
Photo by Pete Turner

San Luis Peak and the surrounding ridges are made up of volcanic tuff (consolidated volcanic ash). The ash was erupted about 27 million years ago from a huge volcanic depression known as the Nelson Mountain Tuff. Much of the ash from the eruption spread out to form tuff layers that cap the surrounding ridges, but much of it fell back to fill the caldera and form the tuff that now forms San Luis Peak and its neighbors. It is only one of more than a dozen similar calderas in the San Juan volcanic field.

TRAILHEAD/ACCESS POINTS

Eddiesville Trailhead: From Saguache on US Highway 285, go west on CO Highway 114 for 36 miles. Turn left onto County Road 17GG and follow it for slightly over 5 miles to a T intersection with County Road NN14. Turn right and follow County Road NN14 for 1.3 miles, then turn left onto County Road 15GG, just before reaching Upper Dome Reservoir.

Alternately, this point can also be reached from the north. From west of Monarch Pass on US Highway 50, turn left (south) on CO 114 just west of Parlin. Travel just over 20 miles on CO 114 and turn right onto County Road NN14 and follow it for 7 miles, then turn right onto County Road 15GG.

From either direction, follow County Road 15GG for slightly over 4 miles, around the west side of the reservoir and then curve to the southwest. Angle left onto FS Road 794/Cochetopa Creek Road (may also be signed County Road 14DD) and follow it for nearly 17 miles to the Eddiesville Trailhead. This road can be very challenging when wet.

San Luis Pass Trail Access: 🚙 See Segment 21 on page 236.

SERVICES, SUPPLIES, AND ACCOMMODATIONS: These amenities are available in Creede; see Segment 21 on page 237.

TRAIL DESCRIPTION: Segment 20 begins at the well-marked Eddiesville Trailhead, **mile 0.0**, near a ranch inholding that is essentially a private island within the La Garita Wilderness. The trailhead is near the junction of Stewart and Cochetopa Creeks, with camping potential in the area. Turn left from the trailhead, travel south on FS Road 794/Cochetopa Creek Road, crossing Stewart Creek at **mile 0.1**. At **mile 0.2**, the road ends at the entrance gate to the private ranch, where the trail turns uphill to the right and continues following the single-track Skyline Trail again. Re-enter the La Garita Wilderness shortly afterward then turn sharply left at the ranch fence corner. Cross a small, seasonal stream at **mile 0.8**.

Pass through a gate at **mile 1.2**, then continue straight at the junction with the Machin Basin Trail at **mile 1.5**. The CT heads south, then bends to the southwest before passing through another gate at **mile 3.6**. A short side trip at **mile 4.6** provides a view of Cochetopa Creek in a boisterous cascade down a rocky gorge

Climbing out of Cochetopa Creek toward the saddle beneath San Luis Peak. Photo by Len Glassner

during good flows. There is good access to water over the next four miles, with several good camping options near **mile 6** and **mile 7** near water. Note the columnar jointing in the volcanic rock on Organ Mountain (13,801') to the north in this area.

Follow along the north side of Cochetopa Creek as the trail climbs and heads to the west, passing the junction with the faint Stewart Creek Trail at **mile 7.4** where camping may be found. Cross Cochetopa Creek at **mile 7.5**, then pass good alpine meadow campsites. This begins a lengthy section above tree line that extends into Segment 24 with limited sections below tree line. Climb to the high saddle at **mile 8.7**, where a well-constructed side trail leads to the summit of San Luis Peak (14,014'). The climb entails 1,400 feet of elevation gain over 1.4 miles to gain expansive views in all directions.

Descend from the saddle, passing under unusual and photogenic rock spires, to a small seasonal spring at **mile 9.0**. Climb to another saddle at **mile 9.9**, then descend into the headwaters of Spring Creek and pass the Bonholder Trail junction

CLIMBING SAN LUIS PEAK

Left: From the saddle, a section-hiker points toward San Luis Peak and the climbing route from the CT. Photo by Bill Manning **Right:** A climber ascends a talus-covered slope. Photo courtesy of Colorado Mountain Expeditions

The Colorado Trail's closest encounter with a fourteener comes when it passes gentle-giant San Luis Peak (14,014 feet) at **mile 8.7** of Segment 20.

Despite the popularity of fourteener bagging, if you elect to climb San Luis Peak while passing by on your trek, you may be lucky enough to have it all to yourself. According to the Colorado Fourteeners Initiative, San Luis Peak is one of the least climbed of the fourteeners. The ascent is not a difficult one, with its Class 1 rating and 1,400 feet of elevation gain in about 1.4 miles. Proceed north from the saddle, following the gentle ridge to the top. Plan on an early start, though, to avoid afternoon storms. Allow 2 to 3 hours round trip.

on the right at **mile 10.4**. Contour around the head of the basin below the sheer and rocky north face of Peak 13,285, then cross a seasonal stream at **mile 10.8** and another seasonal stream at **mile 11.3**. Camping may be found near these streams but select a site carefully to minimize the potential for falling dead trees. Ascend to another saddle at **mile 11.9** located on the Continental Divide, which the trail has not reached since leaving Lujan Pass on Segment 17, then leave the La Garita Wilderness again. Head downhill to San Luis Pass and a 4-way trail junction at **mile 12.6** where Segment 20 ends.

 TRAVEL TIPS

It is a temptation to climb 14,014-foot **San Luis Peak**, but the high incidence of lightning storms in the area can make it a dicey proposition. Be sure to check the cloud patterns and weather before ascending.

It's best to depart from the pass quite early. Drop the bulk of your gear on the pass for the jaunt to the top, then resume your trek before **afternoon thundershowers** move in.

Features

MILEAGE	COMMENTS	ELEVATION
0.0	Begin Segment 20 at Eddiesville TH, left onto FS Rd 794/Cochetopa Creek Rd	10,351'
0.1	Stewart Creek	10,334'
0.2	Right onto single-track at end of FS Rd 794 at ranch gate, enter La Garita Wilderness, then continue left	10,356'
0.8	Seasonal stream	10,363'
1.2	Gate	10,342'
1.5	Straight (Machin Basin Tr to left)	10,362'
3.6	Gate	10,644'
4.6	Waterfall gorge to left (off trail)	10,745'
7.4	Straight (Stewart Creek Tr to right)	11,752'
7.5	Cochetopa Creek	11,758'
8.7	Angle left at San Luis saddle (side trail to San Luis Peak to right)	12,611'
9.0	Seasonal spring	12,543'
9.9	Saddle	12,368'
10.4	Straight (Bonholder Tr to right)	12,137'
10.8	Seasonal stream	12,032'
11.3	Seasonal stream	11,912'
11.9	Continental Divide, leave La Garita Wilderness	12,383'
12.6	End Segment 20 at San Luis Pass (Cascade Creek Tr to right, San Luis Pass Tr [signed W Willow Creek Tr] to left)	11,942'

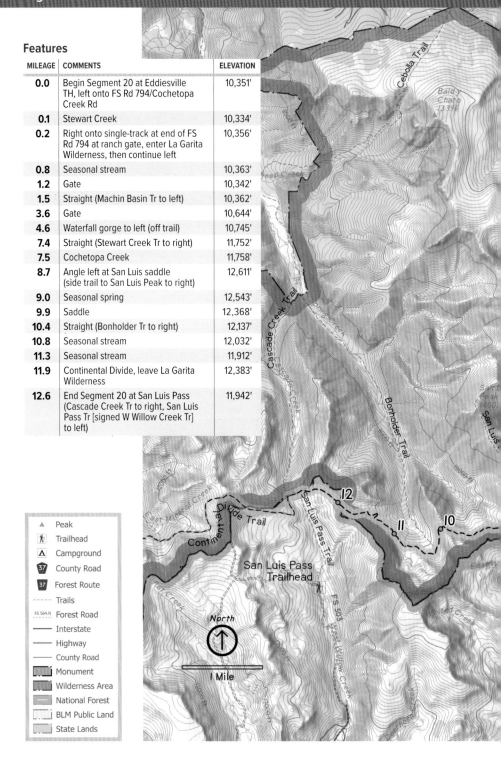

Peak
Trailhead
Campground
37 County Road
37 Forest Route
----- Trails
FS 564.N Forest Road
—— Interstate
—— Highway
—— County Road
Monument
Wilderness Area
National Forest
BLM Public Land
State Lands

North

1 Mile

Continental Divide Trail

794

0
Eddiesville South Trailhead
Stewart Creek
Trailhead

794

1

2

East Fork Cochetopa Creek

Stewart Creek Trail

La Garita Wilderness

Organ
Mountain
13,730

3

4

5

6 Skyline Trail

7

Cutoff Trail

Gunnison
National Forest

Machin Basin Trail

o Grande
onal Forest

Elevation and Distance

13,000'

12,000'

11,000'

10,000'

0   1   2   3   4   5   6   7   8   9   10   11   12 **Miles**

o Creek Trail

SEGMENT 21
San Luis Pass to
Spring Creek Pass Trailhead

CT on Snow Mesa with 1,500 sheep and a cowboy.
Photo by Jeff Sellenrick

Distance	14.7 miles
Elevation Gain	Approx. 3,116 feet
Elevation Loss	Approx. 4,157 feet
USFS Maps	Gunnison and Rio Grande National Forests
The CT Databook, 8th Edition	Pages 52–53
The CT Map Book	Pages 49–51
Trails Illustrated Maps	Nos. 139, 141, 1201
Latitude 40° Map	Southwest Colorado Trails
Jurisdiction	Gunnison and Divide Ranger Districts, Gunnison and Rio Grande National Forests

ACCESS FROM
DENVER END

ACCESS FROM
DURANGO END

AVAILABILITY
OF WATER

BICYCLING

See page 261

Sheepherder on Snow Mesa. Photo by Don Wallace

ABOUT THIS SEGMENT: This segment is quite the rollercoaster. The CT climbs in and out of the East, Middle, and West Mineral Creek drainages and traverses the Continental Divide with a maximum segment elevation of 12,894 feet. The views of the surrounding mountains are equally spectacular from the ridges and saddles as they are from the headwaters of the creeks below. There are many great potential campsites in the forests as the trail rolls in and out of the trees.

Segment 21 ends after crossing Snow Mesa. The trail is high and exposed continuously from **mile 5.5** until reaching tree line around **mile 13.2** after dropping off the west edge of Snow Mesa, so be cautious about crossing this nearly 8-mile stretch if thunderstorms threaten. Even though the mesa looks relatively flat on the map, it does dip into several small creek drainages, oftentimes quite steeply. This is one of the most remote segments of the CT and Snow Mesa can feel completely cut off from civilization. This can be a good thing on clear, windless days, but a scary prospect if there are lightning bolts flashing around you. The last 2 miles of the segment descend more than 1,200 feet to Spring Creek Pass and CO Highway 149.

This segment begins at San Luis Pass, a point that is not accessible by vehicle. 4WD vehicles can approach to within 1 mile of the segment start, and high clearance AWD vehicles can approach to within 2.5 miles, while Creede is 10 miles from the start.

A lamb checks out passing hikers. Photo by Don Wallace

TRAILHEAD/ACCESS POINTS

San Luis Pass Trail Access: From the north end of Creede, follow the gravel and steep FS Rd 503/West Willow Road north into a narrow canyon for 7 miles to the closed Equity Mine and a small parking area. 4WD vehicles with low range gearing can continue 1.1 miles, where the road becomes FS Road 505/Rat Creek Road and switchbacks down to a ford of West Willow Creek. Continue on FS Road 505 for an additional 0.6 mile to where it turns left and uphill and the San Luis Pass Trail continues straight. There is no formal parking available here. From this point, it's a 1.3-mile hike to San Luis Pass and the CT/CDT on a non-motorized trail.

Spring Creek Pass Trailhead: See Segment 22 on page 243.

TRAIL DESCRIPTION: Segment 21 begins at San Luis Pass at **mile 0.0**, where there is a 4-way trail junction with the Cascade Creek and San Luis Pass Trails. Briefly head west, then south, then to the northwest as the trail climbs more steeply up a ridge. At **mile 1.0**, cross the Continental Divide and re-enter the La Garita Wilderness for the third time. Reach a saddle and high point of the segment just north of Peak 13,111 at **mile 1.3**. The trail then descends through the headwaters of East Mineral Creek tributaries, passing seasonal water at **mile 2.1**. At **mile 2.3** is a campsite below the trail near tree line. Pass the East Mineral Creek Trail junction at **mile 2.6** and cross another tributary of East Mineral Creek at **mile 2.7**, which likely has water. Ascend to another saddle along the ridge that divides the East and Middle Mineral Creek drainages at **mile 3.3**.

Downhill from the saddle, cross Middle Mineral Creek at **mile 4.0** with lots of camping potential in scattered trees to the east. There are small tarns in the area where moose are sometimes observed browsing in the willows. After a series of

> **WARNING:** The trail section is largely above tree line. Hikers should consider weather as a major factor when choosing campsites and determining hiking schedules. Snow Mesa can be a very unsettling experience during an electrical storm.

CREEDE

It is about a 10-mile side trip into Creede from San Luis Pass. Walk 1 mile south, descending the San Luis Pass Trail along the headwaters of West Willow Creek until you meet up with FS Road 505, which becomes FS Road 503 after the first crossing of West Willow Creek. Continue on it downhill into town. The parking area at the Equity Mine sits 1.7 miles down this road. This area is often used by people climbing nearby San Luis Peak, hunters during hunting season, and people on a self-guided mine tour. On a busy weekend, a backpacker may find an easy hitch into town. Note that Creede can also be reached, if with difficulty due to the 33-mile distance and low traffic, from the Spring Creek Pass Trailhead that is described at the start of Segment 22 (page 243). Creede is an old mining town with various watering holes that recall the town's rip-roaring past.

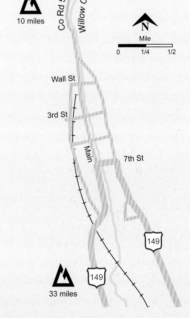

Distance from CT: 10 miles
Elevation: 8,852 feet
Zip code: 81130
Area code: 719

Dining
Several locations in town

Gear (including fuel canisters)
San Juan Sports
102 S. Main St.
(719) 658-2359

Groceries
Kentucky Belle Market
103 W. 2nd St.
(719) 658-2526

Info
Chamber of Commerce
904 S. Main St.
(719) 658-2374

Laundry
Kip's Grill
101 E. 5th St.
(719) 658-0220

Lodging
Several locations in town

Post Office
Creede Post Office
10 S. Main St.
(719) 658-2615

Medical
Mineral County Public Health/
Creede Family Practice
802 Rio Grande Ave.
(719) 658-2416
(719) 658-0929

Showers
Snowshoe Lodge
202 E. 8th St.
(719) 658-2315

Left: Trail users are treated to astounding views of fourteeners in the distance. Photo by Andrew Skurka **Right:** Wildflowers blanket a slope above Miners Creek. Photo by Aaron Locander

uphill switchbacks, gain the ridge that separates the Middle and West Mineral Creek drainages at **mile 4.9** where there's a dry campsite. There may be water at **mile 5.3**, but it is not reliable and camping is challenging, although it is the last sheltered campsite until reaching the end of the segment near Spring Creek Pass Trailhead.

Pass the Mineral Creek Trail at **mile 6.3** and cross the Continental Divide and exit the La Garita Wilderness for the last time **at mile 6.9**. Climb gently and pass south around Peak 12,813 and catch a stunning view of Snow Mesa and the white volcanic tuff exposed on the slopes below the mesa.

At a saddle at **mile 8.4**, the Skyline Trail, followed by the CT and CDT since reaching Cochetopa Creek on Segment 19, continues north into the headwaters of Rough Creek while the CT and CDT turn left and head south toward Snow Mesa. At **mile 9.3**, a carsonite post to the left marks the faint La Garita Stock Driveway, which allows motorcycles and mountain bikes, both of which are also allowed to the west on the CT/CDT across Snow Mesa to Spring Creek Pass. A pond at **mile 9.5** is generally a reliable source of water, although it may be hard to reach the water because of mud flats when water levels are low. A more accessible water source may

---

Take in the **views from Snow Mesa** above Spring Creek. You can see the Rio Grande Pyramid and the Uncompahgre Mountains, where Ute Indians once hunted.

TRAVEL TIPS

Ahead is a great U-shaped bend of the Continental Divide that holds the **headwaters** of the mighty Rio Grande.

be at the crossing of Willow Creek at **mile 9.8**. There are potential campsites with big sky views on top of Snow Mesa but no shelter of any kind. Continue west, climbing in and out of several small drainages before reaching the edge of the mesa at **mile 12.7**. Drop off the mesa and reach the shelter of tree line in another one-half mile, then the end of the segment at the Spring Creek Pass Trailhead on the west side of lightly traveled CO Highway 149, **mile 14.7**. The trailhead offers parking and a bathroom but no camping.

VIEWING PTARMIGAN

VIEWING
OPPORTUNITY

The white-tailed ptarmigan is a small alpine grouse that inhabits open tundra in summer, resorting to willows and other sheltered areas in winter. It is the only bird species in Colorado to spend the entire year above tree line. The extensive alpine terrain along CT Segment 21 is perfect habitat for this hardy ground bird.

Left: Ptarmigan can be tricky to spot. Photo by Terry Root **Right:** Photographers can sometimes get close. Photo by Julie Vida and Mark Tabb

The ptarmigan's near-perfect seasonal camouflage helps it escape detection from predators (and even sharp-eyed trail users). Its mottled-brown summer plumage makes it almost invisible amid the scattered rocks and alpine plants. In winter, only the bird's black eyes and bill stand out against its pure white coloration.

Ptarmigan are weak flyers and are as likely to scurry away when disturbed as to burst into a short, low sail over the tundra. Despite that, they still manage to travel surprising distances in early winter to congregate in areas that harbor their favorite winter sustenance: dormant willow buds. In summer they add insects, seeds, and berries to their diet.

Nesting occurs in June with four to eight buff, spotted eggs laid in a lined depression in open ground. During breeding, males are sometimes aggressive toward interlopers passing through their territory, flying around erratically and making hooting noises, or approaching to peck comically at the boot of a resting hiker.

A study by ecologist James Larison of Cornell University raised a warning flag about the future of these fascinating birds. In areas of Colorado where metals from mining operations have leached into the soil, ptarmigan have accumulated high levels of cadmium in their bodies. Ultimately, this causes calcium loss, and the birds can suffer broken bones in their brittle wings and legs.

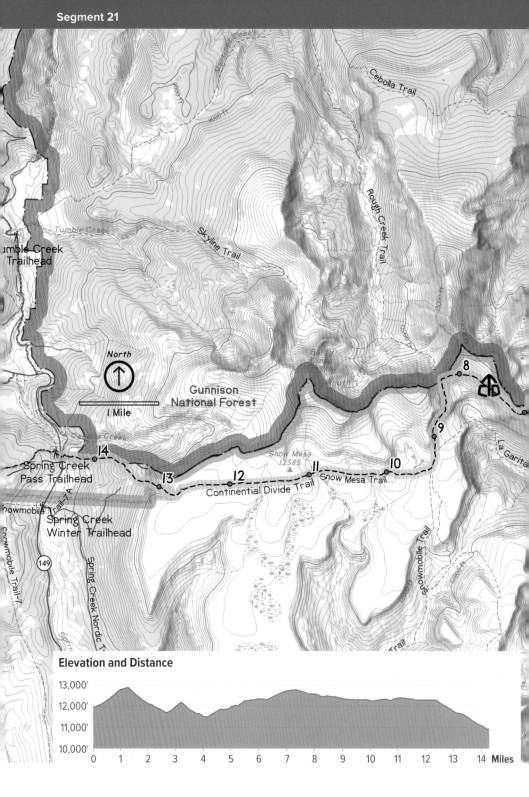

Elevation and Distance

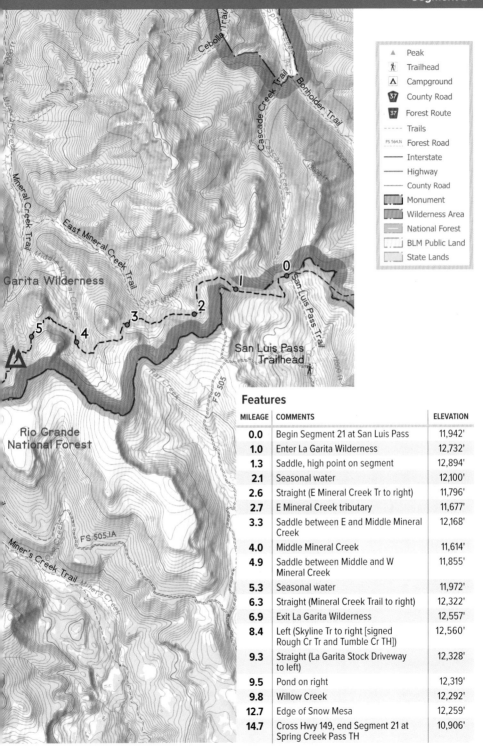

Features

MILEAGE	COMMENTS	ELEVATION
0.0	Begin Segment 21 at San Luis Pass	11,942'
1.0	Enter La Garita Wilderness	12,732'
1.3	Saddle, high point on segment	12,894'
2.1	Seasonal water	12,100'
2.6	Straight (E Mineral Creek Tr to right)	11,796'
2.7	E Mineral Creek tributary	11,677'
3.3	Saddle between E and Middle Mineral Creek	12,168'
4.0	Middle Mineral Creek	11,614'
4.9	Saddle between Middle and W Mineral Creek	11,855'
5.3	Seasonal water	11,972'
6.3	Straight (Mineral Creek Trail to right)	12,322'
6.9	Exit La Garita Wilderness	12,557'
8.4	Left (Skyline Tr to right [signed Rough Cr Tr and Tumble Cr TH])	12,560'
9.3	Straight (La Garita Stock Driveway to left)	12,328'
9.5	Pond on right	12,319'
9.8	Willow Creek	12,292'
12.7	Edge of Snow Mesa	12,259'
14.7	Cross Hwy 149, end Segment 21 at Spring Creek Pass TH	10,906'

SEGMENT 22
Spring Creek Pass Trailhead to Carson Saddle

The majestic San Juan Mountains. Photo by Roger Forman

Distance	17.3 miles
Elevation Gain	Approx. 3,829 feet
Elevation Loss	Approx. 2,385 feet
USFS Maps	Gunnison and Rio Grande National Forests
The CT Databook, 8th Edition	Pages 54–55
The CT Map Book	Pages 51–53
Trails Illustrated Maps	Nos. 139, 141, 1201
Latitude 40° Map	Southwest Colorado Trails
Jurisdiction	Gunnison and Divide Ranger Districts, Gunnison and Rio Grande National Forests

ACCESS FROM DENVER END

ACCESS FROM DURANGO END

AVAILABILITY OF WATER

BICYCLING

ABOUT THIS SEGMENT: Segment 22 begins climbing again on a lightly traveled two-track and then single-track to cross Jarosa Mesa. The trail across the mesa is rough with rocks sticking up out of soil that's in short supply. Afterwards, the trail follows a two-track through tundra and then moves through a forested area. The trail becomes single-track again. It climbs into the tundra and passes over two prominent hills as it heads toward Coney Summit and the high point on The Colorado Trail (13,264'). Views from the Coney ridge are fantastic. The trail switchbacks down a steep hillside then joins

Above the clouds. Photo by Pete Kartsounes

a short section of steep 4WD road to Carson Saddle where there's rich mining history.

As the CT descends toward Carson Saddle it affords spectacular views of Lake San Cristobal, Red Mountain, and Redcloud and Sunshine Peaks. The arched course of the Lake Fork valley marks the edge of the Lake City caldera, which erupted about 23 million years ago. High peaks beyond it are carved in volcanic tuff that fills the caldera. Lake San Cristobal first formed when a huge landslide (the Slumgullion Slide) dammed the river about 760 years ago. Parts of the slide are still moving.

Mountain bikers rejoin the CT at the start of this segment after the lengthy La Garita Wilderness detour.

Much of this segment is above tree line with limited sections below tree line and severe weather can be a factor. Plan travel with the weather in mind to stay safe.

TRAILHEAD/ACCESS POINTS

Spring Creek Pass Trailhead: This trailhead is located where CO Highway 149 tops the Continental Divide at Spring Creek Pass. The pass is approximately 17 miles southeast of Lake City and 33 miles northwest of Creede. There is a Forest Service picnic area here with tables and fire rings, a toilet, and an informative kiosk, as well as parking for another half-dozen or so cars, but camping is not allowed. Water is usually available during the summer in a small irrigation ditch on the east side of the highway.

Carson Saddle Trail Access: See Segment 23 on page 250.

TRAIL DESCRIPTION: Segment 22 begins atop Spring Creek Pass on the Continental Divide, **mile 0.0**. Mountain bikers rejoin the trail here after completing the La Garita Wilderness detour. The trail leaves the trailhead west on the two-track

Spring Creek Pass Trailhead to Carson Saddle

A sign marks the highest point on The Colorado Trail. Photo by Felecia Moran

FS Road 547/Jarosa Mesa Road at **mile 0.1**. At **mile 2.7**, bear right off FS Road 547 onto single-track. The route is marked with rock cairns and tall posts with CT and CDT confidence markers, helping guide you for the next 3 miles. Just before the turn onto single-track, a seasonal creek crosses the road with potential campsites nearby.

At **mile 4.1**, reach the high point on Jarosa Mesa. Continue west to a three-way junction of two-tracks at **mile 5.6**, where the trail continues straight across FS Road 547 and follows the intersecting two-track, open for non-motorized and administrative use only. Reach a saddle at **mile 7.0**, then curve to the southwest. Take the right fork onto single-track at **mile 7.9**. At **mile 8.7**, cross a two-track, then a side trail to the Colorado Trail Friends Yurt located 0.1 mile uphill to the right. Water is often available 200 feet to the left and downhill on the side trail.

Continue west on single-track through a short section of forest then reach tree line at **mile 9.3**. The trail will remain above tree line, near the Continental Divide, and exposed to severe weather from this point to midway on Segment 24, a distance of roughly 32 miles. Be aware of weather conditions and plan accordingly to be in safe locations if weather moves in. Proceed through a large patch of willows, then bear left and proceed west on tundra. At **mile 11.5** reach the head of the Ruby Creek cirque with seasonal water in ponds 400 feet below and 0.5 mile off the trail, with a reliable stream farther below. Climb several steep switchbacks through a rocky band that may be problematic for stock and bicyclists at **mile 12.1**. Continue climbing to a high point and then another, enjoying great views. Small tarns, 0.1 mile and 50 feet below the trail at **mile 13.3**, may hold water early season and in wetter years. Descend to a saddle at **mile 14.5** where Kitty Creek ponds can be seen a half-mile and 400 feet below (south).

The Colorado Trail reaches its highest point at **mile 15.7** (13,264') on the slope just beneath Coney Summit. The trail curves to the right below Coney Summit, crossing a closed 4WD road, then switchbacks several times as it starts descending toward Carson Saddle, crossing 4WD FS Road 518/Carson Road twice in quick succession at **mile 16.1**. The trail follows close to the ridge above the road then drops down and joins the steep road at **mile 16.6**. At a junction with a short spur road to the left at **mile 17.2**, curve to the right to continue on FS Road 518. Head uphill to a Y intersection with FS Road 518.1C/North Clear Creek Road just below Carson Saddle and the end of Segment 22, **mile 17.3**.

LAKE CITY

It is approximately 17 miles north and west from Spring Creek Pass to the old mining town of Lake City on CO Highway 149. CT travelers can sometimes catch a ride with town shuttle volunteers at 12:30, but hitching can prove to be a long wait.

Distance from CT: 17 miles
Elevation: 8,671 feet
Zip code: 81235
Area code: 970

Dining
Several locations in town

Gear (including fuel canisters and shuttle)
The Sportsman
238 S. Gunnison Ave.
(970) 944-2526

Groceries
The Country Store
916 N. CO Highway 149
(970) 944-2387

Info
Chamber of Commerce
800 Gunnison Ave.
(970) 944-2527

Laundry
The Lost Sock
808 N. Gunnison Ave.
(970) 944-2401

Lodging (several)
Backcountry Basecamp
720 Gunnison Ave.
(970) 403-6301

The Raven's Rest Hostel
207 Gunnison Ave.
(970) 944-7119

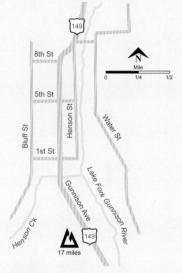

Medical
Lake City Medical Center
700 N. Henson St.
(970) 944-2331

Post Office
Lake City Post Office
803 Gunnison Ave.
(970) 944-2560

Showers
Elkhorn RV Resort
713 N. Bluff St.
(970) 944-2920

Midway through this segment, the CT moves **above tree line** for the next 32 miles, so many hikers choose to camp just below tree line to make an early start the following morning.

TRAVEL
TIP

Features

MILEAGE	COMMENTS	ELEVATION
0.0	Begin Segment 22 at Spring Creek Pass TH	10,906'
0.1	Follow FS Rd 547/Jarosa Mesa Road uphill	10,897'
2.7	Seasonal creek, then angle right onto single-track (FS Rd 547 continues straight)	11,385'
4.1	Jarosa Mesa high point	12,035'
5.6	Cross FS Rd 547 then angle left onto closed 2-track	11,734'
7.0	Saddle	12,056'
7.9	Right onto single-track (2-track continues to left)	12,020'
8.7	Angle right across 2-track, yurt uphill on right, spring downhill to left	11,718'
11.5	Ruby Creek cirque	12,489'
12.1	Cliff band, may be challenging for stock and bicyclists	12,777'
13.3	Small tarns below trail	12,881'
14.5	Saddle	12,879'
15.7	Highest point on CT	13,264'
16.1	Cross FS Rd 518/Carson Road, then right and cross again shortly after	13,131'
16.6	Right onto FS Rd 518	12,788'
17.2	Right on FS Rd 518 (dirt road to left)	12,336'
17.3	End Segment 22 at Carson Saddle at Y intx of FS Rds 518 and 518.1C/North Clear Creek Road	12,352'

Elevation and Distance

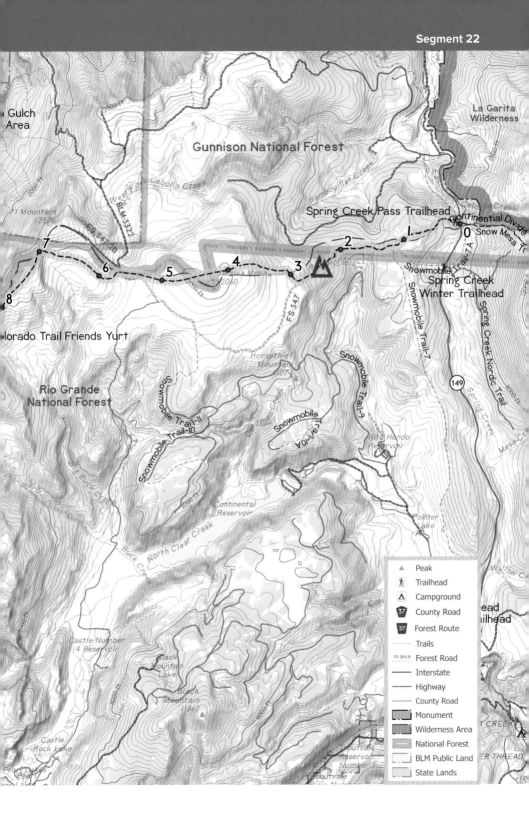

SEGMENT 23
Carson Saddle to Stony Pass Trailhead

Segment 23 is nearly all above 12,000 feet. Photo by Julie Vida and Mark Tabb

Distance	16.1 miles
Elevation Gain	Approx. 3,515 feet
Elevation Loss	Approx. 3,339 feet
USFS Maps	Gunnison, Rio Grande, and San Juan National Forests
The CT Databook, 8th Edition	Pages 56–57
The CT Map Book	Pages 53–55
Trails Illustrated Maps	No. 141, 1201
Latitude 40° Map	Southwest Colorado Trails
Jurisdiction	Gunnison and Divide Ranger Districts, Gunnison and Rio Grande National Forests

ABOUT THIS SEGMENT: Segment 23 is remote, high, physically demanding, and rewarding. The Colorado Trail leaves the popular motorized area at Carson Saddle and heads west on non-motorized single-track up the Lost Trail Creek watershed, passing fields of summer wildflowers and eventually reaching an unnamed pass that is often snowy until late June. While heading down the back side of the pass, Cataract Lake eventually comes into view below and the trail reaches a trail junction that is the beginning of a major historical rerouting of the CT/CDT. The trail originally dropped into the Pole Creek drainage on a motorized trail and then followed a road and trail to regain the Continental Divide near the head of Elk Creek in Segment 24. Forest Service staff and CTF Trail Crew volunteers developed a non-motorized route that now stays above timberline and closer to the Continental Divide with its spectacular views. Forest Service staff decided to not construct continuous tread in this section but have CTF volunteers build huge rock cairns to mark the trail instead. In many places, trail users have worn a fairly continuous path that now comprises the tread between the large cairns.

Segment 23 is above tree line for its entire length, remains close to the Continental Divide, and almost all of the segment is at an elevation of 12,000 feet or higher—severe weather is common and must be taken into account when traveling this segment. This is one of the most remote segments of the CT and vehicle access to each end, especially Carson Saddle, can be quite challenging.

A small pond offers a good spot to camp. Photo by Roger Forman

One of many striking views along Cataract Ridge. Photo by Debbie Abbott-Brown

TRAILHEAD/ACCESS POINTS

Carson Saddle Trail Access: 🚙 From Lake City, drive south on CO Highway 149 about 2 miles to a Y in the road. Follow County Road 30 to the right, passing Lake San Cristobal. After 9.1 miles, reach a turnoff to County Road 36 on the left. Turn left onto County Road 36, which becomes FS Road 568/Carson Road higher up. This is not a road for the squeamish; it is very steep, rocky, and narrow, with many tight switchbacks and some significant exposure. In mid-summer, expect to encounter 4WD vehicles, ATVs/UTVs, and motorcycles. Follow this road for about 5 miles to Carson Saddle, a low point on the Continental Divide about 1.5 miles above the abandoned mining town of Carson. Segment 23 begins on the south side of Carson Saddle at the intersection of FS Road 518.1C/North Clear Creek Road and FS Road 518/Carson Road.

Stony Pass Trailhead: 🚙 See Segment 24 on page 259.

SERVICES, SUPPLIES, AND ACCOMMODATIONS: These amenities are available in Lake City; see Segment 22 on page 245.

Bighorn sheep look down from a ridgeline. Photo by Pete Turner

TRAIL DESCRIPTION: Begin Segment 23 at the east leg of the Y intersection of FS Roads 518/Carson Road and 518.1C/North Clear Creek Road on the south side of Carson Saddle, **mile 0.0**. Follow FS Road 518.1C to the southwest and angle right onto non-motorized single-track at **mile 0.5**. After a short climb, the trail turns to the west and crosses a small stream at **mile 1.2**. There is a good campsite about 50 feet below the trail. Begin a long climb up the Lost Trail Creek drainage, crossing a seasonal stream with campsite nearby at **mile 1.7** and a larger stream at **mile 2.4**. Reach a small, unnamed pass at **mile 3.8** and drop into the Pole Creek drainage to the west.

The trail continues straight and briefly joins the Pole Creek Trail at a junction with the West Lost Trail at **mile 4.9**, then leaves the Pole Creek Trail to the right at **mile 5.1**. Because the Pole Creek and West Lost Trails are motorized single-track trails, motorcycles might be seen on this short section of the CT.

The **Cataract Lakes** are among the most spectacular on the entire CT. Be sure to camp more than 200 feet from the water to protect this delicate alpine ecosystem.

Enjoy the spectacular **above-tree line views** from the Continental Divide on this segment but be cautious in conditions of poor visibility.

TRAVEL TIPS

Volunteer-built cairns mark the trail to Stony Pass. Photo by Mick Gigone

The trail heads west from here, then descends steeply to the north where it turns sharply left at a junction with the Cataract Creek Trail at **mile 5.7**. Continue along a small lake with several good campsites. There are also excellent campsites at Cataract Lake, about a quarter mile to the northeast. Follow the trail as it heads back west, passing several more potential but unprotected campsites, staying right at a junction with a faint trail at **mile 6.1**. Cross a stream at **mile 6.2**, then a couple more seasonal streams in the next half-mile. After gaining a saddle at **mile 7.0**, the trail bears to the right and continues climbing, crossing a wide field where elk are commonly seen. Contour around the north side of Peak 13,164 and begin to follow a long string of cairns at **mile 7.9**, where the trail turns to the southwest. The cairns are tall and easy to follow and the trail is much more distinct as a result of use since the trail reroute was first completed.

Descend to a low saddle and junction with the faint East Fork Middle Pole Trail at **mile 8.6**, then continue westerly, crossing a small stream at **mile 9.0**. Reach a small pass and cross the Continental Divide above Cuba Gulch, then contour above Cuba Gulch and continue straight at a trail junction at **mile 10.2**. Pass a junction with the Cuba Gulch Trail (faint) at **mile 10.5** with seasonal streams and unprotected camping at the head of the basin.

The cairns continue to mark the trail as it climbs to gain a ridge at a junction with a trail at **mile 10.9**. Water may be available at seasonal tarns to the north-

THE STONY PASS ROAD

The historic Stony Pass Road was constructed in 1872 as a means to transport supplies in and ore out of the booming Silverton mining district. For a few short years, it was a busy and important route for miners and others attracted by news of new-found wealth in the San Juans. After a couple years, however, the difficult route was eclipsed by the Denver & Rio Grande Western's rail route through Animas Canyon. The road quickly fell into a sorry state and gained a reputation as a "pretty rough ride."

Stony Pass Road (left) beneath Canby Mountain divides Segments 23 and 24.
Photo by Jeff Sellenrick

Robert M. Ormes, of early guidebook fame, recalls struggling up it in his car after being assured that the first car into Silverton came in this way. Finding it a lot more than his auto could handle, he encountered a man on the road who told him, "Sure it came in this way . . . but, it was in some wagons."

west below the distinctive Cuba Peak. Continue south through the head of Minnie Gulch, then pass the Minnie Gulch Trail junction at **mile 11.7** and the Middle Pole Trail junction soon after. Climb steeply up several switchbacks to a high point on the ridge at **mile 12.1**. Drop down to a saddle at **mile 12.9** and continue straight where the West Pole Trail heads left and the Pole Creek Connector Trail heads right. Continuing along the ridge, travelers will pass a small pond and potential campsite at **mile 13.8**. Follow switchbacks along a narrow ridge to a saddle and the intersection with the Maggie Gulch Trail at **mile 14.4**. Turn left and begin descending the headwaters of the Rio Grande and travel around the base of rugged Canby Mountain. Cross a creek at **mile 14.7** and stay high on the hillside through braided trails resulting from large herds of grazing sheep. The trail drops down to FS Road 520/Rio Grande Reservoir Road at **mile 15.8**. Turn right and follow the road to **mile 16.1** and the end of Segment 23 where the trail leaves the road to the left at Stony Pass Trailhead, 0.2 mile below Stony Pass.

The Weminuche Wilderness Bike Detour begins here and rejoins the CT at Molas Pass and the beginning of Segment 24. See page 261 for a description of the route.

Elevation and Distance

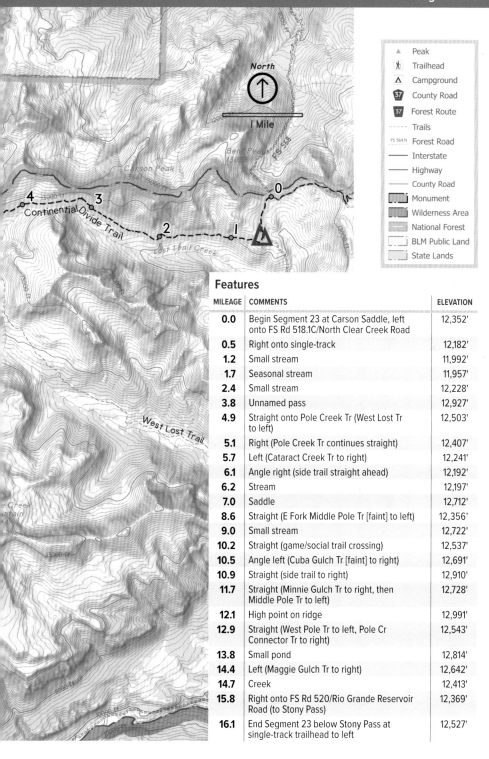

Features

MILEAGE	COMMENTS	ELEVATION
0.0	Begin Segment 23 at Carson Saddle, left onto FS Rd 518.1C/North Clear Creek Road	12,352'
0.5	Right onto single-track	12,182'
1.2	Small stream	11,992'
1.7	Seasonal stream	11,957'
2.4	Small stream	12,228'
3.8	Unnamed pass	12,927'
4.9	Straight onto Pole Creek Tr (West Lost Tr to left)	12,503'
5.1	Right (Pole Creek Tr continues straight)	12,407'
5.7	Left (Cataract Creek Tr to right)	12,241'
6.1	Angle right (side trail straight ahead)	12,192'
6.2	Stream	12,197'
7.0	Saddle	12,712'
8.6	Straight (E Fork Middle Pole Tr [faint] to left)	12,356'
9.0	Small stream	12,722'
10.2	Straight (game/social trail crossing)	12,537'
10.5	Angle left (Cuba Gulch Tr [faint] to right)	12,691'
10.9	Straight (side trail to right)	12,910'
11.7	Straight (Minnie Gulch Tr to right, then Middle Pole Tr to left)	12,728'
12.1	High point on ridge	12,991'
12.9	Straight (West Pole Tr to left, Pole Cr Connector Tr to right)	12,543'
13.8	Small pond	12,814'
14.4	Left (Maggie Gulch Tr to right)	12,642'
14.7	Creek	12,413'
15.8	Right onto FS Rd 520/Rio Grande Reservoir Road (to Stony Pass)	12,369'
16.1	End Segment 23 below Stony Pass at single-track trailhead to left	12,527'

SEGMENT 24
Stony Pass Trailhead to Molas Pass

CT Volunteer Adopter Jody Furtney carries a pulaski toward the next trail maintenance project. Photo by Seth Furtney

ACCESS FROM
DENVER END

ACCESS FROM
DURANGO END

AVAILABILITY
OF WATER

BICYCLING

See page 261

Distance	20.9 miles
Elevation Gain	Approx. 3,475 feet
Elevation Loss	Approx. 5,119 feet
USFS Maps	Rio Grande and San Juan National Forests
The CT Databook, 8th Edition	Pages 58–59
The CT Map Book	Pages 55–58
Trails Illustrated Maps	No. 140, 1201
Latitude 40° Map	Southwest Colorado Trails
Jurisdiction	Columbine and Divide Ranger Districts, San Juan and Rio Grande National Forests

ABOUT THIS SEGMENT: Segment 24 enters the Weminuche Wilderness just south of FS Road 520/Rio Grande Reservoir Road below Stony Pass and follows the trail toward Arrow and Vestal Peaks, the two most prominent mountains ahead. The route is along the Continental Divide and is co-located with the CDT. About 2 miles south of Stony Pass it passes out of the San Juan volcanic rocks and into 1.7-billion-year-old basement rocks and light- and dark-colored layered gneiss. After passing several small lakes, the trail follows a relatively flat plateau switching between two-track and single-track. Eventually, the CT diverges from the CDT and drops into the Elk Creek drainage. As it begins this descent, it suddenly enters completely different rocks, quartzite interleaved with thin layers of maroon to blue-gray slate, rocks that are part of the Uncompahgre Formation. Rocks like these are found nowhere else along the CT. They are metamorphic rocks, but they have never been subjected to the high temperatures like those that produced the other metamorphic basement rocks. They were clearly deposited as sandstone and shale after the 1.7-billion-year-old basement rocks were formed but were lightly metamorphosed and squeezed into a series of tight accordionlike folds before nearby bodies of 1.4-billion-year-old granite were injected into them. The towering peaks of the Grenadier Range that loom south of the trail are all carved from a thick north-sloping layer of the quartzite.

Wildflowers in late July at 12,500 feet in the San Juan Mountains. Photo by Seth Furtney

Stony Pass Trailhead to Molas Pass

Dramatic descent into Elk Creek from the Continental Divide. Photo by Todd Wolter

Because the quartzite is particularly resistant to weathering, it preserves the smooth polished and striated rock outcrops shaped by the glacier that occupied this valley until about 12,000 years ago.

This is one of the most impressive sections of trail, descending a series of long switchbacks until reaching the headwaters of Elk Creek and the remnants of old mining operations below. The trail follows the creek down steeply at first, eventually reaching tree line. Travelers will pass four large avalanche paths and debris piles resulting from the March 2019 avalanche cycle while descending the valley. (See sidebar on page 125.) It took four trail seasons for CTF Adopters and trail crew volunteers, as well Forest Service staff and other partner organizations, to clear a path through the massive debris piles and re-establish the trail tread.

The trail continues generally westward until leaving the Weminuche Wilderness, crossing the train tracks for the Durango & Silverton Narrow Gauge Railroad, and passing over the Animas River on a large bridge.

 WARNING: Don't miss the turnoff point for the CT where it drops off the CDT.

As the CT climbs out of the canyon and approaches Molas Lake, it passes out of quartzite and into nearly horizontal beds of early Paleozoic sandstone, shale, and limestone. From Molas Lake, access to Molas Pass, US Highway 550, and Silverton is easy.

The southbound CT diverges from the CDT in Segment 24. Photo by Patty Laushman

TRAILHEAD/ACCESS POINTS

Stony Pass Trailhead: Drive to the north end of Silverton on Greene Street, then angle right on Blair Street/County Road 2 and drive 6.9 miles (paved then gravel) to Howardsville, an area with old mining buildings. Turn right on the gravel County Road 4 and drive uphill about 1.7 miles to a Y intersection. Angle left onto gravel County Road 3 and drive southeast 4.1 steep miles to reach Stony Pass. Continue, now on FS Road 520/Rio Grande Reservoir Road, for 0.2 mile to the Stony Pass Trailhead, a wide shoulder on the right with trail sign where CT Segment 24 leaves the road to the south on single-track.

Molas Pass Trail Access: See Segment 25 on page 267.

SERVICES, SUPPLIES, AND ACCOMMODATIONS: These amenities are available in Silverton; see Segment 25, page 269.

TRAIL DESCRIPTION: Begin Segment 24 at the Stony Pass Trailhead on the south side of FS Road 520/Rio Grande Reservoir Road, **mile 0.0**. Pass remnants of mining activity and enter the Weminuche Wilderness at **mile 0.1**. Follow the trail south, crossing several seasonal streams, as it drops and then rises back up to the Continental Divide. Descend switchbacks to a small valley and cross a side trail at **mile 2.2**. Climb past a small knob to the west of the trail and turn sharply left at the Cunningham Gulch Trail junction at **mile 2.5**. Cross a small stream at **mile 3.0**, then several small tarns near the trail. Stay left at the junction with the Whitehead Trail at **mile 3.7**.

The trail continues with several cairns marking the way and several small lakes on either side of the trail until reaching an intersection where there are more small

Before ending Segment 24, southbounders look back on Elk Park and the Animas River with Mt. Garfield behind. Photo by Jeff McGarvin

lakes at **mile 5.6**, where the CT stays left. Small streams are crossed at **mile 5.9** and at **mile 6.3** before reaching a critical intersection at **mile 6.4**. The CT and CDT go their separate ways for good at this junction after having been co-located for 319 miles from Georgia Pass in Segment 6 by way of the CT Collegiate West (just over 235 miles in two sections by way of the CT Collegiate East).

Turn right (uphill) at this signed intersection and angle right onto an old two-track at **mile 6.5**. Continue straight where a faint single-track joins the two-track from the right at **mile 6.7** and continue south, enjoying one of the most memorable views on the entire CT. At **mile 7.0** and another critical intersection, leave the two-track and turn sharply to the right onto single-track and descend a steep hillside on a series of magnificently constructed switchbacks into the Elk Creek drainage.

Once over the Divide and into the Weminuche Wilderness Area, the Elk Creek drainage and its dramatic geologic walls are topped off with views of **Arrow and Vestal Peaks**.

TRAVEL TIPS

This short, impressive range of peaks is known as the **Grenadiers**. If you have time, the short (but steep) climbers' trail into the Vestal valley that begins at the beaver ponds **(mile 12.4)** is an interesting side trip. See if you can spot rock climbers on the famous Wham Ridge.

WEMINUCHE WILDERNESS BICYCLE DETOUR

MOUNTAIN BIKING

This detour goes through Silverton, offering cyclists good opportunity to resupply. Begin at the division between Segments 23 and 24 at the Stony Pass Trailhead. Ride up FS Road 520/Rio Grande Reservoir Road northwest 0.2 mile to the summit of Stony Pass. Descend northwest on County

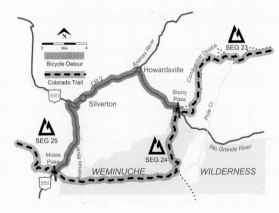

Road 3 to an intersection at **mile 2.8** and angle left, continuing downhill. At another intersection at **mile 4.4**, angle left, downhill, onto County Road 4. At **mile 5.9**, continue ahead at side road on the right. At the mining buildings at Howardsville, **mile 6.1**, turn left (southwest) onto County Road 2 and cross the Animas River (gravel then paved). Arrive in Silverton at **mile 10.1** and angle left onto County Road 110/Greene Street. Pass through town southwest and continue straight onto US Highway 550 (south) at **mile 11.4**. Pedal up the highway, which can be busy with traffic, including large trucks and recreational vehicles. Just before reaching Molas Pass, note the trail sign where the CT crosses the highway, **mile 17.5**. This is the start of Segment 25 where bikers rejoin the CT.

Cross a small stream at **mile 7.8**, then cross the head of Elk Creek and pass near an old mining shed above the trail at **mile 8.0**. After a narrow section next to a cliff that might be challenging for stock, cross to the south side of Elk Creek at **mile 8.2**, then back to the north side at **mile 8.4**, where a waterfall may be visible on the north side of the canyon.

Continue west and down as the canyon narrows. Be mindful of your footing as the trail drops steeply through a spectacular notch. Continue above the creek and, after entering the trees, drop back down close to Elk Creek and the uppermost avalanche debris in the valley at **mile 9.6**. Camping may be found in the area. Reach another access point to Elk Creek and the toe of the largest avalanche path in the canyon at **mile 9.8**. It is easy to appreciate the amount of effort that it took to clear the avalanche debris and rebuild the trail through the tangle of trees as you pass through it.

Molas Lake and Campground near the end of Segment 24 where CT travelers might enjoy a shower. Photo by Bill Bloomquist

Cross a side stream with a hidden waterfall upstream at **mile 10.5**. The canyon begins to widen out from here, with more camping possibilities. Reach a beaver pond at **mile 12.4** with a classic view of Arrow and Vestal Peaks. There are good campsites on the east side of the pond, the last good ones until reaching the Animas River. A steep climbers' trail leads from the ponds into the spectacular Vestal valley for an ambitious side trip.

Continuing west through thick forest, the trail traverses hillsides high above Elk Creek and then descends steeply to rejoin the creek, passing through three more avalanche debris piles. At **mile 15.2**, the CT leaves the gorge and wilderness, passing a trail register, interpretive sign, and Weminuche Wilderness sign. Pass a side trail at **mile 15.3** that leads to the Elk Park loading and unloading point for Durango & Silverton Narrow Gauge Railroad passengers.

After descending a short switchback, cross the railroad tracks near the Animas River at **mile 15.9**. Continue northwest between the tracks and the river and, after passing several potential campsites, cross the Animas River on a long bridge at **mile 16.1**. Looking downstream, the prominent peak is Mount Garfield. At **mile 16.2**, cross Molas Creek on a log bridge. Climb dozens of switchbacks and, at the top, bear right at an intersection with a side trail at **mile 18.2**. Continue straight ahead at another side trail at **mile 18.9**, where there is potential camping nearby and water at Molas Creek. At **mile 19.1**, turn to the right at a side trail to a waterfall on Molas Creek, then climb switchbacks through a rocky section. Stay left at a side trail to Molas Lake at **mile 19.2**, then continue straight at another side trail to Molas Lake at **mile 19.5**. Angle left at a large sign and a junction with the Molas Trail (leading to the Molas Trailhead) at **mile 19.6**.

Cross a side stream and then Molas Creek at **mile 19.9** and curve to the right at another side trail junction at **mile 20.0**. Continue to climb until reaching US Highway 550 near the top of Molas Pass at **mile 20.9**. This is the end of Segment 24. There is a small parking area with toilets 600 feet to the south.

THE GRENADIERS

VIEWING
OPPORTUNITY

Soaring faces of hard quartzite, tumbling brooks, and remote campsites characterize the beautiful Grenadier Range in the western portion of the Weminuche Wilderness. When the CT plunges off the Continental Divide into the Elk Creek Basin, it enters a world that is legendary with generations of Colorado mountaineers.

The Grenadiers were among the last high peaks in Colorado to be summited; most were not

The Durango & Silverton Narrow Gauge train approaches the Elk Creek hiker stop. Photo by Ernie Norris

climbed until the 1930s on Colorado Mountain Club excursions and by members of the legendary San Juan Mountaineers group. The Grenadiers are unusual in that they are made up of quartzite, which is relatively rare in the Southern Rockies. Quartzite is a hard and resistant rock that weathers into clean, steep north faces that often require technical climbing with ropes. From the beaver ponds at **mile 12.4** of Segment 24, there are excellent views of Arrow (13,803') and Vestal (13,864') Peaks, the most famous of the Grenadiers and members of Colorado's Highest Hundred (hundred highest peaks). The climbers' trail begins here, ascending steeply into the basin beneath Wham Ridge, one of the most prized climbs in the state.

The western endpoint of the short but dramatic Grenadier Range is Mount Garfield. It looms 4,000 feet over the Animas River and Durango & Silverton Narrow Gauge Railroad tracks and is a constant companion as you labor up the switchbacks to Molas Pass.

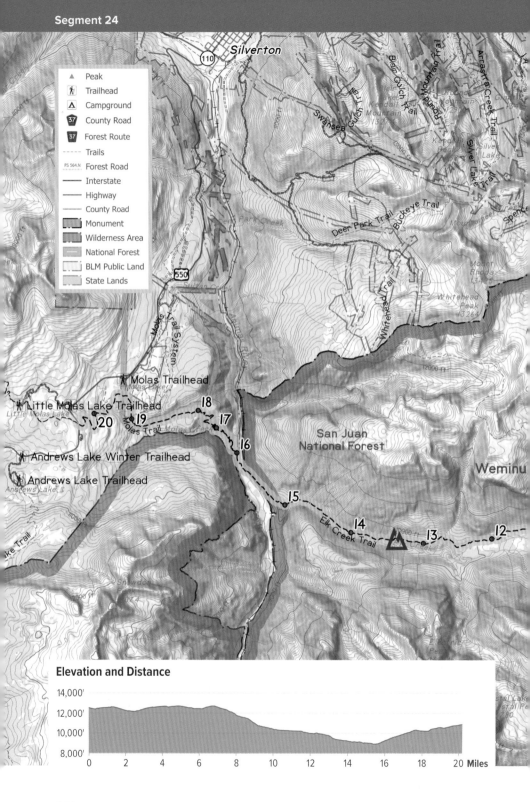

Peak
Trailhead
Campground
County Road
Forest Route
Trails
FS 564.N Forest Road
Interstate
Highway
County Road
Monument
Wilderness Area
National Forest
BLM Public Land
State Lands

Silverton

110

550

Molas Trail System

Molas Trailhead

Little Molas Lake Trailhead

20   19

18

17

16

Molas Trail

Andrews Lake Winter Trailhead

Andrews Lake Trailhead

San Juan
National Forest

Weminu

15

14   13   12

Elk Creek Trail

Elevation and Distance

14,000'
12,000'
10,000'
8,000'

0   2   4   6   8   10   12   14   16   18   20   Miles

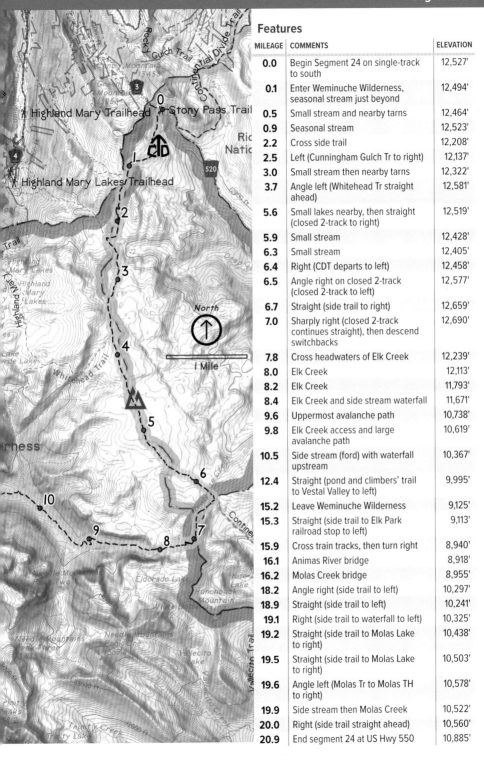

Features

MILEAGE	COMMENTS	ELEVATION
0.0	Begin Segment 24 on single-track to south	12,527'
0.1	Enter Weminuche Wilderness, seasonal stream just beyond	12,494'
0.5	Small stream and nearby tarns	12,464'
0.9	Seasonal stream	12,523'
2.2	Cross side trail	12,208'
2.5	Left (Cunningham Gulch Tr to right)	12,137'
3.0	Small stream then nearby tarns	12,322'
3.7	Angle left (Whitehead Tr straight ahead)	12,581'
5.6	Small lakes nearby, then straight (closed 2-track to right)	12,519'
5.9	Small stream	12,428'
6.3	Small stream	12,405'
6.4	Right (CDT departs to left)	12,458'
6.5	Angle right on closed 2-track (closed 2-track to left)	12,577'
6.7	Straight (side trail to right)	12,659'
7.0	Sharply right (closed 2-track continues straight), then descend switchbacks	12,690'
7.8	Cross headwaters of Elk Creek	12,239'
8.0	Elk Creek	12,113'
8.2	Elk Creek	11,793'
8.4	Elk Creek and side stream waterfall	11,671'
9.6	Uppermost avalanche path	10,738'
9.8	Elk Creek access and large avalanche path	10,619'
10.5	Side stream (ford) with waterfall upstream	10,367'
12.4	Straight (pond and climbers' trail to Vestal Valley to left)	9,995'
15.2	Leave Weminuche Wilderness	9,125'
15.3	Straight (side trail to Elk Park railroad stop to left)	9,113'
15.9	Cross train tracks, then turn right	8,940'
16.1	Animas River bridge	8,918'
16.2	Molas Creek bridge	8,955'
18.2	Angle right (side trail to left)	10,297'
18.9	Straight (side trail to left)	10,241'
19.1	Right (side trail to waterfall to left)	10,325'
19.2	Straight (side trail to Molas Lake to right)	10,438'
19.5	Straight (side trail to Molas Lake to right)	10,503'
19.6	Angle left (Molas Tr to Molas TH to right)	10,578'
19.9	Side stream then Molas Creek	10,522'
20.0	Right (side trail straight ahead)	10,560'
20.9	End segment 24 at US Hwy 550	10,885'

Stony Pass Trailhead to Molas Pass

SEGMENT 25
Molas Pass to Hermosa Park Road

Mid-segment descent beyond saddle near Rolling Mountain. Photo by Katie Quinn

ACCESS FROM DENVER END

ACCESS FROM DURANGO END

AVAILABILITY OF WATER

BICYCLING

Distance	20.7 miles
Elevation Gain	Approx. 3,799 feet
Elevation Loss	Approx. 3,578 feet
USFS Map	San Juan National Forest
The CT Databook, 8th Edition	Pages 60–61
The CT Map Book	Pages 58–60
Trails Illustrated Maps	Nos. 140, 141, 1201
Latitude 40° Maps	Southwest Colorado Trails, Durango Trails
Jurisdiction	Columbine and Dolores Ranger Districts, San Juan National Forest

ABOUT THIS SEGMENT: The segment starts at US Highway 550, just north of Molas Pass, and passes near Little Molas Lake, Little Molas Lake Trailhead, and Little Molas Lake Campground. In this area, the trail passes over gently inclined beds of gray shale, sandstone, and limestone of the Hermosa Formation, which was deposited in a shallow sea that flanked the rising Ancestral Rockies between 312 and 305 million years ago. The limestone layers contain abundant fossils.

Cascade Creek. Photo by Morgan and Robyn Wilkinson

After passing the trailhead, the trail climbs to the Upper Lime Creek drainage, which was heavily forested until a fire roared through in 1879. The forest has not returned to this high-elevation area since then. In the summer months, when the wildflowers along the next few miles of trail are in full bloom, the CT is ablaze in various shades of yellows and purples. The views are second to none.

At about **mile 9**, the trail crosses into redbeds of the Cutler Formation, deposited in lowlands flanking the Ancestral Rockies between 300 and 285 million years ago. The spectacular cliffs on the slopes above this part of the trail are conglomerate deposited on the post-Laramide land surface before the San Juan volcanic rocks, which cap the peaks and ridges, were erupted. Large blocks that have tumbled from the conglomerate layer are conspicuous in several places along this part of the trail. As the trail descends toward Cascade Creek, it encounters an irregular body of light-colored granite and porphyry that makes up most of Grizzly Peak. A ledge of this rock forms a nice waterfall worth visiting uphill from the CT at **mile 14.1**, just before crossing Cascade Creek. After another climb, the distinctive Lizard Head Peak comes into view. The segment is largely above tree line, with intermittent patches of forest, so travel during safe weather periods and try to avoid the inevitable summer afternoon thunderstorms.

TRAILHEAD/ACCESS POINTS

Molas Pass Trail Access: 🚗 Segment 25 begins at a trail sign where the CT crosses US Highway 550 about 0.1 mile north of the Molas Pass summit and 7 miles south of Silverton. There is no parking where the trail crosses the highway. Close by at the pass summit, there is a scenic pullout, bathrooms, and limited daytime-only parking.

A cyclist enjoys a near perfect day. Photo by Nate Hebenstreit

Molas Trailhead: 🚗 The Molas Trailhead, where overnight parking is allowed, is located off US Highway 550 on the right one mile north of the CT crossing of the highway. From the trailhead, the Molas Trail leads south about 0.2 mile and connects to the CT on Segment 24, 1.3 miles from the beginning of Segment 25.

Little Molas Lake Trailhead: 🚗 From Molas Pass on US Highway 550, drive north 0.4 mile, turn left (west) on FS Road 584, and continue 1 mile to the improved Little Molas Lake Trailhead. There are vault toilets and a campground nearby. The CT passes just south of the trailhead 1 mile into Segment 25.

Hermosa Park Road Trail Access: 🚜 See Segment 26 on page 275.

TRAIL DESCRIPTION: Segment 25 begins on the west side of US Highway 550 at a large, weathered Colorado Trail interpretive sign 0.2 mile north of the Molas Pass summit. Because there's no parking here, some trail users start from nearby parking locations, including the scenic pullout at the Molas Pass summit (not recommended, day use only), the Molas Trailhead (1.5 miles from the start of Segment 25 via the end of Segment 24), or Little Molas Lake Trailhead (1.0 mile into Segment 25).

After leaving US 550, **mile 0.0**, pass around the west shore of Little Molas Lake to a trail junction at **mile 0.7**. The CT angles left where a side trail continues straight along the lake and to the Little Molas Campground. The trail heads northwest then turns sharply left and passes by the Little Molas Lake Trailhead with vault toilet at **mile 1.0**. Cross a seasonal stream at **mile 1.7**, join an old roadbed shortly after, then cross another seasonal stream at **mile 2.0**. Leave the old roadbed, angling uphill to the right onto single-track at **mile 2.2**, then turn sharply right and continue uphill just east of the ridge dividing the East Lime Creek and North Lime Creek drainages. Enjoy the big views of the Grenadier Range, the Needle Mountains, the West Needle Mountains, the distant La Plata Mountains (to be viewed up close on Segments 27 and 28), and Engineer Mountain, among others, in a clockwise panorama. High on the ridge at **mile 3.0**, the trail angles left and begins a long traverse around the head of multiple forks of Lime Creek, with more panoramic views.

Reach a saddle with rocky ledges dividing the North Lime Creek and Bear Creek drainages at **mile 4.1** where the trail turns to the west. After crossing a seasonal stream at **mile 4.7**, reach a scenic viewpoint at the end of a ridge at **mile 5.1**. It is possible to camp near reliable ponds 0.3 mile to the south in good weather. The trail passes a treed area where camping is possible just before crossing a small stream on a wet rock ledge at **mile 5.4**. More camping is possible in scattered trees before crossing Lime Creek at **mile 6.2**.

SILVERTON

SERVICES, SUPPLIES, AND ACCOMMODATIONS

Silverton is approximately 7 miles north of Molas Pass on US Highway 550. Closer, about 1 mile from the CT, is Molas Lake Campground (molaslake.com). They handle maildrop via UPS, offer hot showers, and carry a number of items of interest to trail travelers in their tiny store.

Distance from CT: 7 miles
Elevation: 9,318 feet
Zip code: 81433
Area code: 970

Dining
Several locations in town

Groceries
Silverton Grocery
717 Greene St.
(970) 387-5652

Info
Chamber of Commerce
414 Greene St.
(970) 387-5654

Laundry
A & B RV Park
1445 Mineral St.
(970) 387-5347

Lodging (several including)
Prospector Motel
1015 Greene St.
(970) 387-5466

Medical
Silverton Clinic
1315 Snowden St.
(970) 387-5114

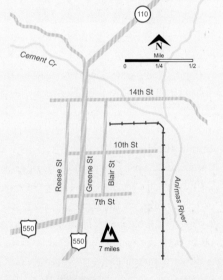

Post Office
Silverton Post Office
138 W. 12th St.
(970) 387-5402

Train Depot
Durango & Silverton
Narrow Gauge Railroad
Blair and W. 12th streets
(970) 247-2733
(888) 872-4607

Saddling up after a day of trail work. Photo by Pete Turner

Continue generally westward and around another ridge and below Twin Sisters, with numerous creek crossings over the next several miles. Pass a campsite in the trees below the trail at **mile 8.1** with water 0.1 mile farther. The trail turns sharply to the right then passes a large lake at the intersection with the Engineer Mountain Trail at **mile 10.3**. Climb up the rocky (and sometimes snowy) trail and continue straight at the intersection with the Rico-Silverton Trail at **mile 11.1**. Shortly after, the trail turns sharply left at a switchback and climbs to a saddle south of Rolling Mountain at **mile 11.3**.

Descend several switchbacks through a basin that can be lush with wildflowers in July with a stunning view of Grizzly Peak across the Cascade Creek valley. At **mile 12.7**, bear to the left at an intersection with a side trail that goes to a small lake with camping potential 0.2 mile from the trail. Turn right at the unsigned junction with the White Creek Trail at **mile 12.8**. Cross a small stream at **mile 12.9**, then down a series of short switchbacks. Cross more streams at **mile 14.1**, with an impressive cascade just uphill from the trail and another stream shortly after. Good campsites can be found along this stretch to Cascade Creek. Cross Cascade Creek on a bridge at **mile 14.6** near a refreshing waterfall. The trail turns south and

> ⊘ **WARNING:** Hikers have reported two places in this segment—at mile points **10.2** and **12.9**—where they have gotten off on the wrong trail. In both cases, they took off to the left because it appeared to be the more heavily traveled trail. At both spots the CT makes a sharp right turn!

In July much of the CT is an alpine garden. Photo by Roger Forman

climbs, crossing numerous creeks in the next several miles. Continue straight at an unsigned junction with a climbers' trail to Grizzly Peak at **mile 16.5**. Cross a large stream at **mile 16.7**, where camping may be possible. Continue straight at **mile 17.1**, where a side trail connects to FS Road 579/Cascade Divide Road. Cross a stream at **mile 17.6** and continue straight at the junction with the Graysill Trail at **mile 17.8**, where there is camping potential.

Cross the ridge south of Grizzly Peak and Sliderock Ridge at **mile 18.7**, where there are large views of Lizard Head Peak ahead, Hermosa Peak to the south, and Engineer Mountain behind. Continue to the right and descend the large meadow in Tin Cup Basin, curving back to the left onto an old roadbed at **mile 19.1**. At **mile 19.9**, turn left onto a short section of the motorized single-track East Fork Trail. Angle left onto the non-motorized single-track CT at **mile 20.5**, leaving the East Fork Trail. Pass through a forested area and reach FS 578/Hermosa Park Road near Celebration Lake and the end of Segment 25 at **mile 20.7**.

Molas Lake Campground near the start of the segment offers thru-travelers the last convenient resupply and shower until Durango. Owned by the Town of Silverton, it's located east of the highway and north of the CT and has reservable campsites for a fee. Showers are also available for a small fee.

Little Molas Lake, west of the highway, has non-reservable free camping with vault toilets. Both campgrounds are typically very busy during peak season.

TRAVEL TIPS

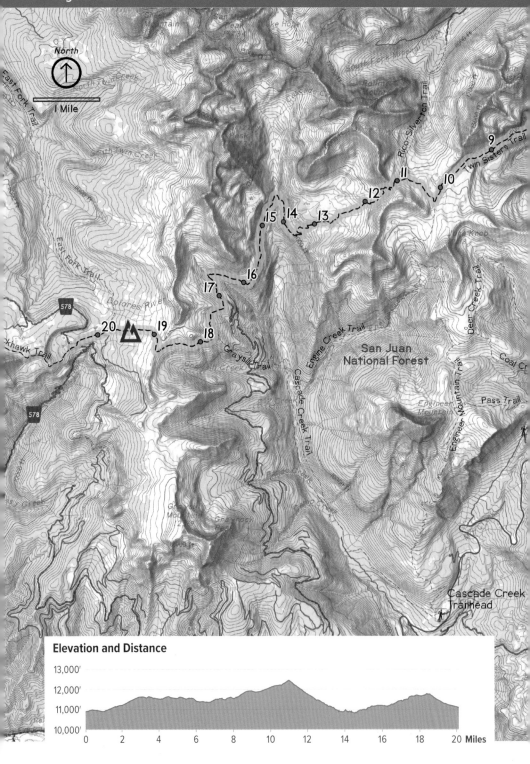

Elevation and Distance

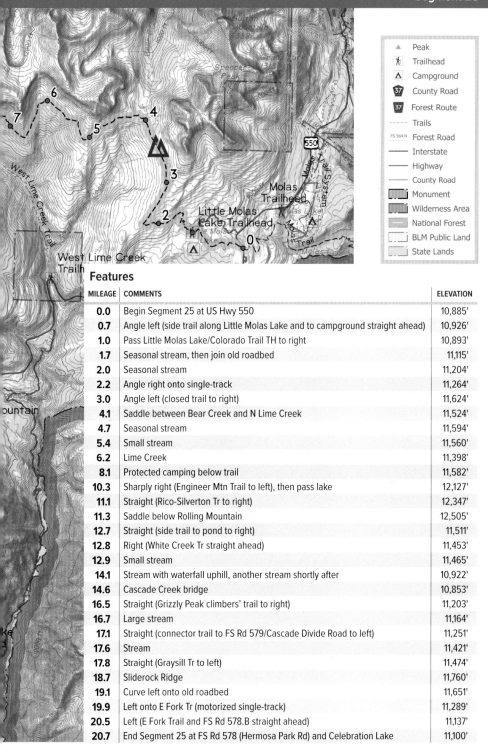

▲	Peak	
𝍐	Trailhead	
Λ	Campground	
37	County Road	
37	Forest Route	
- - - - -	Trails	
FS 564.N	Forest Road	
———	Interstate	
———	Highway	
———	County Road	
▨	Monument	
▨	Wilderness Area	
▨	National Forest	
▨	BLM Public Land	
▨	State Lands	

Features

MILEAGE	COMMENTS	ELEVATION
0.0	Begin Segment 25 at US Hwy 550	10,885'
0.7	Angle left (side trail along Little Molas Lake and to campground straight ahead)	10,926'
1.0	Pass Little Molas Lake/Colorado Trail TH to right	10,893'
1.7	Seasonal stream, then join old roadbed	11,115'
2.0	Seasonal stream	11,204'
2.2	Angle right onto single-track	11,264'
3.0	Angle left (closed trail to right)	11,624'
4.1	Saddle between Bear Creek and N Lime Creek	11,524'
4.7	Seasonal stream	11,594'
5.4	Small stream	11,560'
6.2	Lime Creek	11,398'
8.1	Protected camping below trail	11,582'
10.3	Sharply right (Engineer Mtn Trail to left), then pass lake	12,127'
11.1	Straight (Rico-Silverton Tr to right)	12,347'
11.3	Saddle below Rolling Mountain	12,505'
12.7	Straight (side trail to pond to right)	11,511'
12.8	Right (White Creek Tr straight ahead)	11,453'
12.9	Small stream	11,465'
14.1	Stream with waterfall uphill, another stream shortly after	10,922'
14.6	Cascade Creek bridge	10,853'
16.5	Straight (Grizzly Peak climbers' trail to right)	11,203'
16.7	Large stream	11,164'
17.1	Straight (connector trail to FS Rd 579/Cascade Divide Road to left)	11,251'
17.6	Stream	11,421'
17.8	Straight (Graysill Tr to left)	11,474'
18.7	Sliderock Ridge	11,760'
19.1	Curve left onto old roadbed	11,651'
19.9	Left onto E Fork Tr (motorized single-track)	11,289'
20.5	Left (E Fork Trail and FS Rd 578.B straight ahead)	11,137'
20.7	End Segment 25 at FS Rd 578 (Hermosa Park Rd) and Celebration Lake	11,100'

SEGMENT 26
Hermosa Park Road to Hotel Draw Road

Ascending to Blackhawk Pass. Photo by Nate Hebenstreit

Distance	11.1 miles
Elevation Gain	Approx. 1,827 feet
Elevation Loss	Approx. 2,551 feet
USFS Map	San Juan National Forest
The CT Databook, 8th Edition	Pages 62–63
The CT Map Book	Pages 60–61
Trails Illustrated Maps	Nos. 141, 144, 1201
Latitude 40° Maps	Southwest Colorado Trails, Durango Trails
Jurisdiction	Dolores Ranger District, San Juan National Forest

ACCESS FROM
DENVER END

ACCESS FROM
DURANGO END

AVAILABILITY
OF WATER

BICYCLING

Cornhusk lily. Photo by Nate Hebenstreit

ABOUT THIS SEGMENT: This segment follows the high ground between the Hermosa Creek drainage to the south and east and the Dolores River drainage to the north and west. The trail here is largely in flat-lying beds of the Cutler Formation, cut by dikes and sills of light-colored porphyry. This segment feels very remote, descending and ascending forested ridges until climbing to Blackhawk Pass just east of Blackhawk Mountain. The views from here are outstanding. The CT then drops into the Straight Creek watershed below. There are several potential campsites after entering the forest with good access to the creek. The second crossing of Straight Creek is the last reliable water for over 14 miles.

Much of this segment is near or above tree line, with intermittent patches of forest, so travel during safe weather periods and try to avoid the frequent summer afternoon thunderstorms.

TRAILHEAD/ACCESS POINTS
Hermosa Park Road Trail Access: There are two ways to drive to this access point, both requiring a 4WD vehicle: from US Highway 550 through Purgatory Resort and from CO Highway 145, south of Lizard Head Pass and just north of Rico.

> **WARNING:** Scrutinize the depth of the Hermosa Creek ford and the optimal line before driving into it.

The CT is well signed in most places, but using this guide will help ensure you keep on track.
Photo by Nate Hebenstreit

For the US 550 approach, drive approximately 28 miles north of Durango to the main entrance to Purgatory Resort on the west side of the road. At the upper parking area, bear right onto FS Road 578/Hermosa Park Road. Drive on gravel, staying on FS Road 578, west then north about 9 miles to a ford of Hermosa Creek that can be treacherous after recent rains. Continue straight at an intersection with FS Road 550/ Hotel Draw Road after another mile, then travel nearly 6 more miles on an increasingly steep and rough road to reach a small parking area at Celebration Lake and the CT access point. For the approach from CO 145, drive 6 miles north of Rico and turn right onto FS Road 578 and drive slightly over 6 miles up the Barlow Creek valley. At a Y intersection, take the left branch to stay on FS Road 578, passing the scenic Bolam Pass after another mile, and continuing another mile to reach Celebration Lake and the CT access point.

Hotel Draw Road Trail Access: See Segment 27 on page 283.

SERVICES, SUPPLIES, AND ACCOMMODATIONS: There is no convenient resupply point for this segment.

TRAIL DESCRIPTION: Segment 26 begins in the small parking pullout off of FS 578/Hermosa Park Road at the southwest edge of Celebration Lake, **mile 0.0**. There is camping near here, as well as after crossing a small stream flowing out of the south end of the lake, **mile 0.1**. Begin climbing, first through trees and then across an open slope with expansive views of the now much closer La Plata Mountains to the south and the Needle and West Needle Mountains to the east. Continue a traversing climb to **mile 1.0**, where the trail crests the base of the east ridge below Hermosa Peak. The trail contours to the north beneath the peak and massive talus fields, then passes a seasonal spring at **mile 1.3** with good camping before and after. Turn left onto an old roadbed at **mile 1.7**. Cross a small stream at **mile 1.8**, with camping nearby. Continue traversing around the base of Hermosa Peak, crossing Barlow Creek at **mile 2.8**, and cross a small stream with excellent camping nearby at **mile 3.0**. At **mile 3.1**, leave the old roadbed sharply right and uphill onto single-track.

Pass a small pond below the trail at **mile 3.8**, then reach a small saddle below Section Point (11,940') with great views from the small knob north of the saddle. Descend and turn sharply to the left at the junction with the Circle Trail, **mile 4.1**. Travelers can reach the town of Rico, with lodging, food, and resupply potential via the Circle Trail and Silver Creek Road, approximately 6 miles and 3,000 feet below the CT.

Follow on or slightly below the crest of the ridge leading southwest from Section Point by passing through several forested sections then contouring around the headwaters of Silver Creek before beginning to climb. Cross a small stream at **mile 6.4** with some camping in the area. Continue climbing and gain Blackhawk Pass at **mile 6.9**. Descend to the seasonal headwaters of Straight Creek at **mile 7.7**. There is a large campsite 0.1 mile to the south. Continue heading downhill

---

The north side of **Blackhawk Pass** is a valley of enchantment with vast herds of elk. **Verdant alpine meadows** near the pass, filled with lush mid-summer growth, attract wildlife—elk and mule deer, marmots, and pika—and hikers drawn by the wildflowers and lovely vistas. Have your camera ready. Famous Lizard Head Peak is in view near the pass.

TRAVEL TIP

MAINTAINING THE TRAIL: CTF VOLUNTEERS

Left: CTF volunteers ready to make trail improvements. Photo by Colin McKenna
Right: Teamwork is key to improving the trail. Photo by Bill Bloomquist

Maintaining all 567 miles of The Colorado Trail is an immense undertaking, requiring the efforts of hundreds of dedicated CTF Trail Crew and Adopt-A-Trail volunteers each year.

Every summer, The Colorado Trail Foundation organizes approximately 20 volunteer trail crews. The efforts vary from one-day to weeklong, with 15 to 25 volunteers staffing each. CT crews work on trail improvement projects including bridges, retaining walls, trail reroutes, rebuilding tread, and constructing water diversions. Volunteers receive trail work, tool use, and safety training. They value spending time in the outdoors and giving back to The Colorado Trail. Volunteers enjoy camping in the Colorado mountains, learning about the trail, sharing meals, and building friendships. Trail crews are rewarding work and a lot of fun.

Adopters and their helpers are the trail's frontline volunteers, keeping the CT passable and reporting trail conditions to the Foundation. Approximately 80 Adopters care for their own 3-to-15-mile section by removing fallen trees, maintaining water diversions, and replacing CT signage. Adopters can be responsible individuals, family groups, Scout troops, hiking clubs,

Left: Reconstructing tread. Photo by Lisa Turner **Right:** Volunteer with a Pulaski and a smile. Photo by Bill Bloomquist

mountain bike groups, horse users, or friends groups. Adopters often stick with the task for many years, even decades, finding fun and a sense of accomplishment in keeping their adopted section in good shape for trail users.

If you are interested and would like more information on CTF trail crews or Adopt-A-Trail, please visit ColoradoTrail.org.

> **WARNING:** Trail users should be aware that the Straight Creek crossing at **mile 8.6** is the last reliable water source until Deer Creek at **mile 11.9** on Segment 27, over 14 miles away.

through the forest, crossing Straight Creek again at **mile 8.6,** the last reliable water source for over 14 miles (see sidebar for additional details). Pass a couple of other seasonal streams at **mile 8.9** and at **mile 9.1**. Continue southeast, passing several potential dry campsites over the next 2 miles. At **mile 10.3,** the trail joins an old roadbed on the ridge and reaches the end of Segment 26 at **mile 11.1**, 75 feet before FS Road 550/Hotel Draw Road and a small, undeveloped parking area.

Features

MILEAGE	COMMENTS	ELEVATION
0.0	Begin Segment 26 at FS Rd 578/ Hermosa Park Road and Celebration Lake	11,100'
0.1	Celebration Lake outlet creek	11,081'
1.0	Base of E ridge Hermosa Peak	11,533'
1.3	Seasonal spring	11,449'
1.7	Left onto old roadbed	11,565'
1.8	Stream	11,482'
2.8	Barlow Creek	11,487'
3.0	Small stream	11,521'
3.1	Right onto single-track	11,561'
3.8	Pond below trail	11,720'
4.1	Sharp left (Circle Tr straight ahead)	11,759'
6.4	Small stream	11,605'
6.9	Blackhawk Pass	11,984'
7.7	Straight Creek	11,470'
8.6	Straight Creek	11,037'
8.9	Seasonal stream	10,882'
9.1	Seasonal stream	10,809'
10.3	Join old roadbed	10,660'
11.1	End Segment 26 at FS Rd 550/Hotel Draw Road	10,393'

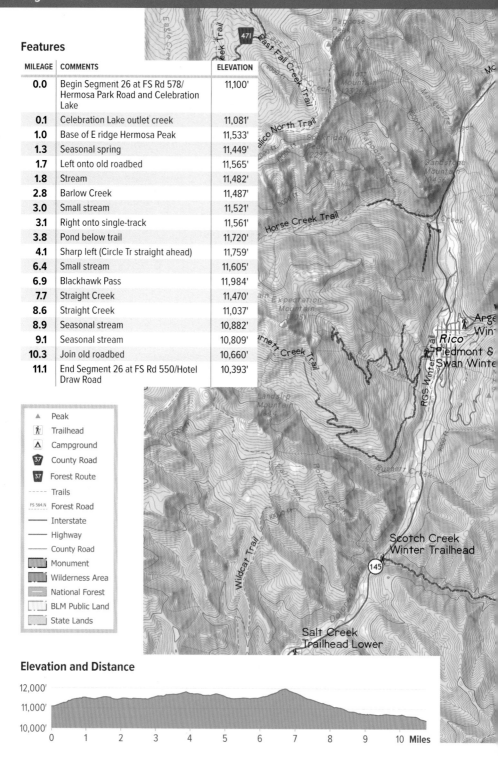

Legend:
- ▲ Peak
- Trailhead
- ⚊ Campground
- 37 County Road
- 37 Forest Route
- ----- Trails
- FS 564.N Forest Road
- Interstate
- Highway
- County Road
- Monument
- Wilderness Area
- National Forest
- BLM Public Land
- State Lands

Elevation and Distance

THE COLORADO TRAIL

SEGMENT 27
Hotel Draw Road to Kennebec Trailhead

Looking south toward the La Plata Mountains. Photo by Nate Hebenstreit

ACCESS FROM
DENVER END

ACCESS FROM
DURANGO END

AVAILABILITY
OF WATER

BICYCLING

Distance	20.8 miles
Elevation Gain	Approx. 4,186 feet
Elevation Loss	Approx. 2,922 feet
USFS Map	San Juan National Forest
The CT Databook, 8th Edition	Pages 64–65
The CT Map Book	Pages 61–64
Trails Illustrated Maps	No. 144, 1201
Latitude 40° Maps	Southwest Colorado Trails, Durango Trails
Jurisdiction	Columbine Ranger District, San Juan National Forest

ABOUT THIS SEGMENT: The first 9 miles of Segment 27 pass through and along numerous Forest Service roads and closed logging roads, along with single-track sections. There are numerous intersections, but, thanks to both CTF volunteers and US Forest Service personnel, they are well-marked with wooden posts, signs, or confidence markers. For the most part, the trail stays near the ridgeline dividing the Dolores River and Hermosa Creek watersheds, here chiefly made up of rocks of the Cutler Formation. The trail then climbs as it leaves the roads and logged forests behind. At **mile 4**, it crosses into red sandstone shale and siltstone of the Dolores Formation, deposited by streams, lakes, and winds between about 230 and 200 million years ago, after the destruction of the Ancestral Rockies. As the trail climbs toward the Cape of Good Hope, it passes into still younger rocks, sandstone, shale, and limestone deposited shortly before the inundation by the Cretaceous seaway.

Once the trail passes the junction with the Grindstone Trail, it enters the tundra and traverses Indian Trail Ridge, which is made up of a thick layer of sandstone that belongs to this group of younger rocks. From here, there are fantastic views of the surrounding mountains and drainages below. It is common to see large herds of elk below the ridge to the west. Between **mile 15.2** and **mile 19.6**, the trail is sometimes rocky and precipitous, where horseback riders will want to be especially cautious. The trail stays above tree line on this section, with no easy means of escape from sudden storms. All travelers will want to watch the weather patterns before committing to this section. Taylor Lake at **mile 19.6** is a spectacular sight from above for trail users.

TRAILHEAD/ACCESS POINTS: There are three ways to drive to the beginning of Segment 27. Two require a 4WD vehicle: from US Highway 550 through Purgatory Resort and from CO Highway 145, south of Lizard Head Pass and just south of Rico. The 2WD approach via FS Roads 435/564/550 is much longer but usually accessible by regular passenger cars.

Hotel Draw Road Trail Access (from US Highway 550): Drive approximately 28 miles north of Durango to the main entrance of Purgatory Resort on the west side of the road. At the upper parking area, bear right onto FS Road 578/

From **Indian Trail Ridge**, views of cascading wildflowers, the Hermosa valley, and the La Plata Mountains are extraordinary. This segment features sweeping vistas, culminating in a dramatic, 5-mile walk atop an alpine ridge at more than 12,000 feet. Wildflower enthusiasts will find the incredible displays at their peak starting in mid-July.

TRAVEL TIP

Taylor Lake is a welcome sight at the south end of Indian Trail Ridge. Photo by Ben Kraushaar

Hermosa Park Road. Drive on gravel, staying on FS Road 578, west then north about 9 miles to a ford of Hermosa Creek that can be treacherous after recent rains. About a mile after the ford, make a sharp left turn onto FS Road 550/Hotel Draw Road. After 3.7 miles, reach a small parking area on the right where the CT comes down from the north and intersects the Hotel Draw Road.

Hotel Draw Road Trail Access (4WD from CO Highway 145): Drive 3 miles south of Rico and turn left onto FS Road 550/Scotch Creek Road. Proceed about 6 miles to an intersection with FS Road 564/Divide Road to the left and FS Road 550/Hotel Draw Road straight ahead. Continue on FS Road 550 for 1.1 miles to reach a small parking area on the left where the CT comes down from the north and intersects the Hotel Draw Road.

Hotel Draw Road Trail Access (2WD from CO Highway 145): Drive 8.5 miles south of Rico and turn left onto FS Road 435/Roaring Fork Road. After nearly

> **WARNING:** Scrutinize the depth of the Hermosa Creek ford and the optimal line before driving into it.

7 miles, make a sharp left turn onto FS Road 564/Divide Road. Continue slightly over 12 miles to an intersection with FS Road 550.1/Scotch Creek Road to the left and FS Road 550/Hotel Draw Road to the right. Turn right onto FS Road 550 and follow it for 1.1 mile to a small parking area on the left and the beginning of the segment.

Kennebec Trailhead: See Segment 28 on page 294.

SERVICES, SUPPLIES, AND ACCOMMODATIONS: There is no convenient resupply point for this segment.

TRAIL DESCRIPTION: Segment 27 begins 75 feet north of a small parking area on FS Road 550/Hotel Draw Road at **mile 0.0**. Angle right and head southwest on single-track that parallels the road. At **mile 0.1**, the trail joins an old roadbed to the right, then bear left at a fork after another 400 feet. At **mile 0.7**, the CT curves to the left at a junction with an old roadbed. Stay right on single-track where a spur two-track leads left to FS Road 550/Hotel Draw Road at **mile 1.2**. The trail angles left to briefly join FS Road 550 at **mile 1.3**, passing a closed road to the right. Shortly after, angle left onto FS Road 564/Divide Road where FS Road 550.1/Scotch Creek Road continues straight ahead. Leave FS Road 564 and angle left onto single-track at **mile 1.4**.

Climb a forested ridge with good views to the south ahead, then pass through a 4-way junction with the Corral Draw Trail at **mile 2.9**. Continue following the scenic ridge, passing several potential dry campsites before meeting FS Road 564 again at **mile 3.9**. Angle left onto the road and follow it briefly before leaving it to the left onto single-track at **mile 4.1**, then cross the road shortly after. Cross the road again at **mile 4.2**. After following the ridge for nearly a mile, join the road again at **mile 5.0** and then leave it to the left after 250 feet. Pass straight across a two-track and campsite at **mile 5.3**, then join FS Road 564 one last time at **mile 5.6**, again for another 250 feet before angling left back onto single-track. At **mile 6.5**, reach a square steel signpost at the former Big Bend Trail junction, where water might be found via a faint trail 200 yards downhill (southeast) in a grove of trees. Pass near FS Road 564 at **mile 7.0**. Water may be flowing from a piped spring 0.1 mile west on the road (south side). The trail turns sharply left and follows an old roadbed at **mile 7.1**. Leave the roadbed and angle left at a junction with the Salt Creek Trail (Dolores

Early morning along the Indian Trail Ridge. Photo by Kingdon Hawes

River side) at **mile 7.2**. Continue straight at a junction with another Salt Creek Trail (Hermosa Creek side) at **mile 8.0**. Follow the most defined route through a heavily logged area over the next mile, passing to the east of Orphan Butte. At **mile 8.9**, follow a short section of old roadbed to the right and cross another roadbed, continuing on single-track. Follow an old roadbed again from **mile 9.1**, then leave the roadbed for single-track at **mile 9.2**. Skirt the edges of several more logged clearings, then leave the logged areas behind.

Begin a steady climb up a ridge then reach the base of a talus slope at **mile 11.9**, where water may surface just below the trail. Seasonal water may also be flowing out of a culvert a few hundred feet up the trail. Deer Creek is a reliable water source but may require 0.2 mile of off-trail travel to reach good flow in the main drainage in dry years. Camp with caution in this area as evidence of fallen trees is widespread.

At **mile 12.5,** the trail reaches a junction with a side trail on the right that leads to expansive views and dry campsites. The trail continues left (northwest) from here, passing a seasonal spring at **mile 12.7**, then turns sharply back as it climbs up a gentle ridge. Reach a steel marker post at a former trail junction at **mile 13.4**, where the Cape of Good Hope extends to the east.

Turn left at an intersection with the Grindstone Trail at **mile 15.2**, the last downhill exit from the high ridge for more than 3.5 miles. Enter tundra shortly after and begin ascending a series of very exposed high points on Indian Trail Ridge. Reach a high point on the ridge at **mile 18.5** (12,308'), though not the last high point on the ridge. Shortly after the last summit can be one of the most stunning displays of wildflowers on the CT, with the La Plata Mountains as a backdrop. When photographing the wildflower panorama, avoid trampling the vegetation so that others may also enjoy the display.

After a brief descent, turn left and head downhill toward Taylor Lake and Cumberland Basin below. After a steep, rocky descent particularly troublesome for horseback riders, pass the Sharkstooth Trail leading to Taylor Lake and camping potential on the right at **mile 19.6**. Continue to the southeast, eventually reaching the Kennebec Trailhead and the end of Segment 27 at **mile 20.8**.

 WARNING: Indian Trail Ridge can be dangerous during afternoon thunderstorms.

TRAIL PHOTO TIPS

VIEWING
OPPORTUNITY

A hiker against the sky, Collegiate West near Cottonwood Pass. Photo by Dean Krakel

The Colorado Trail is a spectacular but challenging environment to take photographs in, especially photographs that capture the beauty and uniqueness of your trip.

- The most important thing is to take your time. Take your time. Most hikers snap shoot. Go beyond that by investing a minute or two in making your photographs.
- Think about what you're taking a picture of and why. What attracted your attention? Compose the frame so that element is the most important part of the image.
- When something catches your attention, whether it's the scenic beauty or a camp moment, stop whatever you're doing and take the photo.
- Take more than one shot. Take lots of pictures. Take risks. Experiment with exposure. Shoot even when you don't think there's any chance of a frame coming out.
- Shoot in rain and snow. Use boulders and trees to steady your hands. Change lenses. Zoom in and out.
- Use the light. Morning and evening light is best, but even in direct sunlight there's a way to find light that will enhance your subject. Shoot the quiet before the sunrise and the twilight after the sunset.

- Never pass by something you want to photograph just because the light is poor or because you think you'll see another similar scene or object on down the trail. When something catches your eye, take the picture. Make the best use of what's available.
- Change your point of view. Walk a few feet or yards off the trail. Lie down. Bend over. Squat. Stand up on something or get beneath something. Don't shoot everything from eye level.
- Keep your camera handy. If you're not wearing it around your neck, stow it within easy reach in a pocket or pouch. Then, when a spectacular ray of light touches the peaks or a moose strolls onto the trail, you won't have to fumble around and miss the moment.
- Photograph people as well as the scenery. Candid photos and portraits add human interest to the photo report. Act naturally when you're being photographed, candid and cool. If you're photographing people, don't become a director. Natural moments are the best.
- Good photography, on the trail or off, isn't a matter of what kind of camera you carry. Making good photographs is up to the photographer.

Left: Hiker shadows and trail marker, Camp Hale, Segment 8. **Right:** Columbines, Kennebec Pass, Segment 28. Photos by Dean Krakel

Scotch Creek
Winter Trailhead

Salt Creek
Trailhead Lower

Upper Hermosa
Creek Trailhead

Ryman Creek Trail

Salt Creek Trail

Lower Ryman Trail

FS 564

Salt Creek
Trailhead Upper

FS 564

Blackhawk Trail

FS 550

FS 550.1

FS 578

BIG CREEK

West Cross Trail

Highline Trail

Corral Draw Trail

Big Bend Creek

North

1 Mile

Salt Creek Trail

Elbert Creek Trail

Elbert Creek Trail

Big Lick Trail

San Juan
National Forest

Little Elk Trail

Hermosa Creek Trail

North Hope Creek

Hermosa Creek
Wilderness

Haviland
Winter Trail

Dutch Creek Trail

Gouldings Creek Trail

Pinkerton-Flagstaff Trail

Highline Trail

Grindstone Trail

Bear Creek Trail

Clear Creek
Trailhead

Kennebec
Trailhead

Clear Creek Trail

Lower Hermosa Creek Trailhead

LOWER HERMOSA

Jones Creek Trail

Sliderock Trail

FS 171N

Junction Creek Trail

171

576

124

Sawtooth Trail

Map Legend

- ▲ Peak
- 👤 Trailhead
- ⊼ Campground
- [37] County Road
- [37] Forest Route
- ‑ ‑ Trails
- FS 564 N Forest Road
- — Interstate
- — Highway
- — County Road
- Monument
- Wilderness Area
- National Forest
- BLM Public Land
- State Lands

Map labels: Cascade Creek Trailhead, Lake Trailhead, Purgatory Creek, Purgatory Trail, Cas, Haviland Trailhead, Tacoma, CHRIS PARK GROUP, wood, Ridge, Crater Lake, Grasshopper Creek

Features

MILEAGE	COMMENTS	ELEVATION
0.0	Begin Segment 27 at FS Rd 550/Hotel Draw Road, angle right on single-track	10,393'
0.1	Right onto old roadbed	10,371'
0.7	Curve left on roadbed	10,408'
1.2	Right on single-track (spur 2-track to FS Rd 550 to left)	10,444'
1.3	Angle left onto FS Rd 550, then angle left onto FS Rd 564/Divide Rd (FS Rd 550.1/ Scotch Creek Rd straight ahead)	10,420'
1.4	Angle left onto single-track (FS Rd 564 angles right)	10,410'
2.9	Cross Corral Draw Trail	10,829'
3.9	Angle left onto FS Rd 564	10,791'
4.1	Angle left onto single-track, then cross FS Rd 564	10,771'
4.2	Angle left across FS Rd 564	10,827'
5.0	Straight onto FS Rd 564, then left onto single-track after 250 ft	10,737'
5.3	Straight across 2-track and campsite	10,769'
5.6	Straight onto FS Rd 564, then left onto single-track after 250 ft	10,713'
6.5	Steel post at former trail jct	10,625'
7.0	Pass near FS Rd 564	10,698'
7.1	Angle left (closed road to right)	10,764'
7.2	Angle left (Salt Creek Tr to right)	10,772'
8.0	Straight (Salt Creek Tr to left)	10,852'
8.9	Angle right onto closed road, cross another closed road, then continue on single-track	10,913'
9.1	Follow old roadbed	10,848'
9.2	Leave roadbed on single-track	10,820'
11.9	Seep at base of talus, more water at Deer Creek below	11,102'
12.5	Straight (side trail to right for view and dry camping)	11,332'
12.7	Seep	11,394'
13.4	Steel post at former trail jct	11,617'
15.2	Left (Grindstone Tr to right)	11,686'
18.5	High point on segment	12,308'
19.6	Straight (Sharkstooth Tr and Taylor Lake to right)	11,644'
20.8	End Segment 27 at Kennebec TH	11,642'

Elevation and Distance

Elevation profile ranging from 10,000' to 13,000' over 0 to 20 Miles.

Hotel Draw Road to Kennebec Trailhead

SEGMENT 28
Kennebec Trailhead to
Junction Creek Trailhead

Gudy's Rest at mile 17.7 honors Gudy Gaskill. Photo by Julie Vida and Mark Tabb

Distance	21.7 miles
Elevation Gain	Approx. 1,897 feet
Elevation Loss	Approx. 6,557 feet
USFS Map	San Juan National Forest
The CT Databook, 8th Edition	Pages 66–67
The CT Map Book	Pages 64–67
Trails Illustrated Maps	No. 144, 1201
Latitude 40° Maps	Southwest Colorado Trails, Durango Trails
Jurisdiction	Columbine Ranger District, San Juan National Forest

ACCESS FROM
DENVER END

ACCESS FROM
DURANGO END

AVAILABILITY
OF WATER

BICYCLING

ABOUT THIS SEGMENT: The final segment of The Colorado Trail begins at the Kennebec Trailhead, rises very slightly to Kennebec Pass, and then descends thousands of feet to the Junction Creek Trailhead near Durango. The segment is not all downhill, though, with a significant climb starting about one-third of the way through the segment. Beyond the pass, the CT descends a section of "sliderock." This steep hillside is most impressive and constantly changing under natural forces including gravity. CTF volunteers work every year to rebuild the trail bench and reestablish it as user-friendly.

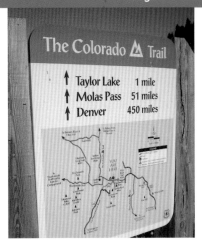

Trailhead sign below Kennebec Pass.
Photo by Lawton "Disco" Grinter

This is an incredibly diverse segment, starting above tree line, passing through stands of spruce, fir, and pine, and crossing Junction Creek at its headwaters and again where there are sturdy bridges. There is dense vegetation in the Junction Creek drainage, which stands in sharp contrast to the alpine basin filled with summer wildflowers at the beginning of the segment. The views are magnificent from Kennebec Pass but quickly disappear as the trail enters the narrow canyon below. Around Kennebec Pass and along the trail as it descends to the creek, rocks of the Dolores and Cutler Formations are cut by numerous dikes, sills, and irregular bodies of white porphyry that were emplaced during the Laramide Orogeny. Trail users pass several mines and prospects that explored mineral deposits related to the porphyry.

A miner's cabin sits atop redbeds of the Cutler Formation opposite a large talus slope known as Sliderock. Photo by Roger Forman

 WARNING: Camping is not allowed beyond **mile 17.3** of this segment (except at Junction Creek Campground, less than a half mile from **mile 20.6**).

East of Kennebec Pass and the Sliderock section, these cyclists push uphill. Photo by Adam Lisonbee

Campsites are limited in this segment. There is plenty of water when first entering the canyon, but flat spots for camping are rare. Later in the segment, when the CT climbs out of the canyon, there are flat spots but water is scarce. Camping is not permitted after **mile 17.3** due to easy accessibility and heavy day use; plan your trip down this segment carefully and stop early before all the best camping sites are taken.

This segment of the CT has the most vertical travel of any segment of the trail: more than 6,500 feet of vertical in one direction and nearly 1,900 feet in the other. Tired muscles from big elevation are often forgotten during celebrations upon completion of The Colorado Trail.

TRAILHEAD/ACCESS POINTS

Kennebec Trailhead: From the intersection of US Highways 550 and 160 at the south end of Durango, drive west on US 160 about 11 miles (0.5 mile beyond the CO Highway 140 turnoff to Hesperus). Turn right on County Road 124 (paved for 4.5 miles, then gravel becoming 4WD dirt) and travel 14 miles to reach the Kennebec Trailhead. The last 2 miles are rough and steep, a section where a 4WD vehicle is strongly recommended.

Cyclists at Champion Venture Road. Photo by Bill Manning

Sliderock Trail Access Point: The CT can be accessed by 2WD vehicles at Segment 28, **mile 2.5**. From the Junction Creek Trailhead previously described, continue on the gravel-improved FS Road 171/Junction Creek Road for nearly 18 miles to FS Road 171.N/Champion Venture Road on the left. Turn left and proceed 0.7 mile on this more rugged road to where the CT crosses the road. To the right, uphill, the CT leads 2.5 miles to the Kennebec Pass Trailhead via the Sliderock Trail portion of this segment. To the left, downhill, the CT leads to the Junction Creek Trailhead 19.2 miles away.

Junction Creek Trailhead: Drive on north Main Avenue in Durango to 25th Street and turn west. After a couple of blocks the street bears right and becomes Junction Street, then County Road 204 after a few more blocks as the street leaves the city limits. Follow it for 3 miles to an intersection with County Road 205 and take the left road to continue on County Road 204. Travel another 0.6 mile to reach the Junction

If you didn't stop for a **shower** in one of the falls in Junction Canyon, grab one at the large, modern recreation center in Durango, located three blocks north of Junction Creek Road and Main Avenue. There is bus service along Main Avenue.

TRAVEL TIP

The moon shines bright looking west from Kennebec Pass. Photo by Jared Champion

Creek Trailhead, featuring a very busy and frequently full parking lot with vault toilets and the southern terminus of The Colorado Trail. The road continues as FS Road 171/ Junction Creek Road. In about another mile, there is an even smaller parking area just before the road switchbacks. The CT can be accessed via a 100-yard-long connector trail that leaves the road to the north at the switchback.

TRAIL DESCRIPTION: Segment 28 begins at the Kennebec Trailhead, **mile 0.0**. The trailhead is a potentially confusing area with a network of roads and side trails. Pay attention to the signs and maps to ensure you're on the CT as it travels east on single-track. (Avoid the dead-end road that leads to a notch in the ridge above, which is not the CT.) Pass by a seasonal seep at **mile 0.4**. After reaching Kennebec Pass at **mile 0.6**, head downhill then sharply left at a trail junction at **mile 0.7**. The CT soon crosses a large talus slope appropriately referred to as the Sliderock section. Below, enter a spruce forest and descend switchbacks until reaching FS Road 171.N/ Champion Venture Road at **mile 2.5**. Cross the road, pass a dry campsite, and continue heading downhill into Fassbinder Gulch. There is a seasonal creek at **mile 3.9**. The trail leaves the bottom of the gulch and crosses two small tributaries in the next half mile, then a larger stream at **mile 4.8**. Camping in this area is generally poor due to thick vegetation.

DURANGO

Durango, an old railroad town and now the commercial center for southwestern Colorado, is approximately 3.5 miles from the Junction Creek Trailhead. The town is connected to Denver via airline and bus service, and to Silverton by the Durango & Silverton Narrow Gauge Railroad.

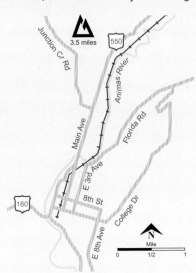

Distance from CT: 3.5 miles
Elevation: 6,512 feet
Zip code: 81301
Area code: 970

Bus
Durango Transit Center
250 W. 8th St.
(970) 259-5438

Dining (several)
Carver Bakery & Brewing Co.
1022 Main Ave.
(970) 259-2545

Gear (including fuel canisters)
Backcountry Experience
1205 Camino del Rio
(970) 247-5830

Gardenswartz Outdoors
780 Main Ave.
(970) 259-6696

Pine Needle Mountaineering
835 Main Ave.
(970) 247-8728

Groceries (several)
City Market
South 6 Town Plaza
(970) 247-4475

Info
Chamber of Commerce
111 S. Camino del Rio
(970) 247-0312

Laundry (several)
North Main Laundry
2980 Main Ave.
(970) 799-6246

Lodging (several)
Check rates etc. online;
consider options on N. Main Ave.

Medical
Durango Urgent Care
2577 N. Main Ave.
(970) 247-8382

Mercy Regional Medical Center
1010 Three Springs Blvd.
(970) 247-4311

Post Office
Durango Post Office
222 W. 8th St.
(970) 247-3434

Showers
Durango Recreation Center
2700 Main Ave.
(970) 375-7300

Train Depot
Durango & Silverton Narrow Gauge
Railroad
479 Main Ave.
(970) 247-2733
(888) 872-4607

Two hikers celebrate the end of their thru-hike at the Junction Creek Trailhead. Photo courtesy of Sarah Luetkenhaus

Pass the Gaines Gulch waterfall at **mile 5.6**. Cross Flagler Fork of Junction Creek at **mile 5.8** and three more times before Flagler Fork joins Junction Creek; there are no bridges at these crossings. Pass limited camping just upstream of a stout bridge over Junction Creek at **mile 7.2**.

Begin the last significant climb on The Colorado Trail after crossing the bridge. This 4-mile climb gains more than 1,000 feet through beautiful, rugged terrain, with steep slopes dropping into the Junction Creek gorge. The trail reaches a ridge, where there is good camping, with a small creek 0.2 mile farther at **mile 8.3**. There is also reliable water in Sliderock Canyon at **mile 9.4** and First Trail Canyon at **mile 10.4**. The trail begins following an old mining road at about **mile 11.0**, then reaches the top of the climb at "High Point" at **mile 11.4**. From here, the trail begins its final descent toward the Junction Creek Trailhead near Durango.

At a sharp left bend in the trail at **mile 11.8**, there is an excellent small campsite on a bench above the trail and seasonal water in a small stream 200 feet below the trail. Continue downhill and pass through a gate at **mile 14.6**. Shortly after the gate, angle left at the junction with the Dry Fork Trail, **mile 14.9**. At **mile 17.3**, there are small campsites and possible spring water from a pipe, though this area is often

VIEWING DIPPERS

A chunky, drab, wrenlike bird, the water ouzel, or dipper, would hardly attract anyone's attention if not for its unusual manner of earning a living. Dippers reside along rushing mountain streams, often perched atop a rock in the foaming center of the torrent. From this vantage point, it constantly bobs up and down, looking for aquatic insects or even small fish to eat. Spotting

American dipper. Photo by Dan Garber

a tasty morsel, it then dives headlong into the water, opens its wings, and "flies" or walks submerged through the flow. Birds stake out a 75- to 200-yard length of stream for their territory, rarely venturing far from its banks.

When disturbed, dippers fly low and rapidly up and down the stream, sounding a high, ringing alarm. During winter, they move to lower levels. Their nests are a bulky ball of moss open on one side, built just above the waterline in inaccessible places such as on a rock wall or behind a waterfall.

Dippers can be found along the streams and rivers throughout western Colorado. In Segment 28, you are as likely to spot one along the lush banks of little Quinn Creek as perched on a boulder in the middle of the Animas River in downtown Durango.

used heavily by cows and the spring can be seasonal. This is the last location where camping is allowed on the remainder of the CT. (Off-trail, camping is available at the Junction Creek Campground (fee), 0.5 mile east of the intersection of FS Road 171 and the CT at **mile 20.6.**)

At the junction with Hoffheins Trail at **mile 17.5**, bear left and continue to Gudy's Rest at **mile 17.7**. This is a scenic overlook with a bench placed in honor of Gudy Gaskill, the remarkable woman who made The Colorado Trail a reality. After descending a series of switchbacks, cross Junction Creek on a bridge (informally known as Ted's Crossing) at **mile 19.1**. Stay right at a trail junction at **mile 20.6**. (Going left on this connector trail leads 100 yards to FS Road 171/Junction Creek Road.) Continue on the CT down the narrow canyon paralleling the stream, eventually reaching the Junction Creek Trailhead and the southern terminus of The Colorado Trail at **mile 21.7**. The trailhead is about 3.5 miles on paved road from Durango's Main Avenue and 25th Street where there are several motels nearby. Downtown Durango is about 1.5 miles south on Main.

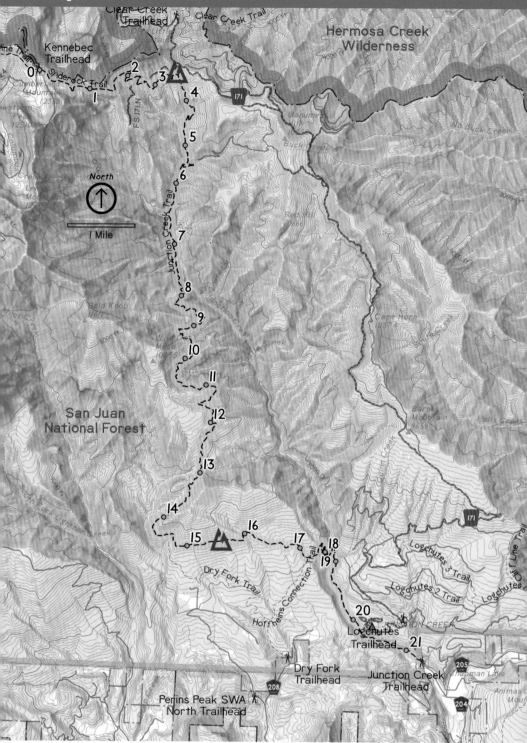

Kennebec
Trailhead

Clear Creek
Trailhead

Clear Creek Trail

Hermosa Creek
Wilderness

No Buck Creek

0

Sliderock Trail

1

2

3

4

5

6

7

8

9

10

11

12

13

14

15

16

17

18

19

20

21

FS 171N

171

Junction Creek Trail

Cape Horn

Barnes
Mountain

Falls Creek

Quinn Creek

North

↑

1 Mile

San Juan
National Forest

Bald Knob

Dry Fork Trail

Hoffheins Connection Trail

171

Logchutes 3 Trail

Logchutes 2 Trail

Logchutes 1

Dutton Cliff Line Trail

Logchutes
Trailhead

Junction Creek
Trailhead

JUNCTION CREEK

205

Chapman Lake

Dry Fork
Trailhead

208

Perins Peak SWA
North Trailhead

204

Legend

▲	Peak
🚶	Trailhead
⋀	Campground
37	County Road
37	Forest Route
- - - -	Trails
FS 564.N	Forest Road
——	Interstate
——	Highway
——	County Road
▦	Monument
▦	Wilderness Area
▦	National Forest
▦	BLM Public Land
▦	State Lands

Features

MILEAGE	COMMENTS	ELEVATION
0.0	Begin Segment 28 at Kennebec TH	11,642'
0.4	Seasonal seep	11,677'
0.6	Kennebec Pass	11,760'
0.7	Sharply left (side trail straight ahead)	11,717'
2.5	Angle sharply left across FS Rd 171.N/ Champion Venture Road	10,359'
3.9	Seasonal stream	9,937'
4.8	Stream	9,474'
5.6	Gaines Gulch waterfall	9,239'
5.8	Flagler Fork	9,026'
7.2	Junction Creek bridge	8,523'
8.3	Small stream	8,987'
9.4	Small stream at Sliderock Canyon	9,061'
10.4	Stream at First Trail Canyon	9,433'
11.0	Join old roadbed	9,516'
11.4	Top of climb at "High Point"	9,568'
11.8	Small Stream	9,425'
14.6	Gate	8,662'
14.9	Angle left (Dry Fork Tr angles to right)	8,608'
17.3	Seasonal spring and stock pond	8,138'
17.5	Left (Hoffheins Tr to right)	7,997'
17.7	Gudy's Rest bench and overlook	7,976'
19.1	Junction Creek bridge (informally Ted's Crossing)	7,433'
20.6	Right (side trail to FS Rd 171/Junction Creek Road and upper Junction Creek TH straight ahead)	7,181'
21.7	End Segment 28 at Junction Creek TH	6,978'

Elevation and Distance

SEGMENT CW01
Twin Lakes to Sheep Gulch

Southbound beneath Hope Pass. Photo by Roger O'Doherty

		ACCESS FROM DENVER END
Distance	9.9 miles	
Elevation Gain	Approx. 3,606 feet	ACCESS FROM DURANGO END
Elevation Loss	Approx. 2,644 feet	
USFS Map	San Isabel National Forest	AVAILABILITY OF WATER
The CT Databook, 8th Edition	Pages 68–69	
The CT Map Book	Pages 68–69	BICYCLING
Trails Illustrated Maps	Nos. 110, 127, 129, 148, 1203	
Latitude 40° Map	Salida Buena Vista Trails	
Jurisdiction	Leadville Ranger District, San Isabel National Forest	

ABOUT THIS SEGMENT: The 85-mile Collegiate West route, co-located with the Continental Divide Trail, became part of The Colorado Trail in 2012. When combined with the Collegiate East route, it creates the 163.3-mile Collegiate Loop, a multi-day hike that is growing in popularity in part because it doesn't require shuttling of vehicles. Users can park anywhere with access to the loop and return to the same spot upon completion.

The beginning of Segment CW01 generally parallels the southern shoreline of Twin Lakes Reservoir through a forest of evergreens and aspen. The historic Interlaken Resort (see page 307) is less than a mile from the beginning of the segment. Several of the resort's original buildings, dating to the late 19th century, are in various states of preservation. Wandering through them takes one back to an earlier era when tourists arrived not by automobile but by train and stagecoach.

For another 2 miles the trail passes through gently rolling sagebrush- and forest-covered hills before beginning a challenging 4-mile, 3,300-foot ascent to 12,548-foot Hope Pass, nestled between Mount Hope and Quail Mountain. The trail then descends slightly more than 2,300 feet in 2.4 miles to the end of the segment at the junction with the Sheep Gulch/Hope Pass Trail that leads to the Sheep Gulch Trailhead in 0.2 mile. This segment is mostly below tree line, except for approximately 2.5 miles when crossing Hope Pass, and weather conditions should be evaluated before crossing the pass.

From Hope Pass, begin descending into Sheep Gulch and the Clear Creek valley. Photo by Roger O'Doherty

Reaching timberline, high above Twin Lakes. Photo by Bill Manning

TRAILHEAD/ACCESS POINTS

Twin Lakes Trail Access: The northern terminus of the CT Collegiate West can be accessed from a parking area at the southeast corner of Twin Lakes and 1.5 miles off CT Segment 11. From Leadville to the north, take Highway 24 south about 15 miles to the Highway 82 turnoff to Twin Lakes (and Independence Pass). Turn left (west) and continue 0.8 mile, then turn left onto the gravel County Road 25. Follow it about 1 mile, staying left at all intersections. Reach a small trailhead with limited parking where the road is gated. From Buena Vista to the south, drive north on Highway 24 about 19 miles, turn west onto Highway 82, and follow the description above. There are also larger parking lots downhill to the west.

Sheep Gulch Trailhead: See Segment CW02 on page 312.

SERVICES, SUPPLIES, AND ACCOMMODATIONS: There are full services and accommodations available in Leadville and Buena Vista and limited amenities in Twin Lakes. See Segment 10 (page 151) for Leadville services, Segment 11 (page 159) for Twin Lakes, and Segment 13 (page 179) for Buena Vista.

Left: Beneath Mount Hope (13,933') north of the pass. Photo by Mary and Marc Parlange
Right: Hope Pass, a rewarding climb. Photo by Alicia Blank

TRAIL DESCRIPTION: Segment CW01 starts on the southeastern edge of Twin Lakes Reservoir at a trail junction not accessible by vehicle. To reach the start of Segment CW01, begin at the Twin Lakes Trail Access parking area at mile 12.3 of Segment 11 and travel west along the CT to mile 13.8. At this well-marked trail junction, the trail to the left continues on Segment 11 and the traditional CT Collegiate East route. The trail straight ahead is the northern terminus of the CT Collegiate West, Segment CW01, **mile 0.0.**

The trail generally follows the shoreline west for slightly more than a mile. Cross seasonal Flume Creek on a bridge at **mile 0.6**. At **mile 0.7** is a junction: the trail to the left is signed for the CT and CDT, but many trail users follow the trail to the right because it passes through the historic Interlaken Resort (see description on page 307). Both trails are similar in length and rejoin at a 4-way intersection at **mile 1.1**. Turn right at this junction if coming from Interlaken or continue straight if arriving via the bypass.

Even though it can be a strenuous climb and descent, **Hope Pass** is a delight with wildflowers, spectacular views, and a sense of accomplishment. Slowing your pace a little and "taking it all in" will heighten your enjoyment.

TRAVEL TIPS

CT travelers in this segment share the route with **hardy runners** training for, and participating in, the Leadville Trail 100 Run, a torturous mountain ultramarathon held each year.

Twin Lakes to Sheep Gulch

Reflection of Mount Elbert, Colorado's highest peak, in Twin Lakes. Photo by Jim Rahtz

Arrive at another intersection at **mile 1.3**, angle left and briefly join an old two-track then turn left back onto single-track after 100 feet. Continue to another intersection at **mile 2.0** and angle right where another trail joins from the left. Cross a seasonally dry wash on a small bridge at **mile 2.4**. Cross Boswell Creek on a bridge at **mile 2.9**, a typically reliable water source.

The CT turns left onto an old roadbed at a junction with Trail 1471.A (known locally as the Bermuda Triangle Trail, which leads to the Willis Gulch Trailhead), **mile 3.5**. This is the beginning of the climb to Hope Pass, a gain of nearly 3,300 feet over the next 4 miles. Leave the roadbed for single-track at a switchback to the left shortly after.

At a junction with Trail 1471 at **mile 4.3**, continue straight ahead. At **mile 4.8**, at a junction with the Big Willis Gulch Trail, bear left on the CT into Little Willis Gulch. Cross the seasonally dry Cache Creek Ditch at **mile 4.9**. There is a campsite and water available in an avalanche meadow at **mile 5.7**. There is a picturesque old cabin at **mile 5.9**. There is another good water stop at **mile 6.5**, just below tree line, where there is also a campsite nearby.

Hope Pass, at **mile 7.5**, is rewarding and offers spectacular views of the Collegiate Range north and south. Mount Elbert, the highest point in Colorado and second highest in the Continental United States, towers to the northwest. To the

THE LEGACY OF THE INTERLAKEN RESORT

VIEWING
OPPORTUNITY

Seemingly isolated and forgotten today, it's hard to imagine that one of the most popular tourist destinations in Colorado before the twentieth century was Interlaken, nestled on the shores of the present-day Twin Lakes. The complex was started in 1879 and enlarged after James V. Dexter bought the lakeside resort in 1883 and transformed it into a popular summer retreat. Visitors rode the train to a nearby stop, then took the short carriage ride to the south shore location.

Restored history at Interlaken. Photo by Bill Manning

The Interlaken Hotel boasted some of the best amenities of the time, with comfortable rooms and expansive views of the surrounding mountains and lakes. There was a tavern, pool hall, barns and stables, and a unique six-sided outdoor privy. An icehouse, granaries, and laundry rounded out the facility. Guests came to fish, hunt, ride horses, or just relax. Dexter built his own private cabin reflecting his nautical interests, including a cupola atop the second story with views in all directions.

Unfortunately, the resort fell into rapid decline after the turn of the century when the Twin Lakes were enlarged to serve irrigation interests. The entrance road was inundated and the large but now shallow lakes were less attractive to nature lovers. Eventually, the resort was abandoned and the buildings began to deteriorate.

In 1979, the Bureau of Reclamation stepped in to record and stabilize the historic district as the reservoir was enlarged further. Buildings that were to be inundated by the new dam were moved slightly uphill and extensively repaired. For CT hikers, a short side trip to the site provides a glimpse at a slice of Colorado history.

south, from east to west, are additional fourteeners Mount Oxford, Mount Belford, Missouri Mountain, and Huron Peak.

From the pass, descend steeply more than 2,300 feet in 2.4 miles. There is some dry camping potential in the basin as the trail reaches the first scattered trees, with seasonal water usually available at a rockslide at **mile 8.9**. Water may also be available at a small spring at **mile 9.4**. Segment CW01 ends at a trail junction at **mile 9.9**. The CT continues to the right. The Sheep Gulch Trailhead is left, 0.2 mile and 170 feet downhill on the Sheep Gulch/Hope Pass Trail. A major side trip is possible from here to climb Mount Oxford, Mount Belford, and Missouri Mountain.

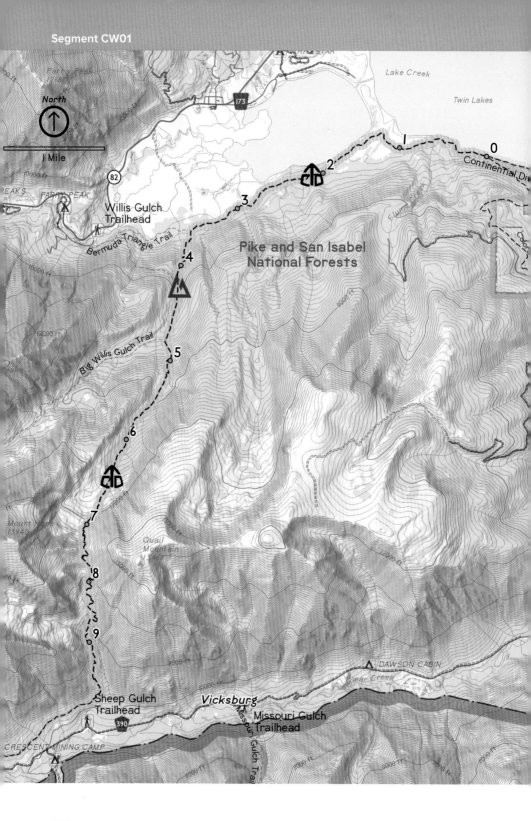

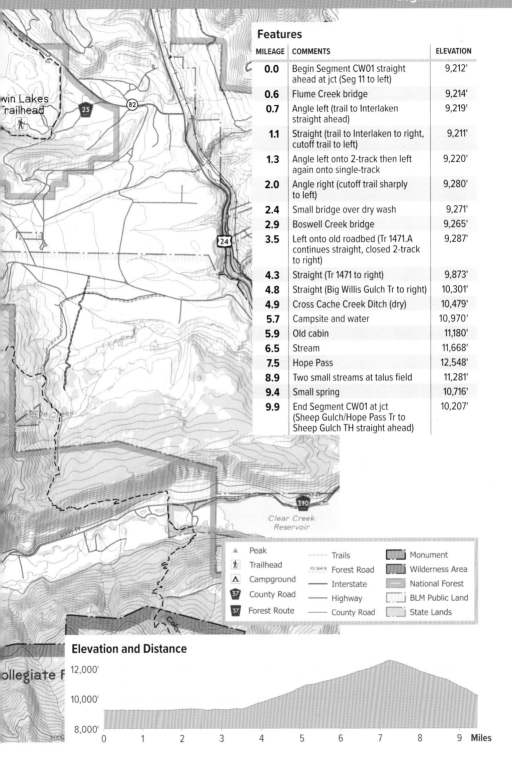

Features

MILEAGE	COMMENTS	ELEVATION
0.0	Begin Segment CW01 straight ahead at jct (Seg 11 to left)	9,212'
0.6	Flume Creek bridge	9,214'
0.7	Angle left (trail to Interlaken straight ahead)	9,219'
1.1	Straight (trail to Interlaken to right, cutoff trail to left)	9,211'
1.3	Angle left onto 2-track then left again onto single-track	9,220'
2.0	Angle right (cutoff trail sharply to left)	9,280'
2.4	Small bridge over dry wash	9,271'
2.9	Boswell Creek bridge	9,265'
3.5	Left onto old roadbed (Tr 1471.A continues straight, closed 2-track to right)	9,287'
4.3	Straight (Tr 1471 to right)	9,873'
4.8	Straight (Big Willis Gulch Tr to right)	10,301'
4.9	Cross Cache Creek Ditch (dry)	10,479'
5.7	Campsite and water	10,970'
5.9	Old cabin	11,180'
6.5	Stream	11,668'
7.5	Hope Pass	12,548'
8.9	Two small streams at talus field	11,281'
9.4	Small spring	10,716'
9.9	End Segment CW01 at jct (Sheep Gulch/Hope Pass Tr to Sheep Gulch TH straight ahead)	10,207'

Symbol	Feature		Symbol	Feature
▲	Peak		-----	Trails			Monument
🚶	Trailhead		FS 564.N	Forest Road			Wilderness Area
Λ	Campground		⎯	Interstate			National Forest
37	County Road		⎯	Highway			BLM Public Land
37	Forest Route		⎯	County Road			State Lands

Elevation and Distance

SEGMENT CW02
Sheep Gulch to Cottonwood Pass Trailhead

The Three Apostles lie ahead of southbound travelers in Segment CW02.
Photo by Sam Parks

Distance	25.9 miles
Elevation Gain	Approx. 6,122 feet
Elevation Loss	Approx. 4,163 feet
USFS Map	San Isabel and Gunnison National Forests
The CT Databook, 8th Edition	Pages 70–71
The CT Map Book	Pages 69–72
Trails Illustrated Maps	Nos. 129, 148, 1203
Latitude 40° Map	Salida Buena Vista Trails
Jurisdiction	Leadville and Gunnison Ranger Districts, San Isabel and Gunnison National Forests

ACCESS FROM
DENVER END

ACCESS FROM
DURANGO END

AVAILABILITY
OF WATER

BICYCLING

See page 171

Lake Ann from above. Photo by David Dolton

ABOUT THIS SEGMENT: Segment CW02 passes in and out of the heart of the Collegiate Peaks Wilderness, which contains more fourteeners and high peaks than any other designated wilderness area in Colorado and the rest of the lower 48 states. The trail crosses the Continental Divide at the rocky and windswept Lake Ann Pass. Huron and La Plata Peaks, both fourteeners, are reasonably accessible from the trail, as are a host of thirteeners, including the Three Apostles east of Lake Ann Pass. Lake Ann itself is one of the jewels of the Collegiate West.

There are several stream crossings and many year-round water sources all along this segment, including the lovely beaver-dammed streams and ponds in the Texas Creek Basin.

While much of this segment is below timberline, trail users are exposed to potential severe weather on the 2-mile crossing of Lake Ann Pass and the last two miles of the segment, with the latter exposure continuing through an extended section above tree line through most of Segment CW03.

> **WARNING:** Parts of the Collegiate West alternative hold deep snowpack into July and are among the last places on the CT to melt off and become passable.
>
> The steep rock slope beneath Lake Ann Pass in Segment CW02 is typically a snowfield until early- or mid-July, as are parts of Segment CW03.

Sheep Gulch to Cottonwood Pass Trailhead

Clear Creek near Winfield, Collegiate West, Segment CW02. Photo by Dave Ankenbauer

TRAILHEAD/ACCESS POINTS

Sheep Gulch Trailhead: The northern terminus of this segment is at a trail junction located above the Sheep Gulch Traihead. The trailhead, located between the old mining towns of Vicksburg and Winfield, is accessible by driving US Highway 24 about 19 miles south of Leadville or 15 miles north of Buena Vista. Turn west on the graveled Clear Creek Road (County Road 390, becoming FS Road 390) and drive about 9.5 miles to the Sheep Gulch Trailhead on the right. Head up the 0.2-mile connector trail to the junction with CT/CDT, where Segment CW02 begins.

Cottonwood Pass Trailhead: See Segment CW03 on page 320.

SERVICES, SUPPLIES, AND ACCOMMODATIONS: Buena Vista, approximately 19 miles from Cottonwood Pass, offers full services. See Segment 13 (page 179) for a more complete description. The Taylor Park Trading Post, about 15 miles west of the pass, offers limited services.

TRAIL DESCRIPTION: Segment CW02 begins at **mile 0.0** at a trail junction above the Sheep Gulch Trailhead. Head southwest and cross a small creek at **mile 0.7**, where water may be available. The trail passes through aspen groves and clearings as it traverses above the Clear Creek valley and angles right at a junction with an old roadbed at **mile 2.1**. Cross another small seasonal stream at **mile 2.4**. Pass through more tall aspen groves and meadows before entering the pines.

Deer in South Fork Texas Creek, Collegiate Peaks Wilderness. Photo by Cornelius Friesen

At **mile 3.1,** the trail crosses FS Road 390.A/North Fork Clear Creek Road. (Those wishing to climb La Plata Peak can diverge from the trail here, following the road west for about a mile, then a faint and difficult trail for 2 miles and 4,100 feet to the top of the 14,361-foot peak.) The trail crosses the North Fork Clear Creek on a bridge at **mile 3.2**. Water is generally available here year-round. There is camping possible between the road and the creek crossing.

Continuing south, trail users are treated to views of the jagged mountains known as the Three Apostles, including Ice Mountain, a high thirteener at 13,951 feet. Cross a seasonal stream at **mile 4.2**, and then enter the Collegiate Peaks Wilderness at **mile 4.8**. Looking back to the north, trail users catch a good view of La Plata Peak as well as great views of Granite Mountain to the south and Huron Peak to the southeast. Angle left at a junction with the Silver Basin Trail at **mile 5.4**, then cross Silver Creek on a bridge at **mile 5.6**. Cross the South Fork Clear Creek bridge at **mile 5.8**. Both creeks offer reliable water sources and camping.

The trail then exits the Collegiate Peaks Wilderness for about a half-mile. At **mile 5.8**, turn right onto an old roadbed, the Lake Ann Trail. (From here, those wishing to climb 14,003-foot Huron Peak can turn left and head northeast for 0.3

TRAVEL TIPS

Volunteers and the US Forest Service have accomplished wonderful **segment CW02 reroutes in recent years**, moving lengthy sections off motorized routes. The single-track for nearly the first 6 miles is an example and, compared to the road walk before, travels a more tranquil setting with stunning views of the Three Apostles.

CTF trail crews, along with Forest Service staff, professional trail crews, and other partner organizations, completed constructing a **new trail section between mile 10.5 and mile 19.3** in 2023. The new section completes another section of non-motorized trail by moving the co-located CT and CDT into the Collegiate Peaks Wilderness and off the Timberline Trail, which allows motorcycles. Final trail data was not available prior to publication and the segment description below describes the old route following the Timberline Trail. Check the CTF website (ColoradoTrail.org) for updated information about the new trail section.

Collegiate Peaks Wilderness Area. Photo by Bill Manning

mile to the South Fork Clear Creek Trailhead and the beginning of the 2.3-mile, 3,400-foot climb to the top of the peak.)

At **mile 6.3**, re-enter the Collegiate Peaks Wilderness after a stream crossing, and begin the increasingly steep climb toward Lake Ann Pass. Shortly after passing a sign to Apostle Basin, cross South Fork Clear Creek on a bridge at **mile 7.0**. There is camping before and after the crossing.

The trail crosses a seasonal stream at **mile 7.4**, then passes potential camping east of the trail at **mile 8.2**. Cross another creek on a log bridge at **mile 8.4**, then cross a third creek, where there is potential camping below the trail shortly after.

The trail then begins the steep climb up to Lake Ann Pass, breaks out of the forest, and reaches a trail junction at **mile 8.8**. A side trail leads left 0.2 mile to Lake Ann and exposed camping, while the CT continues straight ahead. The trail switchbacks through tundra and a large talus field, where pikas scurry and squeak, climbing 800 feet in less than a mile to reach 12,588-foot Lake Ann Pass at **mile 9.7**. The pass sits atop the Continental Divide and provides sweeping vistas of the Collegiate Peaks Wilderness and beyond.

The trail descends more than 1,400 feet over the next 2 miles on switchbacks and meandering tread, with expansive views of the Taylor Park area to the west, and exits the Collegiate Peaks Wilderness at **mile 11.8**. At **mile 11.9**, the southern end of the Lake Ann Trail, turn left onto the Timberline Trail, which allows motorcycles. Cross a seasonal stream at **mile 13.0**, then continue straight at **mile**

Left: A pond midway in South Fork Texas Creek makes for good camping. Photo by Tim Burroughs
Right: Climbing south toward the end of Segment CW02 at Cottonwood Pass. Photo by Bill Manning

13.8 at an intersection with the Texas Ridge Trail. Cross Illinois Creek shortly after where there is camping over the next 0.1 mile. The trail undulates over the next 3 miles, crossing seasonal streams at **mile 14.0** and **mile 15.4**, where there is potential camping above the trail. Descend into Prospector Gulch, crossing the creek at **mile 17.1** and again at **mile 17.6**. After descending to near the end of Prospector Gulch the trail turns to the east and descends diagonally into the Texas Creek valley.

At the Texas Creek Trailhead, located at the end of FS Road 755/Texas Creek Road, **mile 18.7**, leave the Timberline Trail and head east on the Texas Creek Trail, re-entering the Collegiate Peaks Wilderness shortly after. For the next couple of miles, the trail generally parallels Texas Creek and a series of small beaver ponds. At **mile 19.3**, intersect the Waterloo Gulch Trail, which heads north, then cross a stream and continue straight. There is an open meadow nearby where camping is possible. At **mile 20.6**, cross North Texas Creek, a good water source. Turn right, heading due south, onto South Texas Creek Trail at **mile 21.5** and ford Texas Creek, with camping nearby. After over 1,000 feet of elevation gain, there is a small pond to the right of the trail at **mile 23.3**, with camping on the north side. This is the last on-trail, typically reliable water until Segment CW03 mile 7.0, over 9 miles farther.

Continue gaining elevation, crossing several more seasonal streams in the next mile, also with camping potential nearby. Exit the Collegiate Peaks Wilderness at **mile 25.3** just before reaching a saddle. Turn northwest and climb a bit higher along the ridge before reaching County Road 306. Cross the road to the Cottonwood Pass Trailhead and the end of Segment CW02 at **mile 25.9**. There is an exposed campsite near a pond 0.1 mile and 100 feet below the pass to the west.

Sheep Gulch to Cottonwood Pass Trailhead

Features

MILEAGE	COMMENTS	ELEVATION
0.0	Begin Segment CW02 at Sheep Gulch/Hope Pass Tr jct	10,207'
0.7	Small creek	10,095'
2.1	Angle right (side trail angles left)	10,486'
2.4	Seasonal stream	10,506'
3.1	Cross FS Rd 390.A/N Fork Clear Creek Road	10,398'
3.2	N Fork Clear Creek bridge	10,370'
4.2	Seasonal stream	10,608'
4.8	Enter Collegiate Peaks Wilderness	10,644'
5.4	Angle left (Silver Basin Tr angles right)	10,668'
5.6	Silver Creek bridge	10,611'
5.8	S Fk Clear Creek bridge, exit Collegiate Peaks Wilderness, then right on Lake Ann Tr (2-track)	10,589'
6.3	Enter Collegiate Peaks Wilderness	10,713'
7.0	Right (Three Apostles Tr to left), then S Fk Clear Creek bridge	10,830'
7.4	Seasonal stream	10,959'
8.2	Camping to east	11,396'
8.4	Bridge over creek, then another stream	11,526'
8.8	Straight (side trail to Lake Ann to left)	11,776'
9.7	Lake Ann Pass	12,588'
11.8	Exit Collegiate Peaks Wilderness	11,163'
11.9	Left onto Timberline Tr (motorized)	11,159'
13.0	Seasonal stream	11,230'
13.8	Straight (Texas Ridge Tr to right), then Illinois Creek	11,031'
14.0	Seasonal stream	11,088'
15.4	Seasonal stream	11,414'
17.1	Prospector Gulch creek	10,875'
17.6	Prospector Gulch creek	10,653'
18.7	Left on Texas Creek Tr (Texas Cr TH, FS Rd 755/ Texas Creek Road to right), then enter Collegiate Peaks Wilderness	10,010'
19.3	Straight (Waterloo Gulch Tr to left), then cross creek	10,030'
20.6	North Texas Creek	10,178'
21.5	Right on S Texas Creek Tr (Texas Creek Tr straight), cross Texas Creek (ford)	10,345'
23.3	Side trails to small pond to right	11,508'
25.3	Exit Collegiate Peaks Wilderness, then sharply right	12,144'
25.9	Angle right across County Rd 306 to end Segment CW02 at Cottonwood Pass TH	12,142'

Elevation and Distance

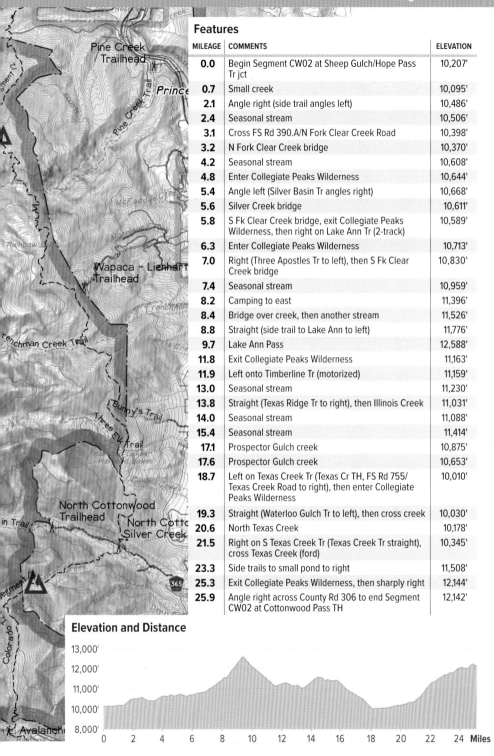

SEGMENT CW03
Cottonwood Pass Trailhead to Tincup Pass Road

From Cottonwood Pass looking north at the Divide, including the Three Apostles. Photo by Mike Fife

Distance	16.1 miles
Elevation Gain	Approx. 3,532 feet
Elevation Loss	Approx. 4,591 feet
USFS Map	San Isabel and Gunnison National Forests
***The CT Databook**, 8th Edition*	Pages 72–73
The CT Map Book	Pages 72–74
Trails Illustrated Maps	Nos. 129, 130, 148, 1203
Latitude 40° Map	Salida Buena Vista Trails
Jurisdiction	Salida and Gunnison Ranger Districts, San Isabel and Gunnison National Forests

ACCESS FROM
DENVER END

ACCESS FROM
DURANGO END

AVAILABILITY
OF WATER

BICYCLING

See page 171

ABOUT THIS SEGMENT: This segment is the highest segment in the Collegiate West, nearly always above 12,000 feet—and approaching 13,000 feet several times—before dropping at the end of the segment to Tincup Pass Road. Because of camping and water limitations, as well as potential weather issues, consider completing this segment in a single day, or plan for limited protected camping along the way.

Even above timberline, Mother Nature is hearty. Photo by Cornelius Friesen

The trail begins climbing immediately from the Cottonwood Pass Trailhead on the Continental Divide, reaching a ridgeline overlooking Taylor Park to the west and the imposing profiles of several fourteeners to the north and east.

Because much of this segment is well above timberline, users are encouraged to avoid exposure to the Colorado high country's frequent and unpredictable lightning storms by traveling early in the day and moving lower as clouds roll in. It is not unusual to encounter cold rain, sleet, heavy fog, and hail—all in the span of a single

Midway in Segment CW03 is South Mineral Basin looking ahead to Emma Burr Mountain. Photo by Rick Stockwell

Cottonwood Pass Trailhead to Tincup Pass Road

Mineral Basin and stunning scenery. Photo by Mal Sillars

day—even in the heart of the summer trail season. Take precautions, especially when lightning is present.

Although this segment does not pass through designated wilderness, it nevertheless is not open to mountain bike travel.

TRAILHEAD/ACCESS POINTS

Cottonwood Pass Trailhead: Cottonwood Pass, the northern terminus of CW03, can be reached from the east and west on Cottonwood Pass Road. From the center of Buena Vista, take County Road 306 west about 19 miles to the top of the pass. From Gunnison, it is approximately 46 miles east on CO Highway 135 and County Roads 742 and 209, passing by Taylor Park Reservoir along the way. The trailhead is on the south side of the pass with a small and very busy parking lot.

Tincup Pass Road Trail Access: See Segment CW04 on page 327.

SERVICES, SUPPLIES, AND ACCOMMODATIONS: Full services are available in Buena Vista (see page 179). Limited services are available at Mount Princeton Hot Springs Resort and Taylor Park Trading Post.

Left: Segment CW03 south of Cottonwood Pass feels like the top of the world. Photo by Mike Fife **Right:** Co-located CDT and CT Collegiate West in Segment CW03 with Mounts Harvard (left) and Columbia (middle) in the far background. Photo by Mal Sillars

TRAIL DESCRIPTION: The segment begins at the Cottonwood Pass Trailhead, **mile 0.0**. There is an exposed campsite near a pond 0.1 mile and 100 feet below the pass to the west. There are many closed social trails over the first mile, so pay close attention to posts with CT and CDT markers identifying the trail.

Ascend more than 400 feet to a high point at **mile 0.7**, with great views of the surrounding Collegiate Peaks and Taylor Park to the west. Lost Lake at **mile 2.1** offers camping and water and is reached 0.5 mile and 700 feet below the trail via off-trail hiking down a steep but straightforward slope. Past this, the trail climbs and then descends for a couple of miles. A few limited stands of trees provide minimal protection in bad weather near mile 4, but the steep terrain limits camping.

Over the next mile and a half or so, the trail ascends more than 700 feet to regain the Continental Divide at a saddle between Sanford Basin on the west and Mineral Basin on the east at **mile 5.5**. Stay to the right (south) of any remaining snow while descending the other side. Descend into Mineral Basin and cross a seasonal stream at **mile 6.4**. During the descent, there are some small grassy areas where exposed camping is possible in good weather.

Carefully plan your travel timing in the above-timberline CW03 to be well situated for any storms. The first 5.6 miles is quite exposed, but it generally faces west, allowing users to monitor incoming weather and reformulate plans.

TRAVEL TIPS

South of 5.6 miles, the trail is east of (and well below) the Divide. This part of the segment is not as exposed but users are less able to see and **gauge approaching storms**.

The off-trail descent to Lost Lake for water and camping. Photo by Rick Stockwell

There is a generally reliable stream at **mile 7.0**, then a small bridge. Some marginally protected camping can be found in areas with small trees as the trail wraps around the base of Mount Kreutzer. Protected camping and water can be found

Indian paintbrush.
Photo by Tim Burroughs

near a pond 0.2 mile and 200 feet below the trail to the southeast from a marker post at **mile 7.7**. Cross small bridges over a couple of seasonal streams at **mile 8.4** and **mile 8.8**. Over the next 1.5 miles, climb about 700 feet through a talus field and a high mountain tundra to top the east ridge of Emma Burr Mountain at **mile 10.2**. There are spectacular views at the top, including of the trail as it drops nearly 600 feet into the head of Morgans Gulch to the south before beginning to climb again.

There is a stream crossing in Morgans Gulch at **mile 11.6**. Signage nearby discourages camping in the area due to sensitive wildlife habitat. From the stream, the trail ascends nearly 700 feet in less than a mile, an unusually steep ascent on this relatively new segment, before topping out at **mile 12.2**. At 12,868 feet, it is the highest point

Hiking ridgeline meadows south of Cottonwood Pass. Photo by Tim Burroughs

on the Collegiate West route, offering great views. The trail then descends into the headwaters of Woodchopper Creek. At **mile 13.4**, diverge off trail, downhill (northeast) 0.4 mile to a pair of small lakes for water and exposed camping.

The final 2.5 miles of the segment descend steadily toward FS Road 267/Tincup Pass Road. Cross a creek on a bridge, then reach the road and the end of Segment CW03 at **mile 16.1**. There is protected camping in the area and water available from nearby North Fork Chalk Creek.

BUILDING THE COLLEGIATE WEST TRAIL

This entire segment is part of a substantial reroute that moved the co-located CDT/CT Collegiate West off of motorized routes. While all 16.1 miles of Segment CW03 was new trail construction where no trail existed before, the reroute also included improvements to existing trails in the Texas Creek and South Texas Creek drainages, starting at the Texas Creek Trailhead, Segment CW02 **mile 18.7**. Work on this 23-mile stretch was completed in 2013 and was officially opened to trail users in 2014. The multi-year project was accomplished by CTF trail crews, Forest Service staff, the Buena Vista Correctional Facility trail crew, and other partner organizations. Of particular note is the tremendous amount of work to develop a stable trail through multiple lengthy talus fields, much of the construction completed by the Buena Vista Correctional Facility trail crew.

209

Cottonwood Pass
Road Trailhead

Cottonwood
Pass Trailhead

North

1 Mile

Cottonwood Pass Road Trailhead

South Texas Trail

Collegiate Peaks
Wilderness

Mount
14193

Mt. Yale Trail

Browns Pass Trail

North Fork Denny

Denny Creek
Hartenstein Lake

Turner Peak
13153

Denny Creek
Trailhead

Middle
COLLEGI

0

1

306

Hill Trail

Gene's Trail

Highlands Trail

Spruce Trail

2

3

Ptarmigan Lake
Trailhead

Ptarmigan Lake Trail

Pike and San Isabel
National Forests

COTTONWOOD

4

Trout
Lake

5

Gunnison
National Forest

Sanford Creek Trail

Hillerton Trail

Ptarmigan
Lake
Yonder
Mountain

6

12000 ft

7

Mount
Kreutzer
12344

FS 344

Cottonwood Creek

Green Timber
Gulch Trailhead

8

Garden Basin
Trailhead

267

MIRROR LAKE - GUNNISON RD

Cottonwood South Trail

9

11000 ft

Mirror Lake

10

Emma Burr
Mountain
13545

11

Poplar Gulch Trail

12

Napoleon Pass Trail

13

Salmon Creek

14

Wonderhopper

Grizzly Gulch
Trailhead

Poplar Gulch Trailhead

IRON CITY

St. Elmo

15

Continental Divide Trail

16.1

North Fork Chalk Creek

FS 267

12000 ft

12000 ft

FS 295

12000 ft

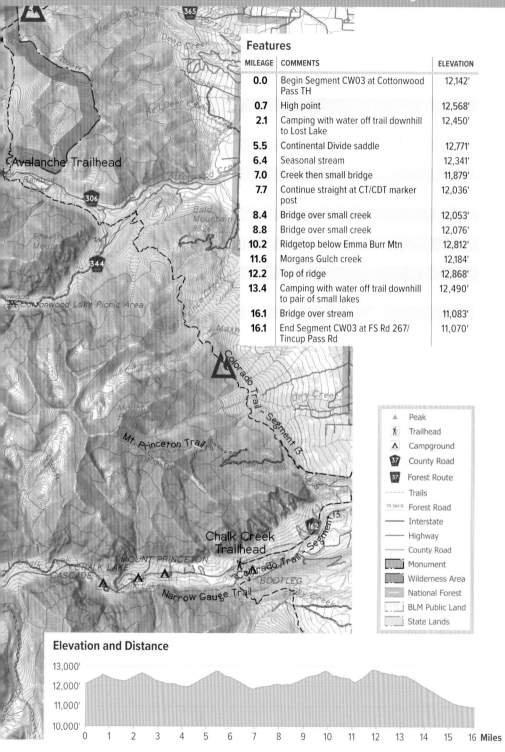

Features

MILEAGE	COMMENTS	ELEVATION
0.0	Begin Segment CW03 at Cottonwood Pass TH	12,142'
0.7	High point	12,568'
2.1	Camping with water off trail downhill to Lost Lake	12,450'
5.5	Continental Divide saddle	12,771'
6.4	Seasonal stream	12,341'
7.0	Creek then small bridge	11,879'
7.7	Continue straight at CT/CDT marker post	12,036'
8.4	Bridge over small creek	12,053'
8.8	Bridge over small creek	12,076'
10.2	Ridgetop below Emma Burr Mtn	12,812'
11.6	Morgans Gulch creek	12,184'
12.2	Top of ridge	12,868'
13.4	Camping with water off trail downhill to pair of small lakes	12,490'
16.1	Bridge over stream	11,083'
16.1	End Segment CW03 at FS Rd 267/ Tincup Pass Rd	11,070'

Legend

- ▲ Peak
- 🚶 Trailhead
- ⛺ Campground
- 37 County Road
- 37 Forest Route
- ----- Trails
- FS 564.N Forest Road
- —— Interstate
- —— Highway
- —— County Road
- Monument
- Wilderness Area
- National Forest
- BLM Public Land
- State Lands

Elevation and Distance

SEGMENT CW04
Tincup Pass Road to Boss Lake Trailhead

Hancock Lake and Chalk Creek Pass. Photo by Cornelius Friesen

Distance	17.0 miles
Elevation Gain	Approx. 2,738 feet
Elevation Loss	Approx. 3,389 feet
USFS Map	San Isabel National Forest
The CT Databook, 8th Edition	Pages 74–75
The CT Map Book	Pages 74–76
Trails Illustrated Maps	No. 130, 1203
Latitude 40° Map	Salida Buena Vista Trails
Jurisdiction	Salida Ranger District, San Isabel National Forest

ACCESS FROM
DENVER END

ACCESS FROM
DURANGO END

AVAILABILITY
OF WATER

BICYCLING

ABOUT THIS SEGMENT: This segment showcases three relatively recent realignments: one near the start that eliminated a steep and eroding section, and two that eliminated road walks up a 4WD road, first near the middle and then one just before the end. Highlights of the segment include the Lower and Upper Hancock Lakes and Chalk Creek Pass. A significant portion of the segment is spent above or near tree line, requiring continued vigilance and planning to avoid being caught by bad weather.

Along the way, trail users encounter remnants of Colorado's mining history, particularly the Alpine Tunnel, a 1,772-foot engineering marvel built in the 1880s for the narrow-gauge Denver, South Park & Pacific Railroad's route from Denver to Gunnison. At an elevation of more than 11,500 feet, it was the first tunnel constructed under the Continental Divide in Colorado. According to the US Forest Service, it "remains the

Segment CW04 begins by crossing this bridge over North Fork Chalk Creek.
Photo by Bill Manning

highest railroad tunnel and the longest narrow-gauge tunnel [ever constructed] in North America." Completed in 1882, it was abandoned in 1910 after minor damage wasn't deemed worth repairing due to the lack of traffic. It is now sealed at both ends. Historical markers at the tunnel's east entrance and farther down the trail built on the old railroad grade recount the history of the tunnel and of the Denver, South Park & Pacific Railroad.

TRAILHEAD/ACCESS POINTS

Tincup Pass Road Trail Access: The CT Collegiate West route and CDT crossing of FS Road 267/Tincup Pass Road can be reached via County Road 162 and FS Road 267 from Nathrop, south of Buena Vista. Take County Road 162/Chalk Creek Drive west about 16 miles to the intersection with FS Rd 267 at the ghost town of St. Elmo. Continue west on the increasingly rough FS Road 267, paralleling North Fork Chalk Creek, for another 4 miles to the intersection with the trail.

Alpine Tunnel Trailhead: From Nathrop, take County Road 162/Chalk Creek Drive west 15.4 miles to where it intersects with FS Road 295/Hancock Road just before the ghost town of St. Elmo. Turn left and continue south on FS Road 295 5.5 miles to the Alpine Tunnel Trailhead. It is 0.7 mile west on the railroad grade to Segment CW04 mile 7.5 or 1.5 miles south on the FS Road 295 (4WD) to Hancock Lakes Trailhead, then 0.1 mile on the Hancock Lakes Trail to Segment CW04 mile 11.0.

Looking north at Hancock Lakes below, CT segment CW04. Photo by Cornelius Friesen

Boss Lake Trailhead: See Segment CW05 on page 335.

SERVICES, SUPPLIES, AND ACCOMMODATIONS: Services are available at Mount Princeton Hot Springs Resort, 15 miles east of the Tincup Pass Road crossing and about 17 miles northeast of the Hancock Trailhead. Limited services are available at Garfield on US 50, about 1.5 miles from the Boss Lake Trailhead.

TRAIL DESCRIPTION: Leave FS Road 267/Tincup Pass Road, **mile 0.0**, to the southwest on single-track following North Fork Chalk Creek. At **mile 0.3**, cross a small bridge over a tributary, then the main creek on a sturdier bridge shortly after. Enter dense forest and climb 600 feet up numerous switchbacks to reach tree line. Cross another stream at **mile 1.6** and begin a 5-mile section above tree line. Cross a small stream at **mile 2.6** as the trail traverses the head of Wildcat Gulch, then cross a small saddle shortly after.

The trail descends slightly, then crosses a spring and two small streams as it climbs to a saddle on the ridge separating Wildcat and Tunnel Gulches at **mile 3.6**. Tunnel Lake comes into view shortly after crossing the pass.

At **mile 4.1**, cross a seasonal stream that feeds Tunnel Lake below, followed by another seasonal stream crossing at **mile 4.5**. Reach a trail junction at a saddle on the Continental Divide at **mile 4.9**. A short trip to the right leads to a view of the

Left: CTF volunteer trail crew working to relocate more trail off of roads. Photo by Cornelius Friesen **Right:** The old railroad grade makes for a friendly path in Tunnel Gulch. Some old ties remain, foreground. Photo by Bill Manning

west side of the Alpine Tunnel where you can see structures restored by volunteers, including the train turntable and several buildings. A side trip to the turntable involves 400 feet of elevation loss over 0.5 mile.

Back at the saddle, the trail turns north above the abandoned Alpine Tunnel and switchbacks down a scree-covered slope to reach the old railroad grade at **mile 5.4**. (Left 200 yards near the tunnel's blocked east entrance is a sign describing the history of the tunnel.) Some small campsites can be found below the cliffs along the railroad grade over the next mile.

The trail begins a 2-mile forested section, then crosses a seasonal stream at **mile 6.5**. The impacts of spruce beetles on mature trees becomes apparent in this forested section and will continue to be visible through Segment 24 (see sidebar on page 197). There is more historical signage at **mile 7.2** about the Denver, South Park & Pacific Railroad, which once traveled the railroad grade and tunnel.

> Users in Collegiate West Segment 04 will enjoy reading the interpretive signs about the **Alpine Tunnel**, an ideal chance to reflect on Colorado mountain history. Traveling along the old railroad grade is a welcome, gentle break from steeper routings elsewhere. You'll be on this old grade for a little over 2 miles, a stretch popular with day-hikers and families. Meeting them can be fun and visiting can sometimes lead to an offer for a ride to, say, Mount Princeton Hot Springs.
>
> TRAVEL TIP

At **mile 7.5**, leave the railroad grade to the right onto the recently completed (2021) single-track reroute. At **mile 7.6**, angle across FS Road 298.A/Williams Pass Road (4WD), open to traffic only during the month of August.

Climb to tree line via gradual switchbacks, where the views become expansive again. The impact of spruce beetles on the Chalk Creek valley forest is once again readily apparent, with significant numbers of dead, mature spruce trees. Observant trail users will notice that the younger spruce trees were more resistant to the beetle, so these will provide a means of recovering the forest in the decades ahead.

Continue a traversing climb, where there is relatively protected and good camping potential just before crossing a stream at **mile 9.4**. The trail leaves the trees and travels across open slopes that have seasonal water before dropping down to a two-track spur just past a mining site at **mile 9.9**. Follow the two-track to the southeast for 100 yards, then turn sharply to the right onto FS Road 299/Hancock Pass Road (4WD) at **mile 10.0**, which can be busy with traffic, particularly on weekends. After 160 feet, turn sharply left off the road and back onto single-track.

Continue climbing through scattered trees and open slopes, then cross a seasonal stream at **mile 10.4**, with potential campsites beyond in the trees below the trail. Cross a talus slope then descend through some trees and reach the large, open, willow-covered upper Chalk Creek valley. Turn right and head up the valley on the Hancock Lake Trail at a junction, **mile 11.0**.

After passing Hancock Lake, where camping is possible, cross a small stream at **mile 11.3**. Cross upper Chalk Creek, then reach a junction with a side trail to Upper Hancock Lake at **mile 11.5**, where camping is also possible. Continue on the main trail and switchback up 400 feet to reach Chalk Creek Pass at **mile 12.0**. Looking back, there are great views of the Hancock Lakes and the Chalk Creek valley. The view ahead overlooks the Middle Fork South Arkansas River valley surrounded by a host of 12,000- and 13,000-foot peaks.

Up close detail is stunning, often worth an extra minute. Photos by Bill Manning

Sunrise from a campsite near Tincup Pass Road. Photo by Bill Manning

Descend south from the pass, crossing a seasonal stream at **mile 12.2**, where there is exposed camping nearby. Continue descending and cross at the toe of a talus field then reach a pond at **mile 12.5**, with protected camping just beyond. The trail continues losing elevation through a mix of trees and open slopes, crossing two seasonal streams, then continues left at a trail junction, **mile 13.8**. (Right 50 yards leads to the end of FS Road 230/Middle Fork Road and a short distance beyond is the Middle Fork South Arkansas River, where water is available and camping potential.)

Angle left across a two-track at **mile 14.4**, then cross two more small seasonal streams. Be sure to notice the ancient Rocky Mountain bristlecone pine in the talus uphill to the left at **mile 14.8**. This hardy, slow-growing, long-lived tree species is resistant to even the harshest weather conditions and can grow in very poor soil.

The trail crosses a large talus field at the base of Mount Aetna, towering nearly 4,000 feet above. At **mile 15.2**, reach FS Road 230 and follow it to the left to **mile 15.4** where the trail leaves the road to the left back onto single-track. The Lost Wonder Hut (lostwonderhut.com) sits one-third mile up the road from **mile 15.2**. The trail switchbacks uphill and crosses two small streams then begins a traversing descent. Cross FS Road 230.C three times (**mile 16.1, mile 16.5,** and **mile 16.8**) on the descent then reach FS Road 230 again at **mile 16.9**. Angle right across the road and continue south toward the Boss Lake Trailhead. (The road continues southwest for 1.5 miles to US Highway 50 and the small town of Garfield, where there are some services available, possibly including mail drop.) At **mile 17.0**, stay right to continue on to CW05. A short spur trail on the left leads to the Boss Lake Trailhead. There is camping in the area with water available nearby at the Middle Fork South Arkansas River at the beginning of Segment CW05.

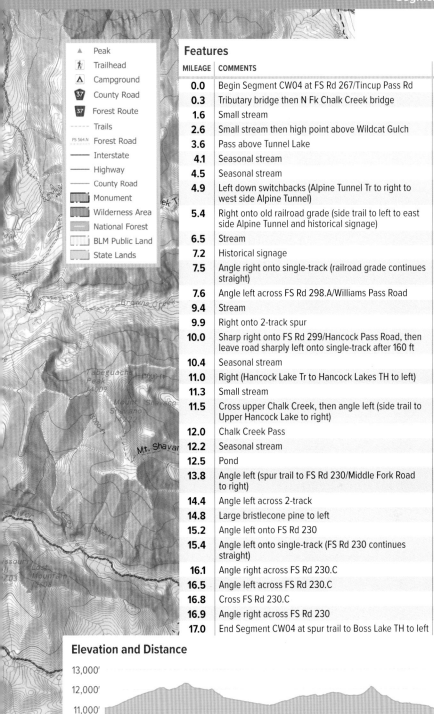

Features

MILEAGE	COMMENTS	ELEVATION
0.0	Begin Segment CW04 at FS Rd 267/Tincup Pass Rd	11,070'
0.3	Tributary bridge then N Fk Chalk Creek bridge	11,104'
1.6	Small stream	11,726'
2.6	Small stream then high point above Wildcat Gulch	12,100'
3.6	Pass above Tunnel Lake	12,326'
4.1	Seasonal stream	12,048'
4.5	Seasonal stream	11,971'
4.9	Left down switchbacks (Alpine Tunnel Tr to right to west side Alpine Tunnel)	11,925'
5.4	Right onto old railroad grade (side trail to left to east side Alpine Tunnel and historical signage)	11,555'
6.5	Stream	11,342'
7.2	Historical signage	11,202'
7.5	Angle right onto single-track (railroad grade continues straight)	11,164'
7.6	Angle left across FS Rd 298.A/Williams Pass Road	11,213'
9.4	Stream	11,718'
9.9	Right onto 2-track spur	11,703'
10.0	Sharp right onto FS Rd 299/Hancock Pass Road, then leave road sharply left onto single-track after 160 ft	11,720'
10.4	Seasonal stream	11,792'
11.0	Right (Hancock Lake Tr to Hancock Lakes TH to left)	11,669'
11.3	Small stream	11,664'
11.5	Cross upper Chalk Creek, then angle left (side trail to Upper Hancock Lake to right)	11,701'
12.0	Chalk Creek Pass	12,105'
12.2	Seasonal stream	11,834'
12.5	Pond	11,628'
13.8	Angle left (spur trail to FS Rd 230/Middle Fork Road to right)	11,234'
14.4	Angle left across 2-track	11,179'
14.8	Large bristlecone pine to left	11,055'
15.2	Angle left onto FS Rd 230	10,786'
15.4	Angle left onto single-track (FS Rd 230 continues straight)	10,743'
16.1	Angle right across FS Rd 230.C	10,840'
16.5	Angle left across FS Rd 230.C	10,665'
16.8	Cross FS Rd 230.C	10,545'
16.9	Angle right across FS Rd 230	10,484'
17.0	End Segment CW04 at spur trail to Boss Lake TH to left	10,438'

Legend:
- ▲ Peak
- 🚶 Trailhead
- ⛺ Campground
- 37 County Road
- 37 Forest Route
- ----- Trails
- FS 564.N Forest Road
- ——— Interstate
- ——— Highway
- ——— County Road
- Monument
- Wilderness Area
- National Forest
- BLM Public Land
- State Lands

Elevation and Distance

13,000'
12,000'
11,000'
10,000'
0 1 2 3 4 5 6 7 8 9 10 11 12 13 14 15 16 **Miles**

SEGMENT CW05

Boss Lake Trailhead to
Ridge Above South Fooses Creek

Evening light hits Mount Aetna and skips off Hunt Lake, Segment CW05.
Photo by Dean Krakel

Distance	16.1 miles
Elevation Gain	Approx. 3,750 feet
Elevation Loss	Approx. 2,271 feet
USFS Map	San Isabel and Gunnison National Forests
The CT Databook, 8th Edition	Pages 76–77
The CT Map Book	Pages 76–77
Trails Illustrated Maps	Nos. 130, 139, 1203
Latitude 40° Map	Salida Buena Vista Trails
Jurisdiction	Salida and Gunnison Ranger Districts, San Isabel and Gunnison National Forests

ACCESS FROM
DENVER END

ACCESS FROM
DURANGO END
No Road Access

AVAILABILITY
OF WATER

BICYCLING

ABOUT THIS SEGMENT: This segment features a climb of more than 2,000 feet to the Continental Divide before descending to Monarch Pass and continuing along a ridgeline to the intersection with the southern end of the CT Collegiate East route (Segment 15, mile 8.6) above South Fooses Creek. It skirts Boss and Hunt Lakes, presents spectacular views from on and near the Divide, passes through the Monarch Mountain ski area, and crosses the only true thoroughfare on the entire CT Collegiate West route, US Highway 50. Though it is south of most the Collegiate Range's fourteeners, it is surrounded by a host of impressive 12,000- and 13,000-foot peaks that repeatedly draw the eye upward.

At its endpoint on the Monarch Crest above South Fooses Creek, trail users can choose to continue in the direction of Durango and the western terminus of The Colorado Trail, or to turn back north toward Twin Lakes, where they can complete the 163.3-mile Collegiate Loop, an option that continues to grow in popularity.

TRAILHEAD/ACCESS POINTS

Boss Lake Trailhead: From Poncha Springs, travel about 12 miles on US Highway 50 to the community of Garfield, sometimes shown as Monarch. Turn right (northwest) on FS Road 230/Middle Fork Road and follow the steep, rocky road for 1.5 miles. The trailhead is down a short spur road to the left of the main road. FS Road 230 lends itself best to a 4WD vehicle with high clearance and low range, though it's not uncommon to see lesser vehicles at the trailhead.

Left: Boss Lake is good for camping or a day outing, great for fishing, and offers access by 4WD vehicles. Photo by Sophie Penniman **Right:** A rock helps steady the camera for a self-timer shot. Photo by Bill Manning

Boss Lake Trailhead to Ridge Above South Fooses Creek

Gaining the Continental Divide in Segment CW05 is breathtaking. Photo by Dean Waits

Monarch Pass Trailhead: Monarch Pass Trailhead is accessed via US Highway 50 from the east or west and is about 18 miles west of Poncha Springs and 42 miles east of Gunnison.

The southern end of Segment CW05 is not accessible by vehicle. The end of the segment can be accessed via either end of Segment 15: 5.7 miles starting from the Fooses Creek Trailhead (**mile 2.9**) or 5.6 miles from the Marshall Pass Trailhead (**mile 14.2**).

SERVICES, SUPPLIES, AND ACCOMMODATIONS: There are full services available in Salida, 22 miles east of Monarch Pass (see page 187), and Gunnison, 42 miles to the west. Monarch at the Crest, located at Monarch Pass, was revamped in 2023 and offers food service, resupply products, package drops, drinking water, and possibly showers and laundry (not finalized at the time of publication). Lodging and a restaurant are available at the Monarch Mountain Lodge at Garfield, about 5.5 miles northeast of Monarch Pass on US Highway 50 or 1.5 miles from the Boss Lake Trailhead on FS Road 230/Middle Fork Road.

Left: Enjoying a well-deserved rest at the top after a big climb from the lakes below. Photo by Bill Manning **Right:** A cairn near the Continental Divide on the Collegiate West, Segment CW05. Photo by Giff Kriebel

TRAIL DESCRIPTION: At the spur trail to the Boss Lake Trailhead, **mile 0.0**, take the trail southwest and cross the Middle Fork South Arkansas River on a bridge. There is camping nearby. The trail climbs several switchbacks then begins a more contouring climb and reaches the Boss Lake Dam at **mile 0.8**. Turn left on the dam and cross a bridge over the lake outlet at **mile 0.9**. There is water available below the bridge, but it can be difficult to access. South of the bridge, continue 100 feet then turn sharply back to the right and follow a switchback as it climbs the low ridge east of Boss Lake. There is camping near the lake.

Descend the ridge and cross FS Road 235/Boss Lake Road at **mile 1.2**, then continue past road closure posts on an old roadbed, passing another road closure point at **mile 1.3**. Follow the trail as it turns west and begins the climb to Hunt Lake. There are campsites just south of Boss Lake near the inlet stream. After a 500-foot climb, reach Hunt Lake at **mile 2.4**, with camping in the area.

Emerge from the trees and follow along the toe of a large talus field below Banana Mountain. There is another small lake, 450 feet higher, at **mile 3.0**. This is the last reliable water source before reaching Monarch Pass, 8 miles ahead. After another 0.7 mile and another 550-foot elevation gain, reach the Continental Divide at a large cairn at **mile 3.7**. Large cairns and expansive views in all directions are

This is the last major road crossing before beginning the least travelled stretch of the Colorado Trail. The Monarch Crest is a great place to resupply (phone ahead to confirm availability) or to have a shuttle pick-up for a resupply in nearby Salida.

TRAVEL TIP

Cyclists enjoy Monarch Crest in CW05 south of US Highway 50. Photo by Ravi Nagarajan

the highlights of the trail for the next three miles. Reach the high point of the segment at **mile 4.4** (12,510') as the trail wraps around the west side of Bald Mountain.

At **mile 6.5**, there is a sign describing how prehistoric tribes built a system of low boulder walls and ambush pits in this area to divert big game herds to awaiting hunters. Evidence suggests this "game drive" was used for thousands of years, perhaps from as early as 3000 B.C. to A.D. 1800. Remnants of the walls are still visible.

At **mile 7.2**, turn right onto a road within the Monarch Mountain ski area. At another intersection at **mile 7.6**, take a right onto another ski area road, staying close to the Continental Divide. Reach a high point at **mile 8.1**, where there is a picnic table at the top of a ski lift. Continue on the ski area road, beginning the descent toward Monarch Pass. At **mile 8.3**, be sure to stop by the very fun Monarch Mountain Pick a Peak directional peak identifier sculpture. As described

THE MONARCH CREST TRAIL

The trail south from Monarch Pass to Marshall Pass is known as the Monarch Crest Trail. This trail is very popular with mountain bikers, especially on weekends, so be on the lookout and ready to share the tread. Motorcycles are also allowed on this trail.

On the Divide, above (and in) the clouds. Photo by Rick Stockwell

on the Monarch Mountain website (skimonarch.com/pick-a-peak/): "Pick A Peak has all the prominent peaks labeled along the outer ridge of the butterfly and a movable dial that can be targeted at unknown summits in the distance. From here you can identify peaks in the Front Range, Sangre de Cristo Range, San Juan Range, Elk Mountains, the Sawatch Range, and other sub-ranges." Continue following the road to the right at **mile 8.5**, where two ski area roads leave to the left. Reach a gate at **mile 9.2** and turn right onto FS Road 237/Old Monarch Pass Road. Shortly after, continue on the road where the motorized Monarch Ridge Trail departs to the left. At the top of Old Monarch Pass, **mile 9.4**, angle left and up onto single-track.

Reach US Highway 50 at **mile 10.8** and go uphill (left) toward Monarch Pass, taking care when crossing the busy highway. Reach the Monarch Pass Trailhead at **mile 11.1**. The souvenir store at the pass, now Monarch at the Crest, has been upgraded and offers more trail user amenities. Be sure to check hours if arriving early or late in the day to avoid disappointment.

From the trailhead, continue south on a service road that is paved for the first 200 feet, beginning between the store and the aerial tram building. Angle off the road and onto single-track to the right at **mile 11.4**. Reach a saddle where the trail joins a two-track to the right at **mile 12.1**. At **mile 12.6**, angle right onto single-track again for the remainder of the segment. Shortly beyond this point, the trail opens up, offering some great views. Because of the exposure, however, keep an eye on the weather.

At **mile 16.1**, reach the southern terminus of the CT Collegiate West route at the junction with CT Collegiate East Segment 15 (mile 8.6). Turn left to continue on the Collegiate East or continue straight to continue on Segment 15.

The Lost
Wonder Hut

0
Boss Lake
Trailhead

3
Hunt Lake
2
1

Garfield

4

Continental Divide Trail

5

Waterdog
Lakes

Waterdog
Lakes

6

Waterdog Lakes
Trailhead

Waterdog Lakes
Trailhead

Pike and San Isabel
National Forests

Fooses Creek
Trailhead

225

7

Monarch Crest Trail

FS 237

MONARCH PARK

Monarch

8 9

237

Colorado Trail – Segment 15

Basin View Trail

11
Monarch Pass
Trailhead

10

12

50

13

Mount Peck

14

Gunnison
National Forest

Monarch Crest Trail

Peel Point

15

Continental Divide Trail

Greens Creek Trail

Agate Creek Trail

North

↑

1 Mile

Agate Creek

Little Cochetopa Trail

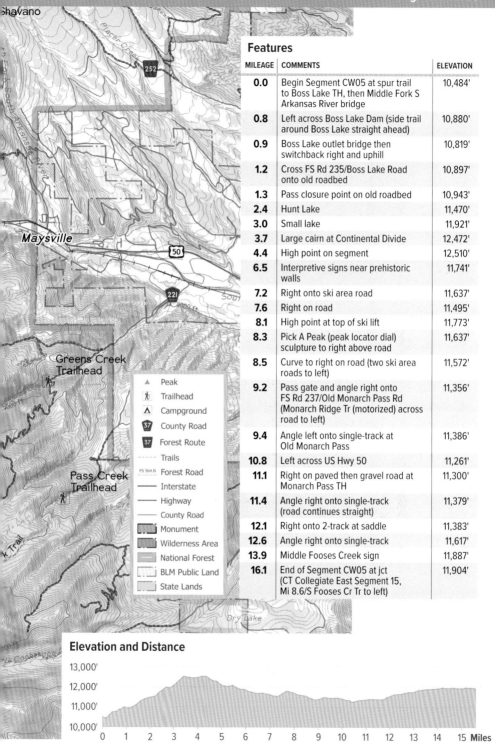

Features

MILEAGE	COMMENTS	ELEVATION
0.0	Begin Segment CW05 at spur trail to Boss Lake TH, then Middle Fork S Arkansas River bridge	10,484'
0.8	Left across Boss Lake Dam (side trail around Boss Lake straight ahead)	10,880'
0.9	Boss Lake outlet bridge then switchback right and uphill	10,819'
1.2	Cross FS Rd 235/Boss Lake Road onto old roadbed	10,897'
1.3	Pass closure point on old roadbed	10,943'
2.4	Hunt Lake	11,470'
3.0	Small lake	11,921'
3.7	Large cairn at Continental Divide	12,472'
4.4	High point on segment	12,510'
6.5	Interpretive signs near prehistoric walls	11,741'
7.2	Right onto ski area road	11,637'
7.6	Right on road	11,495'
8.1	High point at top of ski lift	11,773'
8.3	Pick A Peak (peak locator dial) sculpture to right above road	11,637'
8.5	Curve to right on road (two ski area roads to left)	11,572'
9.2	Pass gate and angle right onto FS Rd 237/Old Monarch Pass Rd (Monarch Ridge Tr (motorized) across road to left)	11,356'
9.4	Angle left onto single-track at Old Monarch Pass	11,386'
10.8	Left across US Hwy 50	11,261'
11.1	Right on paved then gravel road at Monarch Pass TH	11,300'
11.4	Angle right onto single-track (road continues straight)	11,379'
12.1	Right onto 2-track at saddle	11,383'
12.6	Angle right onto single-track	11,617'
13.9	Middle Fooses Creek sign	11,887'
16.1	End of Segment CW05 at jct (CT Collegiate East Segment 15, Mi 8.6/S Fooses Cr Tr to left)	11,904'

Legend:
- ▲ Peak
- 🚶 Trailhead
- ⛺ Campground
- 37 County Road
- 37 Forest Route
- ----- Trails
- FS 564.N Forest Road
- —— Interstate
- —— Highway
- —— County Road
- Monument
- Wilderness Area
- National Forest
- BLM Public Land
- State Lands

Elevation and Distance

USEFUL CONTACT INFO

Useful Phone Numbers

The Colorado Trail Foundation
(303) 384-3729

Colorado Division of Wildlife
(303) 297-1192

To activate a rescue group, contact the nearest county sheriff:

Seg. 1–3	Jefferson	(303) 277-0211
Seg. 4–6	Park	(719) 836-2494
Seg. 7–8	Summit	(970) 453-2232
Seg. 8	Eagle	(970) 328-8500
Seg. 9–11	Lake	(719) 486-1249
Seg. 12–15	Chaffee	(719) 539-2596
Seg. 16–20	Saguache	(719) 655-2525
Seg. 21	Mineral	(719) 658-2600
Seg. 22–23	Hinsdale	(970) 944-2291
Seg. 24–25	San Juan	(970) 387-5531
Seg. 26	Dolores	(970) 677-2257
Seg. 27–28	La Plata	(970) 385-2900
Seg. CW01	Lake	(719) 486-1249
Seg. CW02–CW05	Chaffee	(719) 539-2596

Sunset over the San Juan Mountains.
Photo by Len Glassner

Forest Service Offices

United States Forest Service
Rocky Mountain Region Office
1617 Cole Blvd., Building 17
Lakewood, CO 80401
(303) 275-5350

Gunnison National Forest
Gunnison Ranger District
216 N. Colorado St.
Gunnison, CO 81230
(970) 641-0471

Pike National Forest
South Park Ranger District
320 US Highway 285, Box 219
Fairplay, CO 80440
(719) 836-2031

South Platte Ranger District
30403 Kings Valley Dr., Suite 2-115
Conifer, CO 80433
(303) 275-5610

Rio Grande National Forest
Divide Ranger District
304 South Main St., Box 270
Creede, CO 81130
(719) 658-2556

Saguache Ranger District
46525 CO Highway 114, Box 67
Saguache, CO 81149
(719) 655-2547

San Isabel National Forest
Leadville Ranger District
810 Front St.
Leadville, CO 80461
(719) 486-0749

Salida Ranger District
5575 Cleora Road
Salida, CO 81201
(719) 539-3591

San Juan National Forest
Columbine District
367 S. Pearl St., Box 439
Bayfield, CO 81122
(970) 884-2512

Dolores District
29211 CO Highway 184, Box 210
Dolores, CO 81323
(970) 882-7296

White River National Forest
Dillon Ranger District
680 Blue River Parkway
Silverthorne, CO 80498
(970) 468-5400

Holy Cross Ranger District
24747 US Highway 24
Minturn, CO 81645
(970) 827-5715

Snow remains in late July on
Segment 8 near Searle Pass.
Photo by Len Glassner

LEAVE NO TRACE

The Leave No Trace (LNT) program is a message to promote and inspire responsible outdoor recreation through education, research, and partnerships. Managed as a nonprofit educational organization and authorized by the US Forest Service, LNT is about enjoying places like The Colorado Trail, while traveling and camping with care and preserving these places for the future. The seven Leave No Trace principles of outdoor ethics are:

Plan Ahead and Prepare
- Know the regulations and special concerns for the area you'll visit.
- Prepare for extreme weather, hazards, and emergencies.
- Schedule your trip to avoid times of high use.
- Visit in small groups when possible. Consider splitting larger groups into smaller groups.
- Repackage food to minimize waste.
- Use a map and compass to eliminate the use of marking paint, rock cairns, or flagging.

Travel and Camp on Durable Surfaces
- Durable surfaces include established trails and campsites, rock, gravel, dry grasses, or snow. Protect riparian areas by camping at least 200 feet from lakes and streams.
- Good campsites are found, not made. Altering a site is not necessary.

In popular areas:
- Concentrate use on existing trails and campsites.
- Walk single file in the middle of the trail, even when wet or muddy.
- Keep campsites small. Focus activity in areas where vegetation is absent.

In pristine areas:
- Disperse use to prevent the creation of campsites and trails.
- Avoid places where impacts are just beginning.

Dispose of Waste Properly
- Pack it in, pack it out. Inspect your campsite and rest areas for trash or spilled foods. Pack out all trash, leftover food, and litter.
- Deposit solid human waste in catholes dug 6 to 8 inches deep at least 200 feet from water, camp, and trails. Cover and disguise the cathole when finished.
- Pack out toilet paper and hygiene products.
- To wash yourself or your dishes, carry water 200 feet away from streams or lakes and use small amounts of biodegradable soap. Scatter strained dishwater.

Leave What You Find
- Preserve the past: examine, but do not touch, cultural or historic structures and artifacts. Leave rocks, plants, and other natural objects as you find them.
- Avoid introducing or transporting non-native species.
- Do not build structures, furniture, or dig trenches.

Minimize Campfire Impacts
- Campfires can cause lasting impacts to the backcountry. Use a lightweight stove for cooking and enjoy a candle lantern for light.
- Where fires are permitted, use established fire rings, fire pans, or mound fires. Keep fires small. Only use sticks from the ground that can be broken by hand. Burn all wood/coals to ash, put out campfires completely, then scatter cool ashes.

Respect Wildlife
- Never feed animals. Feeding wildlife damages their health, alters natural behaviors, and exposes them to predators or other dangers.
- Protect wildlife and your food by storing rations and trash securely.
- Control pets at all times, or leave them at home.
- Avoid wildlife during sensitive times: mating, nesting, raising young, or winter.

Aspen grove found in Segment 11. Photo by Julie Vida and Mark Tabb

Be Considerate of Other Visitors

- Respect other visitors and protect the quality of their experience. Be courteous. Yield to other users on the trail.
- Step to the downhill side of the trail when encountering pack stock. Take breaks and camp away from trails and other visitors.
- Let nature's sounds prevail. Avoid loud voices and noises.

Leave No Trace publishes an educational booklet, *Outdoor Skills and Ethics,* that specifically covers backcountry recreation in the Rocky Mountains. To obtain a copy of this, or for more information about the LNT program, contact:

Leave No Trace, Inc.
P.O. Box 997
Boulder, CO 80306
(800) 332-4100
LNT.org
info@LNT.org

Aconitum columbianum monkshood. Photo by Lori Brummer

INDEX

San Luis Peak, 63, 153
  climbing, 231
  photo of, 229, 230, 231
San Luis Valley, 47, 48, 52, 70, 153
sand lily (*Leucocrinum montanum*), 62
Sangre de Cristo Mountains, 48
Sargents Mesa, photo of, 207, 208
Sargents Mesa to CO Highway 114, **206–11**
  map of, 210–11
Sawatch Range, 22, 47, 50, 66, 153, 181, 203
  photo of, 45
scrub oak, 57–58
Search and Rescue Fund, 42
Searle Pass, 22, 37
  photo of, 14, 135, 344
seasons, considering, 22–23
Section Point, photo of, 67
sedimentary rocks, 67
  photo of, 67
Seibert, Pete, 137
sheep, photo of, 236
Sheep Gulch, 303
Sheep Gulch to Cottonwood Pass Trailhead,
  310–17
  map of, 316–17
sheepherder, photo of, 235
Shining Mountains, 47
shoes, 24
  photo of, 24
showy prickly poppy (*Argemone polyanthemos*),
  62
Sierra Club, 136
signs, 32–33
silky phacelia (*Phacelia sericea*), 64
Silver Creek Trail, 203
Silver Creek Trailhead to Chalk Creek
  Trailhead, **174–83**
  map of, 182–83
Silverton, 21, 25, 49, 52, 54, 253, 261
  map of, 269
  services/supplies/accommodations at, 269
Ski Cooper, 51
Sliderock, photo of, 293
Sliderock section, photo of, 294
Slumgullion Slide, photo of, 70
snow buttercup (*Ranunculus adoneus*), 62
Snow Mesa, photo of, 66, 234, 235
South Fooses Creek, 192, 197
South Fooses Ridge
  historical highlights of, 52
  wildflowers of, 64
South Fork Texas Creek, photo of, 313, 315
South Mineral Basin, photo of, 319
South Park, 62, 103, 115
  photo of, 100, 108
South Park & Pacific Railroad, 115
South Platte Hotel, 51
South Platte River, 10, 47
  photo of, 72

South Platte River Trailhead to Little Scraggy
  Trailhead, **80–85**
  map of, 84–85
South Texas Creek, 323
Spanish Trail, 47
Spring Creek Pass Trailhead to Carson Saddle,
  242–47
  map of, 246–47
spruce beetles (*Dendroctonus rufipennis*), 197
spruce-fir forest, 58, 59
State Parks Pass, 169
State Wildlife Area (SWA), 169
steam boiler, photo of, 50
Stony Pass, 261
  photo of, 252
Stony Pass Road, 253
  photo of, 253
Stony Pass Trailhead, 261
Stony pass Trailhead to Molas Pass, **256–65**
  map of, 264–65
Strontia Springs Dam, 75, 77
  photo of, 77
Strontia Springs Reservoir, 83
sub-alpine lifezone, 60
Summit Huts Association, 145
Summit Stage, 25
sun protection, 41
SWA. *See* State Wildlife Area
Swan River, 68
symbols, key to, 18 (fig.)

Tabeguache, 45
Tabeguache Peak, 161, 189
Take Pride in America Program, 9
talus fields, 59
Tarryall Mountains, 103
Taylor Lake, photo of, 284
Tenmile Range, 22, 62, 125, 136
  photo of, 118, 120, 122, 130
Tennessee Pass, 22, 49, 51, 66, 67, 133, 137, 145
Tennessee Pass to Timberline Lake Trailhead,
  140–47
  map of, 146–47
10th Mountain Division, 51, 136, 137, 145
10th Mountain Division Hut, 145
10th Mountain Division Hut Association, 145
10th Mountain Division Hut System, 145
  photo of, 145
Texas Creek, 323
Texas Creek Trailhead, 323
Therm-a-Rest, 30
Three Apostles, photo of, 310, 318
thru-hikers, photo of, 21, 26, 213, 216
thru-traveling
  planning for, 23
  resupplying for, 25
Thurber fescue, 59
timberline, 58
  photo of, 304

Illustration by Jesse Crock

Join Today.
Adventure Tomorrow.

COLORADO
MOUNTAIN CLUB

The Colorado Mountain Club is the Rocky Mountain community for mountain education, adventure, and conservation. We bring people together to share our love of the mountains. We value our community and go out of our way to welcome and include all Coloradoans—from the uninitiated to the expert, there is a place for everyone here.

cmc.org